Colloquial
Japanese

Colloquial Japanese provides a step-by-step course in Japanese as it is written and spoken today. This new edition has been completely rewritten by experienced teachers; it combines a user-friendly approach with a thorough treatment of the language, equipping learners with the essential skills needed to communicate confidently and effectively in Japanese in a broad range of situations. No prior knowledge of the language is required.

Key features include:

- progressive coverage of speaking, listening, reading and writing skills
- jargon-free explanations of grammar, with key structures presented through user-friendly diagrams
- coverage of the different writing systems of Japanese: hiragana, katakana and kanji
- an extensive range of focused and stimulating exercises
- realistic and entertaining dialogues covering a broad variety of scenarios
- useful vocabulary lists throughout the text
- additional resources available at the back of the book, including a full answer key, a grammar summary, a verb/adjective list with conjugation aid, bilingual glossaries and English translations of dialogues.

Balanced, comprehensive and rewarding, *Colloquial Japanese* will be an indispensable resource both for independent learners and for students taking courses in Japanese.

Audio material to accompany the course is available to download freely in MP3 format from www.routledge.com/cw/colloquials. Recorded by native speakers, the audio material features the dialogues and texts from the book and will help develop your listening and pronunciation skills. Supplementary exercise sheets for hiragana, katakana and kanji and two additional units can also be downloaded here. These additional units cover more advanced features of Japanese and incorporate a wide assortment of supporting exercises.

By the end of this course, you will be at Level B1 of the Common European Framework for Languages and at the Intermediate-Mid level on the ACTFL proficiency scales.

THE COLLOQUIAL SERIES
Series Adviser: Gary King

The following languages are available in the Colloquial series:

Afrikaans	Greek	Romanian
Albanian	Gujarati	Russian
Amharic	Hebrew	Scottish Gaelic
Arabic (Levantine)	Hindi	Serbian
Arabic of Egypt	Hungarian	Slovak
Arabic of the Gulf	Icelandic	Slovene
Basque	Indonesian	Somali
Bengali	Irish	Spanish
Breton	Italian	Spanish of
Bulgarian	Japanese	Latin America
Cambodian	Kazakh	Swahili
Cantonese	Korean	Swedish
Catalan	Latvian	Tamil
Chinese (Mandarin)	Lithuanian	Thai
Croatian	Malay	Tibetan (forthcoming)
Czech	Mongolian	Turkish
Danish	Norwegian	Ukrainian
Dutch	Panjabi	Urdu
English	Persian	Vietnamese
Estonian	Polish	Welsh
Finnish	Portuguese	Yiddish
French	Portuguese of	Yoruba
German	Brazil	Zulu (forthcoming)

COLLOQUIAL 2s series: *The Next Step in Language Learning*

Chinese	German	Russian
Dutch	Italian	Spanish
French	Portuguese of Brazil	Spanish of Latin America

Colloquials are now supported by FREE AUDIO available online. All audio tracks referenced within the text are free to stream or download from www.routledge.com/cw/colloquials. If you experience any difficulties accessing the audio on the companion website, or still wish to purchase a CD, please contact our customer services team through www.routledge.com/info/contact.

Colloquial
Japanese

The Complete Course for Beginners

Junko Ogawa and Fumitsugu Enokida

Routledge
Taylor & Francis Group

LONDON AND NEW YORK

Third edition published 2014
by Routledge
2 Park Square, Milton Park, Abingdon, Oxon OX14 4RN

and by Routledge
711 Third Avenue, New York, NY 10017

Routledge is an imprint of the Taylor & Francis Group, an informa business

© 2014 Junko Ogawa and Fumitsugu Enokida

The right of Junko Ogawa and Fumitsugu Enokida to be identified as authors of this work has been asserted by them in accordance with sections 77 and 78 of the Copyright, Designs and Patents Act 1988.

First edition published by Routledge 1981
Second edition published by Routledge 2003

British Library Cataloguing in Publication Data
A catalogue record for this book is available from the British Library

Library of Congress Cataloging in Publication Data
Ogawa, Junko author
  Colloquial Japanese : the complete course for beginners / Junko Ogawa and Fumitsugu Enokida. – New Edition.
    audio disc – (The Colloquial Series)
  Previous ed. : Colloquial Japanese, by H.D.B. Ckarke and Motoko Hamamura, 2003; 2nd ed.
  Includes bibliographical references and index.
  1. Japanese language–Textbooks for foreign speakers–English. 2. Japanese language–Spoken Japanese. 3. Japanese language–Sound recordings for English speakers.
  4. Japanese language–Self-instruction. I. Enokida, Fumitsugu author. II. Title.
  PL539.O323 2014
  495.683'421–dc23

                                                                    2013012026

ISBN: 978-1-138-94988-1 (pbk)

Typeset in Avant Garde and Helvetica
by Graphicraft Limited, Hong Kong

MIX
Paper from
responsible sources
FSC   FSC® C013056
www.fsc.org

Printed and bound in Great Britain by
TJ International Ltd, Padstow, Cornwall

Contents

In this unit you will learn about:
- how to introduce yourself (name, nationality, occupation)
- Basic Japanese structure: **X wa Y desu**
- Japanese names and **-san** (Mr, Mrs, Ms, Miss)
- asking and answering yes/no questions
- numbers up to 10
- giving and asking for telephone numbers
- hiragana of Unit 1

      あいうえお   かきくけこ   がぎぐげご

In this unit you will learn about:
- family terms
- numbers 11–99
- how to talk about someone's age
- time-related expressions (date and month, day of the week, etc.)
- how to give and ask for months and dates
- hiragana of Unit 2

      さしすせそ   たちつてと   ざじずぜぞ   だぢづでど

> **In this unit you will learn about:**
> • vocabulary for clothes and accessories
> • how to make the **ta**-form of a verb: [V-**ta**]
> • how to link verb sentences using the [V-**ta**] + **ri** [V-**ta**] +
>   **ri** . . . pattern
> • saying "after . . ." using [V-**ta**] + **ato de**
> • talking about one's experiences in the past
> • kanji of Unit 15
>
> 本、先、生、学、好、何、字、年、車、毎

> **In this unit you will learn about:**
> • talking about one's hobbies and leisure activities
> • how to make the dictionary form of a verb ([V-dic.])
> • how to change a verb into a noun, using [V-dic.] + **koto**
> • describing one's ability or possibility: [V-dic.] + **koto ga
>   dekimasu**
> • kanji of Unit 16
>
> 姉、妹、兄、弟、男、前、後、金、週、曜

Introduction

About Japan and the Japanese language

Japan is a long country with a population of 127 million (in 2013). It consists of four major islands (Hokkaido, Honshu, Shikoku and Kyushu) but the total number of islands is more than 4,000, if smaller ones are included. The area of Japan is 377,950 square kilometres, which is about the same as that of Germany or Zimbabwe. Japan is divided into 47 prefectures including Tokyo, the capital. Japan has four seasons: spring (March–May), summer (June–August), autumn (September–November) and winter (December–February). Each season offers various beautiful scenery and attractions. For example, people enjoy **o-hanami** (cherry blossom viewing parties) in spring, fireworks and local festivals in summer, red leaves in autumn and winter sports in winter. As for language, English is taught as a compulsory foreign language at junior and high schools and bilingual signs can be seen in big cities. However, the primary language is still Japanese. Therefore, if you would like to appreciate Japan and its cultural heritage, it is best to learn Japanese.

Japanese has various dialects such as the Kansai dialect and the Tohoku dialect but the Tokyo dialect is recognized as standard and taught in Japanese language classes. According to a survey conducted by the Japan Foundation (2009), the number of Japanese language learners has continued to increase since 1979 and over 36.5 million people are learning Japanese worldwide. The motivation to learn Japanese varies from "I am interested in the Japanese language itself" to "I want to communicate with people in Japanese," to "I am a big fan of Japanese anime/manga." Whatever your reason for learning Japanese, knowledge of the language will give you a passport to access the rich Japanese culture and broaden your horizons!

Colloquial Japanese

Course content

This course is for anyone who wishes to acquire the ability to speak, understand, read and write basic Japanese for daily use. It consists of 16 units, covering a wide range of topics including introducing yourself, family, food, transportation, work, hobbies, etc. Each unit has two or three dialogues which introduce frequently used vocabulary and grammar points. You will notice the majority of the grammar points are explained not only explicitly but also visually with diagrams which indicate the key structure. This is to help you to grasp the structure at a glance. The grammar explanation is followed by a range of exercises (reading, listening and writing). If you study Japanese in class, we advise you to use the topics given for speaking practice with your classmates, as well.

The textbook uses transliterated Japanese (i.e. romanized Japanese) throughout the units so that you can read and understand Japanese from the beginning. At the same time, you will be gradually introduced to the scripts (hiragana, katakana and kanji) from Unit 1 and the use of Japanese scripts will increase as you study further to encourage you to decode them. We advise you to write the exercise answers in Japanese scripts even if the exercise itself uses transliteration. Writing Japanese scripts will help you to read and write them much more easily and quickly.

The transliteration of Japanese in this course follows the pronunciation, not the actual spelling. Although the majority of Japanese spelling matches its pronunciation, there are some cases where a discrepancy exists between them. See "Long vowel sounds" (pages 7 and 78) for further explanation.

Key features of the Japanese language

- Nouns in Japanese have no singular/plural distinction.
- Japanese predicates have two tenses: past and non-past. The future tense is indicated by the non-past plus a time-related expression such as "tomorrow".

- Japanese predicates have either the affirmative or negative form.
- As for word order, a Japanese sentence always ends with a predicate such as a verb or adjective. Apart from that, the word order is flexible. For example, "I went to the supermarket yesterday" could be [I/yesterday/supermarket/went], [Yesterday/I/supermarket/went], or [I/supermarket/yesterday/went].
- Due to the flexibility of the word order, the function of each word in a sentence is marked by a particle (similar to an English preposition). Particles always come after the word to which they relate.
- Words which are obvious from the context or have already been mentioned are often omitted. For example, when you are asked what your occupation is, the answer could be [teacher/is] as well as [my occupation/teacher/is].
- Japanese has three types of script: **hiragana**, **katakana** and **kanji** (Japanese Chinese characters). The writing can be vertical (from top to bottom) as well as horizontal (from left to right).

Two speech styles: polite and plain style

The Japanese language has two speech styles: the polite style and the plain style. The polite style is used in formal situations such as talking to a stranger or senior whereas the plain style is used in casual situations such as talking with a close friend. While both speech styles are important, this book introduces only the polite style. This is because using plain style speech in an appropriate situation is complicated and using it inappropriately could make you sound impolite and upset the listener. As a beginner in Japanese, it would be advisable to use the polite style in most situations. Once you become confident in elementary Japanese and make Japanese friends, you will gradually learn when you can use plain style speech. You can find more detailed information about the plain style of speech at www.routledge.com/cw/colloquials.

Japanese scripts and pronunciation

Japanese scripts

Japanese has three types of script: **hiragana**, **katakana** and **kanji** (Japanese Chinese characters). Hiragana and katakana are phonetic symbols and each script carries one-syllable-sound, whereas kanji, which was imported to Japan from China in the fifth and sixth centuries, carries both sounds and meanings.

		sound	meaning
Hiragana	わ	**wa**	Ø
Katakana	ワ	**wa**	Ø
Kanji	私	**watashi/shi**	I/private

Hiragana and **katakana** have an identical set of 46 basic characters (see hiragana and katakana tables on pages 3–4). Hiragana is used for the grammatical element (such as a particle, the conjugated part of a verb or adjective), whereas katakana is used for words which originate from foreign words. All three types of script can be seen in one sentence as below:

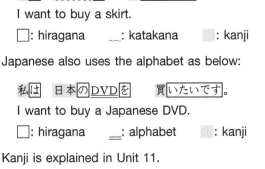

私は スカートを 買いたいです。
I want to buy a skirt.

☐: hiragana ‿: katakana ▓: kanji

Japanese also uses the alphabet as below:

私は 日本のDVDを 買いたいです。
I want to buy a Japanese DVD.

☐: hiragana ‗: alphabet ▓: kanji

Kanji is explained in Unit 11.

Pronunciation

The Japanese language has five vowel sounds: **a**, **i**, **u**, **e** and **o**. Japanese sounds are either a single vowel, a combination of a consonant and vowel, or of a consonant, [**y**] sound plus a vowel, with one exception, **n**, which does not take any vowel.

For example:

consonant + vowel:	**m + a = ma**	**p + o = po**
consonant + y + vowel:	**s + y + u = shu**	**m + y + u = myu**

Each sound has one syllable. Therefore, **a**, **ka** and **kya** take the same length of time to pronounce.

1. Basic syllables: vowel, consonant + vowel and n/m (Audio 1:2–7)

Vowel

a like <u>a</u>h	**akai** red	**aoi** blue
i like <u>i</u>nk	**ima** now	**ishi** stone
u like c<u>oo</u>k (do not round your lips too much)	**uma** horse	**umi** ocean
e like <u>e</u>lephant	**e** picture	**ehon** picture book
o like h<u>o</u>t	**oka** hill	**omoi** heavy

Consonant + vowel

k like <u>c</u>ut	**ka ki ku ke ko**
g like <u>g</u>oal	**ga gi gu ge go**
s like <u>s</u>ea, **sh** like <u>sh</u>e	**sa shi su se so**
z like maga<u>z</u>ine, **j** like <u>j</u>uice	**za ji zu ze zo**
t like <u>t</u>able, **ch** like <u>ch</u>eese, **ts** like ca<u>ts</u>	**ta chi tsu te to**
d like <u>d</u>ark, **j** like <u>j</u>uice, **z** like maga<u>z</u>ine	**da ji zu de do**
n like <u>n</u>oodle	**na ni nu ne no**
h like <u>h</u>ut, **f** like blowing out a candle	**ha hi fu he ho**
b like <u>b</u>oy	**ba bi bu be bo**
p like <u>p</u>ink	**pa pi pu pe po**

Consonant + vowel (cont'd)

m like <u>m</u>uffin   **ma mi mu me mo**
y like <u>y</u>ard   **ya yu yo**
r*   **ra ri ru re ro**
w like <u>w</u>ow   **wa (w)o**[†]
n similar to o<u>ne</u> but more nasal   **n**

* Note that when you pronounce the Japanese "r" sound, do not touch your tongue at the back of the front teeth like the English "l" or curl it like the English "r". The tip of your tongue should be lightly tapping the front palate.

† Whereas **wo** used to keep the "w" sound, it no longer keeps it so its pronunciation is identical to the vowel "o". This hiragana is used as an object marker only (Unit 7).

The following tables show Japanese syllable sounds. Each line has one of the five vowels in common, e.g. all sounds under the "**a**-line" have the "**a**" sound.

	a-line			*i*-line			*u*-line			*e*-line			*o*-line		
	Roman letters	Hiragana	Katakana	Roman letters	Hiragana	Katakana	Roman letters	Hiragana	Katakana	Roman letters	Hiragana	Katakana	Roman letters	Hiragana	Katakana
	a	あ	ア	**i**	い	イ	**u**	う	ウ	**e**	え	エ	**o**	お	オ
k	**ka**	か	カ	**ki**	き	キ	**ku**	く	ク	**ke**	け	ケ	**ko**	こ	コ
s	**sa**	さ	サ	**shi**	し	シ	**su**	す	ス	**se**	せ	セ	**so**	そ	ソ
t	**ta**	た	タ	**chi**	ち	チ	**tsu**	つ	ツ	**te**	て	テ	**to**	と	ト
n	**na**	な	ナ	**ni**	に	ニ	**nu**	ぬ	ヌ	**ne**	ね	ネ	**no**	の	ノ
h	**ha**	は	ハ	**hi**	ひ	ヒ	**fu**	ふ	フ	**he**	へ	ヘ	**ho**	ほ	ホ
m	**ma**	ま	マ	**mi**	み	ミ	**mu**	む	ム	**me**	め	メ	**mo**	も	モ
y	**ya**	や	ヤ				**yu**	ゆ	ユ				**yo**	よ	ヨ
r	**ra**	ら	ラ	**ri**	り	リ	**ru**	る	ル	**re**	れ	レ	**ro**	ろ	ロ
w	**wa**	わ	ワ										**(w)o**	を	ヲ
n/m	**n/m**	ん	ン												

	a-line			i-line			u-line			e-line			o-line		
	Roman letters	Hiragana	Katakana	Roman letters	Hiragana	Katakana	Roman letters	Hiragana	Katakana	Roman letters	Hiragana	Katakana	Roman letters	Hiragana	Katakana
g	ga	が	ガ	gi	ぎ	ギ	gu	ぐ	グ	ge	げ	ゲ	go	ご	ゴ
z	za	ざ	ザ	ji	じ	ジ	zu	ず	ズ	ze	ぜ	ゼ	zo	ぞ	ソ
d	da	だ	ダ	ji	ぢ	ヂ	zu	づ	ツ	de	で	デ	do	ど	ド
b	ba	ば	バ	bi	び	ビ	bu	ぶ	ブ	be	べ	ベ	bo	ぼ	ボ
p	pa	ぱ	パ	pi	ぴ	ピ	pu	ぶ	ブ	pe	ぺ	ベ	po	ぽ	ボ

2. Combined sounds: consonant + ya, yu, yo
(Audio 1:8)

The semi-vowels **ya**, **yu** and **yo** can attach to the following consonants and create a one-syllable sound.

k + y   **kya** like **ki** and **ya** run together
kyu like c<u>u</u>be
kyo like To<u>kyo</u>

g + y   **gya** like **gi** and **ya** run together
gyu like **gi** and **yu** run together
gyo like **gi** and **yo** run together

s + y   **sha** like <u>sho</u>wer
shu like <u>shoe</u>s
sho like <u>show</u>

j + y   **ja** like <u>Ja</u>pan
ju like <u>Ju</u>liet
jo like <u>jo</u>b

ch + y   **cha** like <u>cha</u>mpion
chu like <u>chew</u>
cho like <u>cho</u>p

n + y   **nya** like **ni** and **ya** run together
nyu like <u>knew</u>
nyo like **ni** and **yo** run together

h + y   **hya** like **hi** and **ya** run together
hyu like **hi** and **yu** run together
hyo like **hi** and **yo** run together

b + y   **bya** like **bi** and **ya** run together
          byu like <u>beau</u>tiful but shorter
          byo like **bi** and **yo** run together

p + y   **pya** like **pi** and **ya** run together
          pyu like <u>pu</u>pil but shorter
          pyo like cham<u>pio</u>n

m + y   **mya** like **mi** and **ya** run together
          myu like <u>mew</u> but shorter
          myo like **mi** and **yo** run together

r + y   **rya** like **ri** and **ya** run together
          ryu like **ri** and **yu** run together
          ryo like **ri** and **yo** run together

	consonant + *ya*			consonant + *yu*			consonant + *yo*		
	Roman letters	Hiragana	Katakana	Roman letters	Hiragana	Katakana	Roman letters	Hiragana	Katakana
k	kya	きゃ	キャ	kyu	きゅ	キュ	kyo	きょ	キョ
sh	sha	しゃ	シャ	shu	しゅ	シュ	sho	しょ	ショ
ch	cha	ちゃ	チャ	chu	ちゅ	チュ	cho	ちょ	チョ
n	nya	にゃ	ニャ	nyu	にゅ	ニュ	nyo	にょ	ニョ
h	hya	ひゃ	ヒャ	hyu	ひゅ	ヒュ	hyo	ひょ	ヒョ
m	mya	みゃ	ミャ	myu	みゅ	ミュ	myo	みょ	ミョ
r	rya	りゃ	リャ	ryu	りゅ	リュ	ryo	りょ	リョ
g	gya	ぎゃ	ギャ	gyu	ぎゅ	ギュ	gyo	ぎょ	ギョ
j	ja	じゃ	ジャ	ju	じゅ	ジュ	jo	じょ	ジョ
b	bya	びゃ	ビャ	byu	びゅ	ビュ	byo	びょ	ビョ
p	pya	ぴゃ	ピャ	pyu	ぴゅ	ピュ	pyo	ぴょ	ピョ

In addition to the above combined sounds, katakana has the following combined sounds.

	a-line Roman letters	a-line Katakana	i-line Roman letters	i-line Katakana	u-line Roman letters	u-line Katakana	e-line Roman letters	e-line Katakana	o-line Roman letters	o-line Katakana
sh							she	シェ		
ch							che	チェ		
ts	tsa	ツァ					tse	ツェ	tso	ツォ
t			ti	ティ	tu	トゥ				
f	fa	ファ	fi	フィ			fe	フェ	fo	フォ
v	va	ヴァ	vi	ヴィ			ve	ヴェ	vo	ヴォ
j							je	ジェ		
d			di	ディ	du	ドゥ				
dy					dyu	デュ				
w			wi	ウィ			we	ウェ	wo	ウォ

3. The double consonant character (Audio 1:9)

The double consonant character, 「っ」 or 「ッ」, indicates that a pause exists between the two sounds.

かった bought	かた shoulder	きって stamp	きて please come
ka t ta	ka ta	ki t te	ki te
● ○ ●	● ●	● ○ ●	● ●

Roman letters	kk, ss, pp, tt, gg, etc.
Hiragana	っ (1/4 size)*
Katakana	ッ (1/4 size)*

* Note that when writing these sounds by hand, they should be one quarter of the usual size.

4. Long vowel sounds (Unit 6) (Audio 1:10)

A horizontal line on top of a vowel (ā, ī, ū, ē, ō) means that the vowel is pronounced twice as long as the normal length.

	a-line	*i-line*	*u-line*	*e-line*	*o-line*
Roman letters	ā (or aa)	ī (or ii)	ū (or uu)	ē (or ee)	ō (or oo)
Hiragana	ああ	いい	うう	ええ	おお
				えい	おう
Katakana	アー	イー	ウー	エー	オー

a	**ob<u>a</u>san** middle-aged woman, aunt	ā	**ob<u>ā</u>san** elderly woman, grandmother
i	**oj<u>i</u>san** middle-aged man, uncle	ī	**oj<u>ī</u>san** elderly man, grandfather
u	**k<u>u</u>ki** stalk, stem	ū	**k<u>ū</u>ki** air
e	**<u>e</u>** picture	ē	**<u>ē</u>** yes
o	**k<u>o</u>i** *koi* carp	ō	**k<u>ō</u>i** action

Note that although pronunciation of the Japanese language tends to follow its spelling, the following vowel sequence is pronounced differently (the first sound is pronounced longer and the second vowel disappears):

		Spelling	Pronunciation
えい	ei → ē	**sens<u>ei</u>** teacher	[sensē]
おう	ou → ō	**arigat<u>ou</u>** thank you	[arigatō]

Also note that when the same vowels appear in sequence, a dash (ー) is used for the second vowel in katakana words (e.g. ステーキ [su te e ki], whereas this is not the case in hiragana words (e.g. いいえ [i i e]).

5. Devoicing the "u" and "i" sounds (Audio 1:11)

When the sounds "u" and "i" appear (1) between unvoiced sounds (k, t, s, ts, ch, h, f, p) or (2) at the end of a word and after an unvoiced sound, they are devoiced (whispered). For example, "u" in **tsuki** "moon" and "i" in **eki** "station" are devoiced.

s<u>u</u>sh<u>i</u> sushi   **ts<u>u</u>kue** desk   **k<u>i</u>ssaten** café

6. The syllable "n" sound (Audio 1:12)

"N" is a syllable which represents nasal sounds. It can be pronounced differently as [m], [n], or [ng] depending on what sound follows it. In the examples below, "n" in **manga** and **ongaku** is [ng], whereas "n" in **tempura** is [m] and "n" in **onna** and **densha** is [n].

te n pu ra   de n sha   ma n ga   o n ga ku

tempura   train   manga   music

When "n" is followed by a vowel but used as a syllable, not a consonant, the symbol **n'** is used.

ki n' e n   ki ne n

non-smoking   commemoration

7. Accent pattern: high-low (Audio 1:13)

Japanese is a language with "pitch accent" (high and low). The first and second syllables always have different pitch as below:

ho n   wa ta shi   Ni ho n   Ni ho n go

book   I   Japan   Japanese language

Some words have the same pronunciation but a different high–low accent.

ame   ame   hashi   hashi   shiken   shiken

candy   rain   bridge   chopsticks   personal view   exam

Unit One
Watashi wa Nihon-jin desu
I am Japanese

In this unit you will learn about:

* how to introduce yourself (name, nationality, occupation)
* Basic Japanese structure: **X wa Y desu**
* Japanese names and **-san** (Mr, Mrs, Ms, Miss)
* asking and answering yes/no questions
* numbers up to 10
* giving and asking for telephone numbers
* hiragana of Unit 1

  あいうえお　　かきくけこ　　がぎぐげご

Dialogue 1

How do you do? I am Honda **(Audio 1:14)**

Miss Honda is introducing herself.

HONDA	Hajimemashite.
	Jikoshōkai shimasu.
	Watashi wa Honda desu.
	(Watashi wa) Nihon-jin desu.
	(Watashi wa) Daigakusē desu.
	Dōzo yoroshiku.

MISS HONDA　*How do you do?*
(I will) introduce (myself).
I am Honda.
(I) am Japanese.
(I) am a university student.
Nice to meet you.

Vocabulary

hajimemashite	how do you do?
jikoshōkai shimasu	introduce (oneself)
watashi	I
wa (particle)	[topic marker]
desu	**desu** can be "am", "are" or "is"
Nihon-jin	Japanese (nationality)
daigakusē	university student
dōzo yoroshiku	pleased to meet you.
ohayō (gozaimasu)	good morning
konnichiwa	good afternoon
konbanwa	good evening

 Language points

Basic Japanese structure: X wa Y desu

One of the basic Japanese structures is "**X wa Y desu**". This is equivalent to the English "X is Y". The word order is different between English and Japanese, as you can see below:

I		am	Honda.
Watashi	**wa**	**Honda**	**desu.**
(topic)	(topic marker)	(comment)	

The topic marker **wa** is the indicator of what the sentence is talking about (X = topic). In the above case, the sentence is talking about

watashi "I". Then, the information about the topic (Y = comment) follows in the comment section, in the above case, **Honda desu** "am Honda".

"**X**" and "**Y**" in the **X wa Y desu** structure can take various nouns, such as:

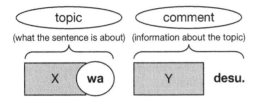

a. **Watashi wa <u>Honda</u> desu.**   I am <u>Honda</u>.
b. **Watashi wa <u>Nihon-jin</u> desu.**   I am <u>Japanese</u>.
c. **Anata wa <u>kaishain</u> desu.**   You are <u>an office worker</u>.

The negative form of **desu** is **dewa arimasen**. Therefore, "I am not Honda" is:

d. **Watashi wa Honda <u>dewa arimasen</u>.**   I <u>am not</u> Honda.

The past affirmative and past negative forms of **desu** are **deshita** and **dewa arimasendeshita** respectively.

Omitting the topic X wa

Once the topic is introduced and shared by the speaker and the listener, it is often omitted in subsequent sentences. In the case of Miss Honda's introduction of herself, she used **watashi wa** the first time but after that, left it out for the second and third sentences. This is because the speaker and listener can assume that both parties know what they are talking about.

Nationality and occupation

Nationality and language (country name + **jin/go**)

To say your nationality, you add **-jin** "people" after the country name. Below is a list of country names. Read them out and you will find how similar many sound to their English equivalents!

Country names

Nihon	Japan	**Kanada**	Canada
Airurando	Ireland	**Kankoku**	South Korea
Amerika	USA	**Marēshia**	Malaysia
Burajiru	Brazil	**Mekishiko**	Mexico
Chūgoku	China	**Nyūjīrando**	New Zealand
Doitsu	Germany	**Oranda**	The Netherlands
Furansu	France	**Ōsutoraria**	Australia
Girisha	Greece	**Porutogaru**	Portugal
Honkon	Hong Kong	**Roshia**	Russia
Igirisu	UK	**Suisu**	Switzerland
Indo	India	**Supein**	Spain
Itaria	Italia	**Toruko**	Turkey

Examples:

Nihon-jin	Japanese	**Igirisu-jin**	British
Chūgoku-jin	Chinese	**Amerika-jin**	American

Watashi wa Kanada-jin desu.   I am Canadian.

A country name followed by **-go** means its language.

Examples:

Nihon-go	Japanese language	**Chūgoku-go**	Chinese language
Furansu-go	French	**Supein-go**	Spanish

Note: "English" is **Ēgo**, not "**Igirisu-go**" or "**Amerika-go**".

Occupation

Here are some occupation-related words:

gakusē	student	**ginkōin**	bank clerk
kyōshi	teacher	**shufu**	housewife
kaishain	office worker	**enjinia**	engineer
isha	doctor	**kankōkyaku**	tourist

Watashi wa gakusē desu.   I am a student.
Watashi wa kōkōsē desu.   I am a high school student.

shōgakusē	primary student	**chūgakusē**	secondary/junior high student
kōkōsē	high school student	**daigakusē**	university student

"○" to make nouns sound politer

Some nouns take "o" in front of them to sound politer.

(o)kuni	country	**(o)namae**	name
(o)sushi	sushi	**(o)mizu**	water
(o)sake	alcohol	**(o)hashi**	chopsticks

Note that when you talk about your country or name, you cannot use **watashi no okuni** or **watashi no onamae** but you should say **watashi no kuni** and **watashi no namae**. (See page 15)

Exercise 1

Translate the following sentences into Japanese.

Example I am Japanese.   *Watashi wa Nihon-jin desu.*

1 I am British.   *Watashi wa*
2 I am a student.
3 I am an office worker.
4 I am not Japanese. I am Chinese.

Exercise 2

Write your self-introduction and say it aloud (try it with your classmates if you have any).

Example *Hajimemashite*.   (How do you do?)

Watashi wa 1. _____ desu.   (your name)
Watashi wa 2. _____ **-jin** desu.   (your nationality)
Watashi wa 3. _____ desu.   (your occupation)
Dōzo 4._____.   (Pleased to meet you.)

Dialogue 2

 What is your occupation? **(Audio 1:15)**

Miss Taylor has recently moved to Japan. To improve her
Japanese, she has found a language exchange partner.
This is her first meeting with her partner.

YAMADA	Hajimemashite. Watashi wa Yamada desu. Anata no (o)namae wa nan desu ka.
TEIRĀ	Hajimemashite. Watashi wa Teirā desu.
YAMADA	Teirā-san wa nani-jin desu ka.
TEIRĀ	Watashi wa Kanada-jin desu.
YAMADA	(Teirā-san no) (o)shigoto wa nan desu ka.
TEIRĀ	Watashi wa ginkōin desu.

MR YAMADA	*How do you do? I am Yamada. What is your name?*
MISS TAYLOR	*How do you do too? I am Taylor.*
MR YAMADA	*Miss Taylor, what is your nationality?*
MISS TAYLOR	*I am Canadian.*
MR YAMADA	*(Miss Taylor,) what is your occupation?*
MISS TAYLOR	*I am a bank clerk.*

 Vocabulary

anata	you
(o)namae	name ("**o**" increases the level of politeness)
nan/nani	what?
-jin	nationality (e.g. -ish -ese, -ian, etc.) person from . . .
ka (particle)	[question marker]
nani-jin	what nationality?
(o)shigoto	work, job, occupation ("**o**" increases the level of politeness)

Language points

Possessive marker no (of)

The marker **no** is equivalent to the English "of" or "s" in "Mike's" and indicates the possessive relationship between two nouns as shown below:

Watashi *no* namae my name
Anata *no* (o)namae your name

Watashi *no* shigoto my occupation
Anata *no* (o)shigoto your occupation

Anata *no* (o)shigoto wa nan desu ka.
What is your occupation?

Japanese names and titles: -san and -sensē

A Japanese name has the surname first, followed by the first name. In the example of "Yamada Takeshi", "Yamada" is his surname and "Takeshi" is his first name. When you speak to this person, you have to add **san** after his name. This **san** is equivalent to English titles such as "Mr", "Mrs", "Ms" and "Miss" and shows your politeness. You can attach **san** after either the surname or first name, or both of them as shown below:

surname + **san**   **Yamada-san**
surname + first name + **san**   **Yamada Takeshi-san**

Note that you cannot use **san** after your own name and the names of your family members.

Another commonly used title is **sensē**. Its original meaning is "teacher" but it is used not only for a teacher but also for a doctor, lawyer, politician, etc. The word **sensē** can be used in the same way as **san** (e.g. **Yamada sensē**) but it can be used alone (e.g. **Sensē, ohayō gozaimasu.**)

Exercise 3

Translate the following English words into Japanese.

1 My name   2 Your occupation
3 Mr Sasaki's occupation   4 My teacher's name

Language point

Asking and answering questions

Yes/no questions

Unlike English, the Japanese sentence does not change its word order when it becomes interrogative. To change "Mr Yamada is a bank clerk" to "Is Mr Yamada/Are you a bank clerk?", you simply add the verbal question marker **ka** at the end of the sentence as below.

a.   **Yamada-san wa ginkōin desu.**
     Mr Yamada is a bank clerk.

b.   **Yamada-san wa ginkōin desu ka.**
     Mr Yamada, <u>are you</u> a bank clerk? / <u>Is Mr Yamada</u> a bank clerk?

How you answer question b is as follows:

b1. **Hai, sō desu.**
     Yes, that is so.

b2. **Hai, ginkōin desu.**
     Yes, (I) am a bank clerk. / Yes, (he) is a bank clerk.

b3. **Īe, ginkōin dewa arimasen.**
     No, (I) am not a bank clerk. / No, (he) is not a bank clerk.

It is common in Japan to address the person to whom you are talking by his or her name (e.g. **Yamada-san**) instead of using **anata** "you", once you know their name. Therefore, sentence b can have two meanings, depending on whether the speaker is asking the question directly to Mr Yamada or not.

Interrogative questions, using "what?"

The Japanese equivalent to the English "what?" has two forms: **nan** and **nani**. Which you should use depends on what sound comes after.

nan: nan-ban what number?, **nan desu ka** what is?, **nan**-sai
how old?, etc.

nani: nani-jin what nationality?, **nani o shimasu ka** do what?, etc.

Similar to the yes/no question, the interrogative question does not
change its word order but you use the interrogative (e.g. **nani, nan**)
in the position of the missing information and add **ka** as shown below:

a. **Yamada-san no (o)shigoto wa ginkōin desu.**
   Mr Yamada's occupation is bank clerk.

b. **Yamada-san no (o)shigoto wa nan desu ka.**
   Mr Yamada, what is your occupation? / What is Mr
   Yamada's occupation?

c. **Yamada-san wa Nihon-jin desu.**
   Mr Yamada is Japanese.

d. **Yamada-san wa nani-jin desu ka.**
   Mr Yamada, what is your nationality? / What is Mr Yamada's
   nationality?

To answer the above questions, you give the answer without either
yes or no.

b1. **Ginkōin desu.**   I am/Mr Yamada is a bank clerk.
d1. **Nihon-jin desu.**   I am/Mr Yamada is Japanese.

Exercise 4

Translate the following sentences into Japanese.

1 Are you an office worker, Mrs Yamada?
2 What is Mr Sasaki's occupation?
3 What is your name?
4 Is your teacher Japanese, Miss Taylor?

Exercise 5

Read out the following questions and then write your own answer in a
full sentence.

1 Anata no (o)namae wa nan desu ka.
2 Anata wa nani-jin desu ka.
3 Anata no (o)shigoto wa nan desu ka.

Dialogue 3

 My telephone number is 093-542-3981 **(Audio 1:16)**

Miss Sato and Mr White are talking.

SATŌ	Howaito-san. Konnichiwa. Genki desu ka.
HOWAITO	Hai, genki desu. Satō-san wa?
SATŌ	Hai, genki desu. Howaito-san no denwa-bangō wa nan-ban desu ka.
HOWAITO	Watashi no denwa-bangō wa 093-542-3981 desu.
SATŌ	093-542-3982 desu ka.
HOWAITO	Īe, 3982 dewa arimasen. 3981 desu.

MISS SATO	*Mr White. Hello. How are you?*
MR WHITE	*Yes, I am fine. What about you, Miss Sato?*
MISS SATO	*Yes, I am fine. What is your telephone number, Mr White?*
MR WHITE	*My telephone number is 093-542-3981.*
MISS SATO	*Is (it) 093-542-3982?*
MR WHITE	*No, (it) is not 3982. (It) is 3981.*

 Vocabulary

konnichiwa	hello, good afternoon	denwa-bangō	telephone number
		nan-ban	what number?
genki desu ka	how are you?	īe	no
hai	yes	dewa	is/am/are not (non-
denwa	telephone	arimasen	past negative
bangō	number		form of verb "be")

 Language points

Numbers (up to ten)

Here, you will learn how to count up to ten. The English words alongside have a similar sound to the number and are there to help you to remember the Japanese numbers. Please note that numbers four and seven have two pronunciations. Most of the time they are interchangeable but sometimes you need to choose a specific one (for example, **shi** and **shichi** are used to say the months April **shi-gatsu** and July **shichi-gatsu**).

0	**zero**	zero	6	**roku**	lock the door
1	**ichi**	witch	7	**nana**	granny, "nana"
2	**ni**	my needle		**shichi**	ship chip
3	**san**	the sun	8	**hachi**	to hatch
4	**yon**	to yawn	9	**kyū**	a long queue
	shi	she	10	**jū**	orange juice
5	**go**	to go			

Giving and asking for telephone numbers

X wa Y desu is used to say "my telephone number is 0123-45-6789" or "Mr Yamada's telephone number is 9876-54-3210" in Japanese, using "my/Mr Yamada's telephone number" as the topic of the sentence as below:

a. **Watashi no denwa-bangō** wa **0123-45-6789** desu.
b. **Yamada-san no denwa-bangō** wa **9876-54-3210** desu.

"**No**" in **watashi no denwa bangō** is the possessive marker **no** as explained on page 15. "-" in "0123-45-6789" is read as **no** as well but does not carry any specific meaning.

0123-45-6789 = **zero ichi ni san no yon go no roku nana hachi kyū**

To ask for a telephone number, you can either simply add the verbal question marker **ka** at the end of the sentence to make a yes/no question (sentence c) or use **nan-ban** (which number) along with **ka** (sentence d).

c. Q: **Anata no denwa-bangō wa 0123-45-6789 desu ka.**
　　 Is your telephone number 0123-45-6789?

　　 A1: **Hai, sō desu.** 　　　　　　　Yes, that is so.
　　 A2: **Īe, sō dewa arimasen.** 　　No, that is not so.

d. Q: **Anata no denwa-bangō wa <u>nan-ban</u> desu <u>ka</u>.**
   <u>What</u> is your telephone number?

A: **(Watashi no denwa-bangō wa) 0123-45-6789 desu.**
   My telephone number is 0123-45-6789.

Exercise 6 (Audio 1:17)

Say the following telephone numbers in Japanese. Then listen to the recording and circle the telephone numbers that you hear.

1 a. 090-824-571   b. 090-824-175
2 a. 080-335-6663   b. 080-335-4443
3 a. 0139-712-4728   b. 0139-712-4782

Exercise 7

Write the answers to the following questions in Japanese. For questions 2 and 3, use the information given below. If you are working with your classmates, ask each other.

1 Anata no denwa-bangō wa nan-ban desu ka.
2 Howaito-san no dewna-bangō wa 784-0394 desu ka. (Mr White: 784-0394)
3 Katō-san no denwa-bangō wa nan-ban desu ka. (Miss Kato: 021-6658)

Exercise 8 (Audio 1:18)

Read out the following text. Then, write ✓ if the statement agrees with the text. Write ✗ if not.

Hajimemashite. Watashi wa Jurī desu. Igirisu-jin desu. XYZ daigaku no gakusē desu. Denwa-bangō wa zero ichi san kyū no roku roku hachi no ni yon ichi nana desu. Dōzo yoroshiku.

1 ( ) Julie is Australian.
2 ( ) She is a university student.
3 ( ) Her telephone number is 0139-667-2417.

Vocabulary

daigaku university

Hiragana of Unit 1

In this unit, you will learn ten new hiragana plus five voiced counterparts. The first five are the Japanese basic vowels and they do not have a voiced version. Practise each hiragana as many times as you want with a spare sheet of paper. To check the stroke order of each hiragana and download an extra exercise sheet, go to www.routledge.com/cw/colloquials.

	1	2	3		1	2	3
a あ	あ	あ	a あ	あ	あ	
i い	い	い	i い	い	い	
u う	う	う	u う	う	う	
e え	え	え	e え	え	え	
o お	お	お	o お	お	お	
ka か	か	か	ga が	が	が	
ki き	き	き	gi ぎ	ぎ	ぎ	
ku く	く	く	gu ぐ	ぐ	ぐ	
ke け	け	け	ge げ	げ	げ	
ko こ	こ	こ	go ご	ご	ご	

Exercise 9

Read out the following Japanese words written in hiragana and write how to read them in the brackets below as shown in the example.

1 あき autumn, fall
(e.g. *a ki*)

2 あい love
(__ __)

3 いけ pond
(__ __)

4 うえ top/above
(__ __)

5 あご jaw
(__ __)

6 かお face
(__ __)

7 きいろ yellow
(__ __ ro)

8 おかね money
(__ __ ne)

9 こむぎこ flour
(__ mu __ __)

Unit Two
Tanjōbi wa itsu desu ka
When is your birthday?

In this unit you will learn about:

- family terms
- numbers 11–99
- how to talk about someone's age
- time-related expressions (date and month, day of the week, etc.)
- how to give and ask for months and dates
- hiragana of Unit 2

さしすせそ　　たちつてと　　ざじずぜぞ　　だぢづでど

Dialogue 1

How old is your father? **(Audio 1:19)**

Mrs Tanaka and Mr Smith are talking about their family members.

TANAKA	Sumisu-san wa nan-sai desu ka.
SUMISU	Watashi wa sanjūsan-sai desu.
TANAKA	Sō desu ka. Jā, Sumisu-san no otōsan wa nan-sai desu ka.
SUMISU	Watashi no chichi wa rokujūgo-sai desu.
TANAKA	Sō desu ka. Watashi no chichi mo rokujūgo-sai desu.

MRS TANAKA	*Mr Smith, how old are you?*
MR SMITH	*I am 33 years old.*
MRS TANAKA	*Really? Then, how old is your father?*
MR SMITH	*My father is 65 years old.*
MRS TANAKA	*Really? My father is also 65 years old.*

Vocabulary

nan	what?	chichi	(one's own) father
-sai	years old	sō desu ka	really?, is that so?,
nan-sai	how old?		I see.
jā	then	mo (particle)	also, too
otōsan	(someone's) father		

Language points

Family terms

Japanese has two words for each family member, one for your own family member and another for someone else's family member.

	Own family member	Other's family member
family	**kazoku**	**gokazoku**
mother	**haha**	**okāsan**
father	**chichi**	**otōsan**
parents	**ryōshin**	**goryōshin**
elder sister	**ane**	**onēsan**
younger sister	**imōto**	**imōtosan**
elder brother	**ani**	**onīsan**
younger brother	**otōto**	**otōtosan**
grandmother	**sobo**	**obāsan**
grandfather	**sofu**	**ojīsan**

Examples:

| **watashi no ane** | my elder sister |
| **Sumisu-san no onēsan** | Mr/Ms Smith's elder sister |

Numbers 11–99

In Unit 1, you learned the numbers from zero to ten (page 18–19). For numbers from 11 to 99, you combine the numbers as below.

11	10 + 1 = **jūichi**			
12	10 + 2 = **jūni**		20	2 × 10 = **nijū**
13	10 + 3 = **jūsan**		30	3 × 10 = **sanjū**
14	10 + 4 = **jūyon**		40	4 × 10 = **yonjū**
15	10 + 5 = **jūgo**		50	5 × 10 = **gojū**
16	10 + 6 = **jūroku**		60	6 × 10 = **rokujū**
17	10 + 7 = **jūshichi**		70	7 × 10 = **nanajū**
18	10 + 8 = **jūhachi**		80	8 × 10 = **hachijū**
19	10 + 9 = **jūkyū**		90	9 × 10 = **kyūjū**

25 = 2 × 10 + 5 = **nijūgo**   68 = 6 × 10 + 8 = **rokujūhachi**

Exercise 1 (Audio 1:20)

Say the following numbers in Japanese. Then listen to the recording and circle the numbers that were read out.

1	23	32	2	41	14	3	17	71
4	85	58	5	60	16	6	19	99

Language point

Talking about someone's age

The Japanese word for "years old" is **-sai** and it attaches to the number.

> a. **Watashi wa <u>29 (nijūkyū)-sai</u> desu.**
> I am <u>29 years old</u>.

To ask Mrs Tanaka whether she is 29 years old or not, you simply add **ka**, the verbal question marker, at the end of the sentence.

> b. **Tanaka-san wa 29 (nijūkyū)-sai desu <u>ka</u>.**
> <u>Are you</u> 29 years old, Mrs Tanaka<u>?</u>

The Japanese word for "how old" is **nan-sai**. To ask someone's age, you do not change the word order but use the **X wa nan-sai desu ka** structure.

   c. Q: **Yamada-san wa <u>nan-sai</u> desu <u>ka</u>.**
      <u>How old</u> is Mr Yamada<u>?</u>

      A: **Yamada-san wa 32 (sanjūni)-sai desu.**
         He is 32 years old.

Note that the pronunciation of the following numbers will change with **-sai**.

   1 year old: **is-sai** (instead of "ichi-sai")

   8 years old: **has-sai** (intead of "hachi-sai")

   10 years old: **jus-sai** (instead of "jū-sai")

   31 years old: **sanjūis-sai**

   18 years old: **jūhas-sai**

   40 years old: **yonjus-sai**

Also note that "20 years old" has two patterns: **nijus-sai** and <u>**hatachi**</u>. This age is very special in Japan because people are treated legally as adults when they reach this age.

Exercise 2

Write how old you and two of your family members are. Remember that you are supposed to use the family term for your own family.

1 (your age)
2
3

Exercise 3 (Audio 1:21)

Suppose you are asking your Japanese friend, Satoshi, how old he and his family members are. First write how you would ask those questions. Then listen to the recording and write their ages in the brackets.

   Example

   Satoshi Q: *Satoshi-san wa nan-sai desu ka.* (28)

   1 Satoshi's father Q: _____ (   )
   2 Satoshi's mother Q: _____ (   )
   3 Satoshi's elder sister Q: _____ (   )
   4 Satoshi's younger brother Q: _____ (   )

Language point

Also mo

Mo means "also". To say "I am also 29 years old", you replace **wa** with **mo** as below.

  a. **Tanaka-san wa 29-sai desu. Watashi <u>mo</u> 29-sai desu.**
    Mr/Mrs Tanaka is 29 years old. I am <u>also</u> 29 years old.

  b. **Watashi wa kaishain desu. Sumisu-san <u>mo</u> kaishain desu.**
    I am a company employee. Mr Smith is <u>also</u> a company
    employee.

 Dialogue 2

 Happy birthday! **(Audio 1:22)**

Mrs Tanaka and Mr Smith are talking in the street.

TANAKA	Sumisu-san, kyō wa Sumisu-san no tanjōbi desu ne. Tanjōbi omedetō gozaimasu.
SUMISU	Arigatō gozaimasu.
TANAKA	Sumisu-san wa nan-sai desu ka.
SUMISU	Watashi wa 33-sai desu. Tanaka-san no tanjōbi wa nan-gatsu nan-nichi desu ka.
TANAKA	Watashi no tanjōbi wa 9-gatsu 17-nichi desu.
SUMISU	Sō desu ka.

MRS TANAKA	*Mr Smith, today is your birthday, isn't it? Happy birthday.*
MR SMITH	*Thank you.*
MRS TANAKA	*How old are you, Mr Smith?*
MR SMITH	*I am 33 years old. What day is your birthday, Mrs Tanaka?*
MRS TANAKA	*My birthday is September 17th.*
MR SMITH	*Is that so?/Really?*

Vocabulary

kyō	today
tanjōbi	birthday
ne (particle)	isn't it?, aren't they?, aren't you? etc.
omedetō (gozaimasu)	congratulations (with **gozaimasu**, this becomes politer)
arigatō (gozaimasu)	thank you (with **gozaimasu**, this becomes politer)
-gatsu	month
nan-gatsu	which month? (*lit.* "what month?")
-nichi	day of the month
nan-nichi	which date? (*lit.* "what date?")

Language points

Date and month

The suffixes for months and dates are **-gatsu** and **-nichi**. In Japanese, the month comes before the date, e.g. **1-gatsu 28-nichi** "January the 28th".

Some months and dates (as marked by *) change their pronunciation as below.

January	**ichi-*gatsu***
February	**ni-*gatsu***
March	**san-*gatsu***
*April	**shi-*gatsu*** (not *yon*-gatsu)
May	**go-*gatsu***
June	**roku-*gatsu***
*July	**shichi-*gatsu*** (not *nana*-gatsu)
August	**hachi-*gatsu***
*September	**ku-*gatsu*** (not *kyū*-gatsu)
October	**jū-*gatsu***
November	**jūichi-*gatsu***
December	**jūni-*gatsu***

*1st	tsuitachi	*17th	jū shichi-*nichi*
*2nd	futsuka	18th	jū hachi-*nichi*
*3rd	mikka	*19th	jū ku-*nichi*
*4th	yokka	*20th	hatsuka/ni jū-*nichi*
*5th	itsuka	21st	ni jū ichi-*nichi*
*6th	muika	22nd	ni jū ni-*nichi*
*7th	nanoka	23rd	ni jū san-*nichi*
*8th	yōka	*24th	ni jū yokka
*9th	kokonoka	25th	ni jū go-*nichi*
*10th	tōka	26th	ni jū roku-*nichi*
11th	jū ichi-*nichi*	27th	ni jū shichi-*nichi*
12th	jū ni-*nichi*	28th	ni jū hachi-*nichi*
13th	jū san-*nichi*	*29th	ni jū ku-*nichi*
*14th	jū yokka	30th	san jū-*nichi*
15th	jū go-*nichi*	31st	san jū ichi-*nichi*
16th	jū roku-*nichi*		

a. **Kyō wa jū-gatsu nijūgo-nichi desu.**
   Today is October 25th.

b. **Watashi no tanjōbi wa shichi-gatsu nijūyokka desu.**
   My birthday is July 24th.

Giving and asking for months and dates: itsu

To give the month and date, you use the **X wa Y desu** structure.
Note that in Japanese, the month comes first, e.g. **10-gatsu** (October)
25-nichi (25th).

a. **Kyō wa 10-gatsu 25-nichi desu.**
   Today is October 25th.

b. **Ashita wa 10-gatsu 26-nichi desu ka.**
   Is tomorrow October 26th?

To ask what the date is, you can use either **nan-gatsu** "what
month?", **nan-nichi** "what day?" or **itsu** "when?". If you use **nan-
gatsu nan-nichi**, the answer should be specifically the month and
date whereas if **itsu** is used, the answer could be date, month, time
or year.

c. Q: **Kinō wa <u>nan-gatsu nan-nichi</u> deshita <u>ka</u>.**
   <u>What date</u> was it yesterday?

   A: **Kinō wa <u>ni-gatsu mikka</u> deshita.**
   Yesterday was <u>February 3rd</u>.

d. Q: **Tomu-san no tanjōbi wa <u>itsu</u> desu <u>ka</u>.**
   <u>When</u> is your birthday, Tom?

   A1: **(Watashi no tanjōbi wa) <u>san-gatsu futsuka</u> desu.**
   My birthday is <u>March 2nd</u>.

   A2: **(Watashi no tanjōbi wa) <u>ashita</u> desu.**
   My birthday is <u>tomorrow</u>.

An interrogative word **itsu** "when?" is also used to ask when something will happen (or happened) like a birthday, national holidays or some specific days.

Exercise 4

Read aloud the following questions. Then say or write the answers in Japanese, using the information below and your own.

1 Anata no tanjōbi wa nan-gatsu nan-nichi desu ka.
2 Anata no okāsan/otōsan no tanjōbi wa itsu desu ka.
3 Jon-san no imōtosan no tanjōbi wa nan-gatsu nan-nichi desu ka.
4 Jon-san no otōsan no tanjōbi wa itsu desu ka.
5 Jon-san no onīsan no tanjōbi wa go-gatsu jūhachi-nichi desu ka.

John's father (November 10th)
John's mother (March 16th)
John's elder brother (April 18th)
John's younger brother (August 14th)
John's elder sister (January 1st)
John's younger sister (December 29th)

Exercise 5 (Audio 1:23)

Listen to the dialogues and write down the birthdays of Tomoko and Satoshi.

1 Tomoko _____
2 Satoshi _____

Dialogue 3

 What date is it next Friday? **(Audio 1:24)**

Mrs Tanaka and Mr Smith are talking about the company's
Christmas party.

SUMISU	Tanaka-san, kaisha no kurisumasu pātī wa itsu desu ka.
TANAKA	Raishū no kin-yōbi desu.
SUMISU	Raishū no kin-yōbi wa nan-gatsu nan-nichi desu ka.
TANAKA	12-gatsu 15-nichi desu.
SUMISU	Sō desu ka. Wakarimashita. Arigatō.

MR SMITH	*Mrs Tanaka, when is (our) company's Christmas party?*
MRS TANAKA	*(It is) next Friday.*
MR SMITH	*Which month and which date is it next Friday?*
MRS TANAKA	*(It is) December 15th.*
MR SMITH	*Really? I see. Thank you.*

 Vocabulary

kaisha	company	**kin-yōbi**	Friday
kurisumasu	Christmas	**wakarimashita**	understand,
pātī	party		understood,
raishū	next week		I see.

 Language point

Days of the week and other time-related words

The suffix for the day of the week is **-yōbi** and "which day of the
week" is **nan-yōbi**.

Sunday	**nichi-*yōbi***
Monday	**getsu-*yōbi***
Tuesday	**ka-*yōbi***
Wednesday	**sui-*yōbi***
Thursday	**moku-*yōbi***
Friday	**kin-*yōbi***
Saturday	**do-*yōbi***
what day of the week	**nan-*yōbi***

day	**kinō** yesterday	**kyō** today	**ashita** tomorrow
week	**senshū**	**konshū**	**raishū**
	last week	this week	next week
month	**sengetsu**	**kongetsu**	**raigetsu**
	last month	this month	next month
year	**kyonen** last year	**kotoshi** this year	**rainen** next year

Senshū <u>no</u> nichi-yōbi   last Sunday
Konshū <u>no</u> getsu-yōbi   this Monday

Exercise 6

Read the following sentences and write ✓ if they agree with the calendar
below and ✗ if not. Today is Thursday, August 14th.

1 ( ) Kyō wa moku-yōbi desu.
2 ( ) Hachi-gatsu mikka wa do-yōbi
    desu.
3 ( ) Raishū no kin-yōbi wa
    nijūni-nichi desu.
4 ( ) Kinō wa getsu-yōbi deshita.
5 ( ) Raigetsu wa ku-gatsu desu.

August						
M	T	W	TH	F	S	S
				1	2	3
4	5	6	7	8	9	10
11	12	13	⑭	15	16	17

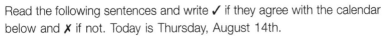

Vocabulary   **A**
C B

deshita   was, were

Exercise 7

Circle the word which does not belong to the category of other words, as in the example.

Example

ashita   kinō   (raishū)   kyō

1	getsu-yōbi	sui-yōbi	kin-yōbi	kotoshi	
2	senshū	ashita	kinō	sengetsu	kyonen
3	nan-yōbi	nan-nichi	moku-yōbi	nan-gatsu	nan-sai
4	raishū	kinō	ashita	raigetsu	rainen

Hint: Are the above words "past" or "non-past"?

Exercise 8 (Audio 1:25)

Read out the following text. Then write ✓ if the statement agrees with the text. Write ✗ if not.

Kyō wa jū-gatsu nijūshichi-nichi desu. Moku-yōbi desu. Kyō wa Yoshiko-san no onīsan no tanjōbi desu. Yoshiko-san no onīsan wa sanjūis-sai desu. Ashita wa tanjōbi pātī desu. Purezento wa chokorēto to kādo desu.

1 ( ) Today is Thursday 17th October.
2 ( ) Today is Yoshiko's elder brother's birthday.
3 ( ) Yoshiko's elder brother is 31 years old.
4 ( ) His birthday party will be held tonight.

Vocabulary

purezento	present
chokorēto	chocolate
to	and (connecting nouns)
kādo	card

Hiragana of Unit 2

In this unit, you will learn ten new Hiragana plus their voiced counterparts. Practise each Hiragana as many times as you want on a spare sheet of paper.

	1	2	3		1	2	3
sa	さ	さ	さ	za	ざ	ざ	ざ
shi	し	し	し	ji	じ	じ	じ
su	す	す	す	zu	ず	ず	ず
se	せ	せ	せ	ze	ぜ	ぜ	ぜ
so	そ	そ	そ	zo	ぞ	ぞ	ぞ
ta	た	た	た	da	だ	だ	だ
chi	ち	ち	ち	ji	ぢ	ぢ	ぢ
tsu	つ	つ	つ	zu	づ	づ	づ
te	て	て	て	de	で	で	で
to	と	と	と	do	ど	ど	ど

Exercise 9

Read out the following Japanese words written in hiragana and write how to read them in the brackets below.

1 すし sushi
(__ __)

2 さしみ sliced raw fish
(__ __ mi)

3 ともだち friend
(__ mo __ __)

4 あした tomorrow
(__ __ __)

5 ちず map
(__ __)

6 すいえい swimming
(__ __ __ __)

7 ちかてつ subway
(__ __ __ __)

8 かぜ cold
(__ __)

9 そうですか Really?
(__ __ __ __ __)

Unit Three

Otearai wa doko desu ka

Where is the toilet?

In this unit you will learn about:

- indicating places: **koko, soko, asoko**
- asking and answering about places: **doko**
- o'clock and minutes: **-ji** and **-pun/-fun**
- telling and asking the time: **nan-ji**
- from and till: **kara** and **made**
- hiragana of Unit 3

  なにぬねの　　はひふへほ　　ばびぶべぼ　　ぱぴぷぺぽ

Dialogue 1

Where is the toilet? **(Audio 1:26)**

Mr White has recently moved to Tokyo to start working for a Japanese company. Today, his friend, Miss Sato, has taken him to her place for the first time.

SATŌ	Howaito-san. Koko wa watashi no uchi desu. Dōzo.
HOWAITO	Dōmo. Anō sumimasen. Otearai wa doko desu ka.
SATŌ	Otearai wa asoko desu.
HOWAITO	Mō ichido yukkuri onegai shimasu.
SATŌ	Hai, otearai wa asoko desu.
HOWAITO	Sō desu ka. Dōmo arigatō gozaimasu.

MISS SATO   *Mr White, here is my home. Please (come in).*
MR WHITE   *Thank you. Um, excuse me but where is the toilet?*
MISS SATO   *The toilet is over there.*
MR WHITE   *Please say it again slowly.*
MISS SATO   *Certainly, the toilet is over there.*
MR WHITE   *I see. Thank you very much.*

Vocabulary

koko	here, this place	**otearai**	toilet
uchi	home, house	**doko**	where?
dōzo	please, here you are	**asoko**	that place over there
dōmo	thank you	**mō ichido**	once more
anō	ah, er, uh, um	**yukkuri**	slowly
sumimasen	excuse me (but)	**onegai shimasu**	please

Language points

Indicating places: koko, soko **and** asoko

Key words for indicating places are **koko** "this place", **soko** "that place near the listener" and **asoko** "that place over there". The **X wa Y desu** structure is used to indicate places.

a. **Otearai wa asoko desu.**   The toilet is over there.
b. **Soko wa watashi no uchi desu.**   That place is my home.
c. **Howaito-san wa watashi no**   Mr White is in my house.
   uchi desu.

Here are some place-related words.

Vocabulary

machi	town, city	**hoteru**	hotel
konbini	convenience store	**eki**	station
sūpā	supermarket	**kūkō**	airport
depāto	department store	**taishikan**	embassy
resutoran	restaurant	**byōin**	hospital
kissaten	coffee shop	**chikatetsu**	underground
ginkō	bank	**yūbinkyoku**	post office
toshokan	library	**kōban**	*koban* (a neighbourhood
gakkō	school		police station)

Asking and answering about places: doko

The Japanese word for "where" is **doko**. To ask where Tokyo station is, you do not change the word order but use the **X wa doko desu ka** structure as below:

a. Q: **Tōkyō eki wa <u>doko</u> desu ka.**
   <u>Where</u> is Tokyo station?

   A: **(Tōkyō eki wa) asoko desu.**
   Tokyo station is over there.

b. Q: **Kimura-san wa <u>doko</u> desu ka.**
   <u>Where</u> is Mr Kimura?

   A: **Kimura-san wa kissaten desu.**
   He is in the coffee shop.

Koko, soko, asoko and **doko** have politer counterparts. The politer versions can often be heard in shops, hotels, restaurants, etc.

	Normal version	*Polite version*
this place	**koko**	**kochira**
that place	**soko**	**sochira**
that place over there	**asoko**	**achira**
where	**doko**	**dochira**

Customer: **Sumimasen. Otearai wa doko desu ka.**
                Excuse me but where is the toilet?

Receptionist: **Otearai wa <u>achira</u> desu.**
                The toilet is <u>over there</u>.

Customer: **Sō desu ka. Dōmo.**
                I see. Thank you.

Exercise 1

Choose the right word and underline it as shown in the example.

> *Example* (Koko <u>Soko</u>) wa otearai desu.
> (<u>That place</u> is a toilet.)

1 Konbini wa (koko asoko) desu.
   (The convenience store is <u>here</u>.)
2 Eki wa (koko soko) dewa arimasen. (Doko Asoko) desu.
   (The train station is not <u>there</u>, but <u>over there</u>.)
3 Igirisu taishikan wa (asoko doko) desu ka?
   (<u>Where</u> is the British Embassy?)
4 Nihon resutoran wa (achira sochira) desu.
   (The Japanese restaurant can be found <u>over there</u>.)
5 Yamamoto-san wa (kochira dochira) desu ka.
   (<u>Where</u> is Mr Yamamoto?)

Exercise 2

Where are they? Answer the questions as shown in the example.

> *Example* Satō-san wa doko desu ka. (in the hotel)
> *Satō-san wa hoteru desu.*

1 Ueda-san wa doko desu ka. (in the hospital)
2 Kimura-san wa doko desu ka. (in the station)
3 Otearai wa doko desu ka. (over there)

Exercise 3 (Audio 1:27)

A male speaker and a female speaker are talking about where Mrs Lee
and Mr Yamada are now. Listen to their conversation and write where
they are in Japanese.

1 Lī-san _____   2 Yamada-san _____

Dialogue 2

What time is it now in Canada? **(Audio 1:28)**

Mr White and Miss Sato are in a cafeteria.

SATŌ	Sumimasen. Howaito-san. Ima nan-ji desu ka.
HOWAITO	Ima, gozen 9-ji han desu.
SATŌ	Sō desu ka. Dōmo arigatō gozaimasu. Howaito-san no (o)kuni wa Kanada desu ne. Kanada wa ima nan-ji desu ka.
HOWAITO	Ēto, Kanada wa ima gogo 5-ji han desu.
SATŌ	Sō desu ka.

MISS SATO	Excuse me, Mr White. What time is it now?
MR WHITE	It is 9:30 a.m.
MISS SATO	Really? Thank you very much. You are from Canada, aren't you? What time is it now in Canada?
MR WHITE	Let me see . . . , it is 5:30 p.m.
MISS SATO	I see./Really?

Vocabulary

ima	now		**han**	half
nan-ji	what time?		**(o)kuni**	country
-ji	o'clock		**ēto**	let me see . . .
gozen	a.m.		**gogo**	p.m.

Language points

O'clock and minutes: -ji and -pun/-fun

"O'clock" and "minute" in Japanese are **ji** and **pun/-fun** respectively. Both come after the number. As for minutes, **fun** is used when the number ends with 2, 5, 7 or 9 and **pun** is used otherwise.

Note that some of the numbers (marked by *) are read differently from what you learned in Unit 1.

O'clock (**-ji**)

1	ichi-*ji*	4	yo-*ji**	7	shichi-*ji**	10	jū-*ji*
2	ni-*ji*	5	go-*ji*	8	hachi-*ji*	11	jū ichi-*ji*
3	san-*ji*	6	roku-*ji*	9	ku-*ji**	12	jū ni-*ji*

Minutes (**-pun**/**-fun**)

-pun				*-fun*			
1	ip-*pun*	6	rop-*pun*	2	ni-*fun*	9	kyū-*fun*
3	san-*pun*	8	hap-*pun*	5	go-*fun*		
4	yon-*pun*	10	jup-*pun*	7	nana-*fun*		

a.m. is **gozen** and p.m. is **gogo**. They come before the time. Sanjup-pun "30 minutes" can be replaced by **han** "half".

2:00 a.m. = *gozen* ni-ji   4:15 p.m. = *gogo* yo-ji jūgo-fun
6:30 a.m. = *gozen* roku-ji sanjup-pun or *gozen* roku-ji han
(**han** means "half")

Telling and asking the time: nan-ji **and** nan-pun

Telling and asking the time uses the **X wa Y desu** pattern, though **X wa** is usually omitted when the local time is asked. "What time?" in Japanese is **nan-ji**. To ask the time, you say **ima nan-ji desu ka**. **Ima** means "now".

X (place) **wa** ima   Y (time)   **desu.**

a. Q: **Sumimasen. Ima <u>nan-ji</u> desu ka.**   Excuse me? <u>What time</u> is
                                                                    it now?
   A: **Ima go-ji desu.**   It is 5 o'clock.

b. Q: **Tōkyō wa ima <u>nan-ji</u> desu ka.**   <u>What time</u> is it now in Tokyo?
   A: **Ima gozen hachi-ji han desu.**   It is 8:30 a.m.

Additional expression:

c. **Ima gozen ku-ji go-fun <u>mae</u> desu.**   It is 5 minutes <u>to</u> 9 a.m.
d. **Ima gogo shichi-ji jup-pun <u>mae</u> desu.**   It is 10 minutes <u>to</u> 7 p.m.

Exercise 4

What time is it now? Read out the time and spell it out, e.g. **ichi-ji**.

1 1:20	2 4:35	3 8:50	4 6:30
5 2:40 p.m.	6 9:05 a.m.	7 11:15 p.m.	8 5:55 p.m.

Exercise 5 (Audio 1:29)

Listen to the conversations and write the time. For 3 and 4, include a.m. or p.m. as well.

1 _____   2 _____

3 _____   4 _____

Exercise 6

Answer the following questions using the information given. If you work with your classmates, ask each other the time in the various places.

Example   UK (1:45 p.m.)
Igirisu wa ima nan-ji desu ka.
Igirisu wa ima gogo 1-ji 45-fun desu.

1 Chūgoku wa ima nan-ji desu ka.
2 Nihon wa ima nan-ji desu ka.
3 Amerika wa ima nan-ji desu ka.
4 Ōsutoraria wa ima nan-ji desu ka.
5 Indo wa ima nan-ji desu ka.

> India (5:40 a.m.), China (7:50 a.m.), Japan (8:25 p.m.),
> America (6:10 a.m.), Australia (3:00 p.m.)

Dialogue 3

From what time to what time are department stores open in Japan? (Audio 1:30)

Mr White plans to go to a Japanese department store this weekend for the first time. Now he asks his friend, Miss Sato, about its opening time.

HOWAITO	Satō-san, Nihon no depāto wa nan-ji kara desu ka.
SATŌ	Futsū gozen 10-ji kara desu.
HOWAITO	Sō desu ka. Jā, nan-ji made desu ka.
SATŌ	Sō desu ne. Futsū gogo 8-ji goro made desu.
HOWAITO	Do-yōbi mo gozen 10-ji kara gogo 8-ji made desu ka.
SATŌ	Īe, do-yōbi wa gogo 8-ji han made desu.

MR WHITE   *Miss Sato, what time do Japanese department stores open?*
MISS SATO   *They usually open at 10 a.m.*
MR WHITE   *Really? Then, until what time are they (open)?*
MISS SATO   *Well . . . , (they are open) until around 8 p.m.*
MR WHITE   *Are they open from 10 a.m. to 8 p.m. on Saturdays as well?*
MISS SATO   *No, they are open until 8.30 p.m. on Saturdays.*

Vocabulary

kara (particle)	from	**made** (particle)	to, until
futsū	usually, normally	**goro**	about, around

Language point

From and till: kara **and** made

Both **kara** "from" and **made** "until" are postpositions.

a. **Ginkō wa gozen 10-ji kara desu.** The bank is (open) <u>from</u> 10 a.m.
b. **Ginkō wa gogo 4-ji made desu.** The bank is (open) <u>until</u> 4 p.m.

To combine the above sentences, you delete the repeated words **desu** and **ginkō** as below:

c. **Ginkō wa gozen 10-ji kara gogo 4-ji made desu.**
    The bank is (open) <u>from</u> 10 a.m. <u>to</u> 4 p.m.

To ask the time, you simply replace the time with **nan-ji** "what time" as shown below:

d. **Ginkō wa <u>nan-ji kara</u> desu ka.**
    <u>From what time</u> is the bank (open)?

Exercise 7 (Audio 1:31)

You will hear a series of conversations about the opening times of the following places. First, write the name of the place in English. Then, listen to the dialogue and write down the time as shown in the example.

Example   Kokura byōin (*Kokura hospital*)
            8:30 a.m.-5:30 p.m.

1 Hoteru no kissaten (   )
2 Sakura toshokan   (   )
3 Sakura sūpā   (   )

Exercise 8

Choose the appropriate interrogatives from the box below and write them in the spaces. You can use the same interrogative more than once.

1 Kissaten wa _____ desu ka.   Asoko desu.
2 Anata no tanjōbi wa _____ desu ka.   11-gatsu 15-nichi desu.
3 Nihon wa ima _____ desu ka.   Gogo 1-ji han desu.
4 Sumisu-san wa _____ desu ka.   Amerika-jin desu.
5 Toshokan wa _____ kara desu ka.   Gozen 9-ji kara desu.
6 Yamada-san wa _____ desu ka.   31-sai desu.

| nan   nan-sai   nan-yōbi   doko   nan-ji   itsu   nani-jin |

Hiragana of Unit 3

In this unit, you will learn ten new hiragana plus their voiced counterparts. Practise each hiragana as many times as you want on a spare sheet of paper.

	1	2	3		1	2	3
na な	な	な	ba ば	ば	ば
ni に	に	に	bi び	び	び
nu ぬ	ぬ	ぬ	bu ぶ	ぶ	ぶ
ne ね	ね	ね	be べ	べ	べ
no の	の	の	bo ぼ	ぼ	ぼ
ha は	は	は	pa ぱ	ぱ	ぱ
hi ひ	ひ	ひ	pi ぴ	ぴ	ぴ
fu ふ	ふ	ふ	pu ぷ	ぷ	ぷ
he へ	へ	へ	pe ぺ	ぺ	ぺ
ho ほ	ほ	ほ	po ぽ	ぽ	ぽ

Exercise 9

Read out the following Japanese words written in Hiragana and write how to read them in the brackets below.

1 なに what
  (__ __)

2 はね wing
  (__ __)

3 にく meat
  (__ __)

4 ねこ cat
  (__ __)

5 ひので sunrise
  (__ __ __)

6 ほうせき jewellery
  (__ __ __ __)

7 せいふく uniform
  (__ __ __ __)

8 ぼうし cap/hat
  (__ __ __)

9 へび snake
  (__ __)

Unit Four

Ano kamera wa ikura desu ka

How much is that camera over there?

In this unit you will learn about:

- indicating things with the demonstrative words **kore** "this", **sore** "that" and **are** "that over there"
- asking questions with the interrogatives **dore** "which one?", **dare** "who?" and **dare no** "whose?"
- giving and asking a price, using **ikura** "how much?"
- numbers up to 1,000,000
- hiragana of Unit 4

  まみむめも　　やゆよ　　らりるれろ　　わをん

Dialogue 1

What is this? (Audio 1:32)

Miss Garcia is working at a Japanese company as an intern. Mr Kimura, her supervisor, is now showing her around one of the rooms, which has many remote controls.

GARUSHIA	Kimura-san. Kore wa nan desu ka.
KIMURA	Sore wa terebi no rimokon desu.
GARUSHIA	Are mo terebi no rimokon desu ka.
KIMURA	Dore desu ka.
GARUSHIA	Are desu.
KIMURA	Ā, are wa eakon no rimokon desu.
GARUSHIA	Sō desu ka. Nite imasu ne.

MISS GARCIA *Mr Kimura. What is this?*
MR KIMURA   *That is a TV remote control.*
MISS GARCIA *Well then, is that one over there also for the TV?*
MR KIMURA   *Which one?*
MISS GARCIA *That one over there.*
MR KIMURA   *Ah, that one over there is for the air conditioning.*
MISS GARCIA *Really? They look similar.*

Vocabulary

kore	this, this one	**are**	that one over there
sore	that, that one (near the listener)	**dore**	which one?
		eakon	air conditioning
terebi	television	**nite imasu**	be similar
rimokon	remote control		

Language points

Indicating things (1): kore, sore **and** are

Kore, **sore** and **are** are demonstrative words which indicate things. Which one you should use is determined by the location of the item from the speaker's viewpoint. The sentence pattern is again **X wa Y desu**, as below:

a. **Kore** wa pen desu.
  This is a pen.

b. **Sore** wa ringo desu.
  That is an apple.

c. **Are** wa Nihon-go no jisho desu.
  That over there is a Japanese dictionary.

Kore, **sore** and **are** can take the position of Y as well.

d. **Watashi no jisho wa kore desu.**
  My dictionary is this one.

Asking questions with interrogatives (1): dore **and** dochira

There are two interrogative words for "which one": **dore** and **dochira**. The former is used when you ask "which one?" among several, while the latter is used when you ask "which one?" out of two. Note that the demonstrative used in the answer is different, as shown in the following examples:

There are *several* remote controls on the table.

Q: **Sumimasen. Terebi no rimokon wa <u>dore</u> desu <u>ka</u>.**
Excuse me. <u>Which one</u> is the remote control for the TV?

A: **(Terebi no rimokon wa) <u>kore</u> desu.**
<u>This one</u> is.

There are *two* remote controls on the table.

Q: **Sumimasen. Terebi no rimokon wa <u>dochira</u> desu <u>ka</u>.**
Excuse me. <u>Which one</u> is the remote control for the TV?

A: **(Terebi no rimokon wa) <u>kochira</u> desu.**
<u>This one</u> is.

The polite versions of **kore, sore, are** and **dore** are **kochira, sochira, achira** and **dochira** respectively. They are also used as the polite versions of **koko** "this place", **soko** "that place", **asoko** "that place over there" and **doko** "where", as learned in Unit 3 (page 36–37).

Various nouns and loan words

Items

pasupōto	passport	**pasokon**	personal computer
tokē	clock, watch	**dejikame**	digital camera
udedokē	wristwatch	**(kētai) denwa**	(mobile) phone
shinbun	newspaper	**hon**	book
megane	(a pair of) glasses	**kaban**	bag
saifu	wallet	**kasa**	umbrella
kutsu	(a pair of) shoes	**bōrupen**	ball-point pen
denchi	battery	**zasshi**	magazine
jisho	dictionary		

Food and drink

kōhī	coffee	**jūsu**	juice
ocha	green tea	**kōcha**	English tea
hanbāgā	hamburger	**niku**	meat
sakana	fish	**yasai**	vegetable
kudamono	fruit	**ringo**	apple

Japanese uses many loan words (i.e. foreign-origin words) and some are used in a shortened form as below:

convenience store	→	**konbiniensu sutoā**	→	**konbini**
personal computer	→	**pāsonaru konpyūta**	→	**pasokon**
digital camera	→	**dejitaru kamera**	→	**dejikame**
remote controller	→	**rimōto kontorōrā**	→	**rimokon**
air conditioner	→	**eā kondishonā**	→	**eakon**

Exercise 1

Translate the following sentences into Japanese.

1 This is my wallet.
2 That one over there is Mr Jones' Japanese book.
3 Which one (out of two) is your dictionary?
4 What is that one over there?
5 This is not my umbrella.

Dialogue 2

That umbrella is mine **(Audio 1:33)**

Miss Garcia found several umbrellas beside her office desk. She wonders whose umbrellas they are and asks questions to Mr Kimura, who is sitting next to her.

GARUSHIA	Kimura-san. Kono kasa wa dare no kasa desu ka.
KIMURA	Sono kasa wa watashi no desu.
GARUSHIA	Sō desu ka. Jā, sono kasa mo Kimura-san no desu ka.
KIMURA	Īe, kono kasa wa watashi no dewa arimasen. Yamada-san no desu.

GARUSHIA	Yamada-san?
KIMURA	Yamada-san wa watashi no tonari no hito desu.

MISS GARCIA	*Mr Kimura. Whose umbrella is this (umbrella)?*
MR KIMURA	*That umbrella is mine.*
MISS GARCIA	*Really? Then, is that umbrella (by your desk) yours, as well?*
MR KIMURA	*No, this umbrella isn't mine. (This is) Mrs Yamada's.*
MISS GARCIA	*Mrs Yamada?*
MR KIMURA	*Mrs Yamada is the person (who is sitting) next to me.*

Vocabulary

kono	this (+ noun)	sono	that (+ noun)
dare	who?	tonari	next to
dare no	whose? (+ noun)	hito	person

Language point

Indicating things (2): kono/sono/ano + noun

When the demonstratives are used with a noun, "re" in **kore/sore/are** becomes "no" as **kono/sono/ano** (+ noun). The interrogative for "which?" is **dono** (+ noun).

kore this + **hon** book	→	**kono** hon this book
sore that + **hon**	→	**sono** hon that book
are that over there + **hon**	→	**ano** hon that over there
dore which + **hon**	→	**dono** hon which book

a. **Kono shinbun wa Nihon no shinbun desu.**
   This newspaper is a Japanese newspaper.

b. **Sono pasokon to ano terebi o kudasai.**
   Please give me that computer and that TV over there.

c. **Yamada-san wa dono tokē o kaimashita ka.**
   Which watch did Mr Yamada buy?

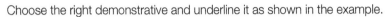

Exercise 2

Choose the right demonstrative and underline it as shown in the example.

Example (Kore <u>Kono</u>) hon wa watashi no hon desu.

1 (Are Ano) hito wa watashi no ane desu.
2 (Sore Sono) wa Nihon no kētai denwa desu ka.
3 Anata no kaban wa (dore dono) kaban desu ka.
4 (Kore Kono) wa nan no denchi desu ka.

Language point

Asking questions with interrogatives (2): dare **and** dare no

The interrogative **dare** is equivalent to the English "who?". When the possessive marker **no** is attached to it (i.e. **dare no**), it means "whose?". The politer counterparts are **donata** and **donata no** respectively. The noun after the possessive marker **no** can be omitted.

a. Q: **Ano hito wa <u>dare (donata)</u> desu <u>ka</u>.**
      <u>Who</u> is that person?

   A: **(Ano hito wa) Yamada-san desu.**
      That person is Mr Yamada.

b. Q: **Kore wa <u>dare no (donata no)</u> hon desu <u>ka</u>.**
      <u>Whose</u> book is this?

   A: **(Sore wa) watashi no (hon) desu.**
      That is my book.

Exercise 3

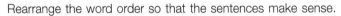

Rearrange the word order so that the sentences make sense.

Example denwa/watashi/no/desu/kono/wa
          Kono denwa wa watashi no desu.

1 desu/ka/kore/wa/no/dare/jūsu *Kore*
2 wa/sono/hito/desu/ka/dare
3 ano/no/jisho/watashi/wa/desu

Exercise 4 (Audio 1:34)

You will hear a series of conversations between a male and a female. They are talking about who owns which item. First write the name of the item in Japanese. Then listen to their conversation and indicate the owner of the item by choosing the correct letter from the box below.

Example   a pair of shoes   *kutsu*   [*c*]

1 a battery   _____   [   ]
2 a pair of glasses   _____   [   ]
3 a watch   _____   [   ]

a. Sumisu-san	b. Yamamoto-san
c. Howaito-san	d. Honda-san

Dialogue 3

How much is that camera over there? (Audio 1:35)

Miss Garcia has come to a department store to buy a new camera. She is now being served by a male shop clerk.

TEN'IN	Irasshaimase.
GARUSHIA	Sumimasen. Ano kamera wa ikura desu ka.
TEN'IN	Ano kamera wa sanman-nisen-en desu.
GARUSHIA	Jā, kono kamera wa ikura desu ka.
TEN'IN	Sono kamera wa niman-kyūsen-kyūhyaku-en desu.
GARUSHIA	Sō desu ka. Jā, kono kamera o kudasai.
TEN'IN	Dōmo arigatō gozaimasu.

SHOP CLERK	*May I help you?*
MISS GARCIA	*Excuse me but how much is that camera over there?*
SHOP CLERK	*That camera over there is 32,000 yen.*
MISS GARCIA	*Then, how much is this camera?*
SHOP CLERK	*That camera is 29,900 yen.*
MISS GARCIA	*Is that so? Well then, can I have this camera, please?*
SHOP CLERK	*Thank you very much indeed.*

Vocabulary

ten'in	shop clerk/assistant	**sen**	(one) thousand
irasshaimase	Welcome, May I help you?	**hyaku**	(one) hundred
		-en	yen (Japanese currency)
ikura	how much?	**-o kudasai**	please give me . . . ,
-man	ten thousand		I will have . . .

Language point

Numbers up to 1,000,000

hyaku (100)   *sen (1000)*   *man (10,000)*

100		**hyaku**	1,000		**sen**	10,000	**ichi** **man**
200	ni	**hyaku**	2,000	ni	**sen**	20,000	**ni** **man**
300*	**san**	**byaku**	3,000*	**san**	**zen**	30,000	**san** **man**
400	yon	**hyaku**	4,000	yon	**sen**	40,000	**yon** **man**
500	go	**hyaku**	5,000	go	**sen**	50,000	**go** **man**
600*	**rop-pyaku**		6,000	roku	**sen**	60,000	**roku** **man**
700	nana	**hyaku**	7,000	nana	**sen**	70,000	**nana** **man**
800*	**hap-pyaku**		8,000*	**has-sen**		80,000	**hachi** **man**
900	**kyū**	**hyaku**	9,000	**kyū**	**sen**	90,000	**kyū** **man**
						100,000	**jū** **man**
						1,000,000	**hyaku** **man**

193 = 100 + 90 + 3   = **hyaku-kyūjū-san**
3,765 = 3000 + 700 + 60 + 5   = **sanzen-nanahyaku-rokujū-go**
84,201 = 80,000 + 4,000 + 200 + 1 = **hachiman-yonsen-nihyaku-ichi**

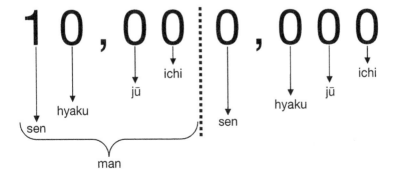

Exercise 5

Read out the following numbers in Japanese and spell them out as shown in the example.

Example 1,204 *sen-nihyaku-yon*

1	159	2	382
3	790	4	1,654
5	3,725	6	98,900

 Language point

Giving and asking a price

The Japanese currency is **en**. To say "This book is 630 yen", you use the **X wa Y desu** structure as below:

a. **Kono hon wa 630(roppyaku-sanjū)-en desu.**
This book is 630 yen.

The Japanese word for "how much?" is **ikura**. To ask the price of a certain item, you do not change the word order but use the **X wa ikura desu ka** structure.

b. A: **Kono hon wa ikura desu ka.**   How much is this book?
B: **(Sono hon wa) 630-en desu.**   That book is 630 yen.

 Exercise 6

Complete the following dialogues between you and a shop clerk as shown in the example.

Example that pair of shoes over there/5,800 yen

YOU   *Sumimasen. Ano kutsu wa ikura desu ka.*
SHOP CLERK   *Ano kutsu wa 5,800-en desu.*
YOU   *Sō desu ka. Jā, ano kutsu o kudasai.*

1 this bag/22,900 yen
   YOU
   SHOP CLERK
   YOU

2 that mobile phone/35,000 yen

YOU

SHOP CLERK

YOU

Exercise 7

Choose the appropriate interrogatives from the box below and write them in the spaces as shown in the example.

Example Kono pasokon wa *dare no* desu ka.
Yamamoto-san no desu.

1 Kore wa _____ no zasshi desu ka.   Kamera no zasshi desu.
2 Sumisu-san no kasa wa _____ desu ka.   Kore desu.
3 Ano hito wa _____ desu ka.   Honda-san desu.
4 Kore wa _____ kamera desu ka.   Nihon no kamera desu.
5 Howaito-san no kōhī wa _____ desu ka.   Kochira desu.
6 Resutoran wa _____ desu ka.   Soko desu.
7 Kono bīru wa _____ desu ka.   480-en desu.

---

nan, ikura, ~~dare no~~, doko, dore, dochira, doko no, dare

Vocabulary

doko no + noun   which company's/country's

Exercise 8 (Audio 1:36)

The following is a monologue by Miss Tanaka. Read it out and complete the following English text accordingly.

Kore wa Nihon no pasokon desu. Kono pasokon wa Kimura-san no desu. Jūniman-en desu. Are wa Igirisu no kētai denwa desu. Ano kētai denwa wa Jonson-san no desu. Kimura-san no kētai denwa dewa arimasen. Ano kētai denwa wa niman-nanasen-en desu.

The item near Miss Tanaka is [1]_____. That item belongs to [2]_____ and cost [3]_____. The item far from Miss Tanaka is [4]_____ and is from [5]_____. Its price is [6]_____.

Hiragana of Unit 4

In this unit, you will learn the last 16 new hiragana. None of them has a voiced counterpart. Practise each Hiragana as many times as you want on a spare sheet of paper.

		1	2	3			1	2	3
ma	ま	ま	ま		ra	ら	ら	ら	
mi	み	み	み		ri	り	り	り	
mu	む	む	む		ru	る	る	る	
me	め	め	め		re	れ	れ	れ	
mo	も	も	も		ro	ろ	ろ	ろ	
ya	や	や	や		wa	わ	わ	わ	
yu	ゆ	ゆ	ゆ		o	を	を	を	
yo	よ	よ	よ		n	ん	ん	ん	

Exercise 9

Read out the following Japanese words written in hiragana and write how to read them in the brackets below.

1 もやし beansprout
(___ ___ ___)

2 ゆみ bow
(___ ___)

3 わに crocodile
(___ ___)

4 わたし I
(___ ___ ___)

5 よぞら night sky
(___ ___ ___)

6 やま mountain
(___ ___)

7 むかし long time ago
(___ ___ ___)

8 ゆうめい famous
(___ ___ ___ ___)

9 ほうれんそう spinach
(___ ___ ___ ___ ___ ___)

10 わたしは　にほんごの　がくせいです。
I am a Japanese language student.
(___ ___ ___ ___ ___ ___ ___ ___ ___ ___ ___ ___ ___ ___ ___。)

Unit Five

Donna ongaku ga suki desu ka

What kind of music do you like?

In this unit you will learn about:

- two types of adjectives: **i**-adjectives and **na**-adjectives
- how to describe things/places/people using adjectives
- adverbs of degree: very/not really . . .
- how to connect sentences using **soshite**, **demo** and **ga**
- how to talk about one's likes and dislikes
- hiragana of Unit 5

きゃ	きゅ	きょ	しゃ	しゅ	しょ	ちゃ	ちゅ	ちょ
にゃ	にゅ	にょ	ひゃ	ひゅ	ひょ	みゃ	みゅ	みょ

Dialogue 1

How is life in Japan? **(Audio 1:37)**

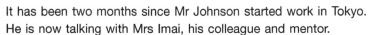

It has been two months since Mr Johnson started work in Tokyo. He is now talking with Mrs Imai, his colleague and mentor.

IMAI	Jonson-san. Nihon no sēkatsu wa dō desu ka.
JONSON	Nihon no sēkatsu wa tanoshī desu.
IMAI	Sō desu ka. Jā, Nihon no tabemono wa dō desu ka.
JONSON	Nihon no kappu rāmen wa totemo oishī desu. Soshite totemo yasui desu.
IMAI	Sō desu ne.

MRS IMAI	*Mr Johnson, how is life in Japan?*
MR JOHNSON	*It is enjoyable.*
MRS IMAI	*Is that so? Then, what do you think of Japanese food?*
MR JOHNSON	*Japanese cup (instant) noodles are very tasty. And they are very cheap.*
MRS IMAI	*That is true/I think so, too.*

Vocabulary

sēkatsu	life		**totemo**	very much
tabemono	food		**oishī** (i-adj.)	delicious, tasty
kappu rāmen	instant noodles		**soshite**	and (sentence link)
tanoshī (i-adj.)	enjoyable		**yasui** (i-adj.)	cheap
dō	how?		**sō desu ne**	That is true, I agree with you.

Language point

Adjectives (1): i-adjectives and na-adjectives

There are two types of Japanese adjective: i-adjectives and na-adjectives. The general rule is that i-adjectives have the "i" sound before **desu**, whereas na-adjectives do not, with a few exceptions (marked by *).

i-adjectives		*na-adjectives*	
ōkī	big	**shinsetsu(na)**	kind
chīsai	small	*[1]**yūmē(na)**	famous
atarashī	new	**nigiyaka(na)**	lively
furui	old	*[2]**kirē(na)**	beautiful,
ī (or **yoi**)	good		clean
warui	bad	**shizuka(na)**	quiet
takai	expensive, high,	**benri(na)**	convenient
	tall	**fuben(na)**	inconvenient
yasui	cheap	**suki(na)**	like
hikui	low	***kirai(na)**	dislike

i-adjectives		*na*-adjectives	
yasashī	easy	**jōzu(na)**	good at
muzukashī	difficult	**heta(na)**	poor at
atsui	hot	**hima(na)**	free (time)
samui	cold (temperature)	***genki(na)**	vigorous,
tsumetai	cold (touch)		lively, fine
omoshiroi	interesting, funny		
tsumaranai	boring, uninteresting		
oishī	delicious, tasty		
mazui	tasteless		

Notes:

*¹ **Yūmē** is spelled as **yuumei** in hiragana.
*² **Kirē** is spelled as **kirei** in hiragana.

Exercise 1

Are they **i**-adjectives or **na**-adjectives? Write "**i**" or "**na**" in the brackets.

Example samui (*I*)

1	jōzu	( )	2	oishī	( )	3	takai	( )
4	shizuka	( )	5	omoshiroi	( )	6	furui	( )
7	shinsetsu	( )	8	nigiyaka	( )	9	fuben	( )
10	ī	( )	11	kirai	( )	12	yasui	( )

Language points

Adjectives (2): non-past/past and affirmative/negative

I-adjectives and **na**-adjectives inflect differently as shown below:

i-adjectives

taka<u>i</u>	**desu**	is/are expensive
taka<u>kunai</u>	**desu**	is/are not expensive
taka<u>katta</u>	**desu**	was/were expensive
taka<u>kunakatta</u>	**desu**	was/were not expensive

Note that "**i**" is dropped from the last three inflections.

na-adjectives

shizuka ~~na~~	desu	is/are quiet
shizuka ~~na~~	dewa* arimasen	is/are not quiet
shizuka ~~na~~	deshita	was/were quiet
shizuka ~~na~~	dewa* arimasendeshita	was/were not quiet

* "**Dewa**" becomes **ja** in colloquial Japanese.

Note that ī as "good" inflects irregularly.

ī desu	good	yokunai desu	not good
yokatta desu	was good	yokunakatta desu	was not good

Adjectives (3): X wa + adjective

A sentence which takes an adjective uses the following pattern:

a. **Kono hon wa** takai desu.
This book is expensive.

b. **Ano hon wa** omoshirokatta desu.
That book was funny.

c. **Yamada-san wa** shinsetsu desu.
Mr Yamada is kind.

The interrogative for adjectives is **dō**, equivalent to English "how".

d. Q: **Sono hon wa** dō desu ka.
How is that book?

A: (**Kono hon wa**) omoshiroi desu.
This book is interesting.

e. Q: **Kinō no pātī wa** dō deshita ka.
How was yesterday's party?

A: (**Kinō no pātī wa**) nigiyaka deshita.
It was lively.

Exercise 2

Complete the following adjective form table.

		Non-past affirmative	Non-past negative	Past affirmative	Past negative
i	atarashī desu		1)	2)	3)
	takai desu		4)	5)	6)
	samui desu		7)	8)	9)
na	hima desu		10)	11)	12)
	genki desu		13)	14)	15)
	benri desu		16)	17)	18)

Exercise 3

Complete the following sentences as shown in the example.

Example Watashi wa ___*genki desu.*___ (I am fine.)

1 Kinō wa _____ (It was cold yesterday.)
2 Kono jisho wa _____ (This dictionary is not good.)
3 (O)sushi wa _____ (Sushi is not cheap.)
4 Tōkyō wa _____ (Tokyo was lively.)
5 Kyōto no hoteru wa _____ (The hotel that I stayed at in Kyoto was not expensive.)

Language point

Adverbs of degree: very/not really . . .

The adverb of degree is placed right before the adjective. Note that **amari** "not so much" and **zenzen** "not at all" always take the negative form of the adjective (★).

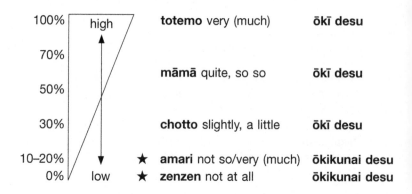

100% high	**totemo** very (much)	**ōkī desu**
70%	**māmā** quite, so so	**ōkī desu**
50%		
30%	**chotto** slightly, a little	**ōkī desu**
10–20%	★ **amari** not so/very (much)	**ōkikunai desu**
0% low	★ **zenzen** not at all	**ōkikunai desu**

a. **Kono machi wa *totemo* ōkī desu.**
This town is *very* big.

b. **Kono machi wa *māmā* ōkī desu.**
This town is *reasonably* big.

c. **Kono machi wa *chotto* ōkī desu.**
This town is *a bit* big.

d. **Kono machi wa *amari* <u>ōkikunai desu</u>.**
This town <u>is *not so* big</u>.

e. **Kono machi wa *zenzen* <u>ōkikunai desu</u>.**
This town <u>is *not* big *at all*</u>.

Exercise 4

Answer the following questions, using the adjectives given in the brackets.
Use the adverbs of degree (**totemo**, **māmā**, **chotto**, **amari** and **zenzen**)
as well.

> *Example* Nihon-go wa omoshiroi desu ka. (yes, very much)
> *Hai, Nihon-go wa totemo omoshiroi desu.*

1 Kinō no tenki wa yokatta desu ka. (no, not good at all)
2 Hiragana wa dō desu ka. (not so difficult)
3 Nihon no tabemono wa dō desu ka. (a little bit expensive)

tenki weather

Dialogue 2

What kind of town is Asakusa? **(Audio 1:38)**

Mr Johnson and Mrs Imai have just finished a meeting and are now walking back to the office.

JONSON	Imai-san no uchi wa doko desu ka.
IMAI	Asakusa desu.
JONSON	Asakusa wa donna machi desu ka.
IMAI	Totemo omoshiroi machi desu. Soshite nigiyakana machi desu.
JONSON	Sō desu ka. Ī desu ne.

MR JOHNSON	*Where is your home, Mrs Imai?*
MRS IMAI	*It is in Asakusa.*
MR JOHNSON	*What kind of town/city is Asakusa?*
MRS IMAI	*It is a very interesting city. And it is a very lively city.*
MR JOHNSON	*Really? That is good.*

Vocabulary

Asakusa	Asakusa, a place in Tokyo
donna + noun	what kind of? (+ noun)

Language point

Adjectives (4): i/na-**adjective + noun**

i-adjective + noun

When i-adjectives modify a noun, **desu** is dropped as below:

<u>omoshiroi</u> **hon**	an <u>interesting</u> book
<u>takai</u> **hon**	an <u>expensive</u> book

na-adjective + noun

When **na**-adjectives modify a noun, **desu** is dropped and **na** is inserted as below:

kirē *na* hon   a <u>beautiful</u> book
yūmē *na* hon   a <u>famous</u> book

The tense and affirmative/negative can be expressed at the end of the sentence.

a. **Ashita wa ī hi <u>desu</u>.**   Tomorrow <u>is</u> a good day.
b. **Kinō wa ī hi <u>deshita</u>.**   Yesterday <u>was</u> a good day.

The interrogative for an adjective + noun is **donna**, equivalent to the English "what kind of". Note that **donna** is always followed by a noun.

c. Q: **Nihon wa <u>donna kuni</u> desu <u>ka</u>.**
   <u>What kind of country</u> is Japan?

   A: **(Nihon wa) kirēna kuni desu.**
   It is a beautiful country.

d. Q: **Kinō no ēga wa <u>donna ēga</u> deshita <u>ka</u>.**
   <u>What kind of film</u> was yesterday's film?

   A: **(Kinō no ēga wa) omoshiroi ēga deshita.**
   It was an enjoyable film.

Exercise 5

Choose the correct answer and circle it.

1 (a. oishī   b. oishīna) tabemono   (*delicious* food)
2 (a. suki   b. sukina) ongaku   (*favourite* music)
3 (a. omoshiroi   b. omoshiroina) ēga   (an *interesting* film)
4 (a. kirē   b. kirēna) hana   (a *beautiful* flower)
5 (a. warui   b. waruina) tenki   (*bad* weather)
6 (a. shinsetsu   b. shinsetsuna) hito   (a *kind* person)

Vocabulary

ongaku	music	**hana**	flower
ēga	film		

Language point

Connecting sentences: soshite, demo **and** ga

Soshite connects sentences which have the same value (i.e. positive–positive or negative–negative) or a casual relationship (i.e. I am Japanese. And I am a student), whereas **demo** and **ga** link sentences which have an opposite or contrastive meaning. Note that a sentence before **soshite** and **demo** must be ended firmly, but this is not the case with **ga**.

   a. **Imai-san wa genki desu. <u>Soshite</u> shinsetsu desu.**
      Mrs Imai is energetic. <u>And</u> she is kind.

   b. **Nihon-go wa omoshiroi desu. <u>Demo</u> muzukashī desu.**
      Japanese is interesting. <u>But</u> it is difficult.

   c. **Nihon-go wa omoshiroi desu <u>ga</u>, muzukashī desu.**
      Japanese is interesting <u>but</u> difficult.

Dialogue 3

Do you like Russian music? **(Audio 1:39)**

During a lunch break, Mr Johnson is browsing in a CD store, when Mrs Imai happens to enter and sees him examining one of the CDs.

IMAI	Ā, Jonson-san. Sore wa doko no ongaku desu ka.
JONSON	Kore wa Roshia no ongaku desu.
IMAI	Jonson-san wa Roshia no ongaku ga suki desu ka.
JONSON	Hai, daisuki desu. Roshia no ongaku wa totemo kirē desu.

MRS IMAI	*Oh, Mr Johnson. What country's music is that?*
MR JOHNSON	*This is Russian music.*
MRS IMAI	*Do you like Russian music, Mr Johnson?*
MR JOHNSON	*Yes, I like it very much. Russian music is very beautiful.*

Vocabulary

ā	oh	**daisuki(na)**	like very much
ga (particle)	[subject marker]	**(na**-adj.)	

Language point

Likes and dislikes

The Japanese equivalent of "like" and "dislike" are **suki(na)** and **kirai(na)** respectively. Unlike English, they are adjectives and inflect in the same way as **na**-adjectives. The **X wa Y ga** adjective structure is used to express one's likes and dislikes, with X indicating who has such a feeling and Y indicating towards what or whom such a feeling is directed. Y is marked by **ga**, the subject marker.

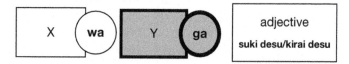

a. **Watashi <u>wa</u> Nihon no ongaku <u>ga suki desu</u>.**
I <u>like</u> Japanese music.

b. **Jonson-san <u>wa</u> (o)sushi <u>ga</u> amari <u>suki dewa arimasen</u>.**
Mr Johnson <u>does not like</u> sushi much.

Jōzu(na) and **heta(na)**, which mean "be good at" and "be poor at", also take the above pattern.

c. **Imai-san <u>wa</u> Ēgo <u>ga</u> totemo <u>jōzu desu</u>.**
Mrs Imai <u>is</u> very <u>good at</u> English.

Exercise 6

What does Karen like/dislike? What is she good/poor at?

Example (like/tennis) *Karen-san wa tenisu ga suki desu.*

1 (like/music)
2 (dislike/TV)
3 (be good at/piano)
4 (be poor at/sports)

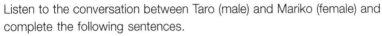

tenisu	tennis	supōtsu	sports
piano	piano		

Exercise 7 (Audio 1:40)

Listen to the conversation between Taro (male) and Mariko (female) and complete the following sentences.

1 Taro likes _____ but dislikes _____.
2 Mariko is good at _____ but poor at _____.

Exercise 8 (Audio 1:41)

Michael (Maikeru) sent the following postcard to Michiko, his Japanese friend. Read out his letter and write ✓ if the statement agrees with the content and ✗ if not.

> Michiko-san e,
>
> Genki desu ka. Watashi wa genki desu. Tōkyō wa dō desu ka. Watashi wa ima Ōsaka desu. Ōsaka wa totemo omoshiroi machi desu. Tenki wa māmā desu. Kinō wa samukatta desu ga, kyō wa samukunai desu. Watashi wa kinō okonomiyaki o tabemashita. Totemo oishikatta desu. Soshite yasukatta desu. Watashi wa ashita Kyōto desu. Tanoshimi desu.
>
> Jā, mata.
>
>   Maikeru yori

[name] + e	dear (used in a letter)	o tabemashita	ate (something)
		tanoshimi(na)	to look forward to
Tōkyō	Tokyo	(na-adj.)	
Ōsaka	Osaka	mata	again
okonomiyaki	Japanese pizza	[name] + yori	from (used in a letter)

1 ( ) Michael thinks Osaka is a very interesting place.
2 ( ) The weather has been good for the last couple of days in
  Osaka.
3 ( ) Michael tried Japanese pizza, which he thought was tasty
  but slightly expensive.

Hiragana of Unit 5

"や" "ゆ" and "よ" can be attached to another hiragana to create a
combined sound. For example, き (**ki**) + や (**ya**) becomes きゃ (**kya**)
and に (**ni**) + ゆ (**yu**) becomes にゅ (**nyu**). In such cases, "や", "ゆ" and
"よ" are written one quarter of the usual size.

	1	2	3		1	2	3
kya	きゃ	きゃ	きゃ	nya	にゃ	にゃ	にゃ
kyu	きゅ	きゅ	きゅ	nyu	にゅ	にゅ	にゅ
kyo	きょ	きょ	きょ	nyo	にょ	にょ	にょ
sha	しゃ	しゃ	しゃ	hya	ひゃ	ひゃ	ひゃ
shu	しゅ	しゅ	しゅ	hyu	ひゅ	ひゅ	ひゅ
sho	しょ	しょ	しょ	hyo	ひょ	ひょ	ひょ
cha	ちゃ	ちゃ	ちゃ	mya	みゃ	みゃ	みゃ
chu	ちゅ	ちゅ	ちゅ	myu	みゅ	みゅ	みゅ
cho	ちょ	ちょ	ちょ	myo	みょ	みょ	みょ

Exercise 9

Read out the following Japanese words written in hiragana and write how to read them in the brackets below.

1 かしゅ singer
 (__ __)

2 きょう today
 (__ __)

3 しゃちょう company CEO
 (__ __ __)

4 ぎゅうにゅう milk
 (__ __ __ __)

5 きょうかしょ textbook
 (__ __ __ __)

6 ちゅうしゃじょう car park
 (__ __ __ __ __)

Unit Six

Watashi wa rainen Nihon e ikimasu

I will go to Japan next year

In this unit you will learn about:

- how to conjugate a verb (non-past and past)
- how to talk about where one goes, comes and returns to
- saying "to" (somewhere), "by" (method of transportation) and "with" (someone)
- terms for places, methods of transportation and time
- hiragana: double consonant sound and long vowel sound

Dialogue 1

Where will you go this winter? (Audio 1:42)

Miss Walker is an exchange student at a Japanese university in Tokyo. She is now talking with her Japanese friend, Mr Suzuki, about the winter holiday.

SUZUKI	Wōkā-san wa kotoshi no fuyu doko e ikimasu ka.
WŌKĀ	Watashi wa Igirisu e kaerimasu. Suzuki-san wa?
SUZUKI	Watashi wa doko(e)mo ikimasen. Demo watashi wa rainen Igirisu e ikimasu.
WŌKĀ	Itsu ikimasu ka.
SUZUKI	Rainen no natsu ikimasu.

MR SUZUKI	*Where are you going this winter, Miss Walker?*
MISS WALKER	*I am going back to the UK. How about you?*

MR SUZUKI	*I am not going anywhere. But I am going to the UK next year.*
MISS WALKER	*When are you going?*
MR SUZUKI	*I am going (there) next summer.*

Vocabulary

fuyu	winter	**doko(e)mo**	nowhere, anywhere
e (particle)	to [direction marker]	**ikimasen**	do not (does not) go
ikimasu	to go	**natsu**	summer
kaerimasu	to go back, return		

Language points

Places

In Units 1 and 3 you learned various "place" nouns such as those below:

Nihon	Japan	**yūbinkyoku**	post office
Igirisu	UK	**gakkō**	school
Amerika	USA	**kaisha**	company
Chūgoku	China	**uchi**	house

In this unit, you will learn more place-related nouns.

Buildings		*Area*	
dōbutsuen	zoo	**ajia**	Asia
suizokukan	aquarium	**yōroppa**	Europe
hakubutsukan	museum	**gaikoku**	foreign country
bijutsukan	art gallery		
kenchō	prefectural office		
shiyakusho	city hall, town hall		

Going places (1): verb conjugation

Unit 6 introduces three Japanese verbs:

ikimasu	to go
kimasu	to come
kaerimasu	to go back, return

Iki-, **ki-** and **kaeri-** are the verb stems and remain unchanged whereas **masu** changes according to the meaning as shown below:

iki *masu*	go	(non-past affirmative)
iki *masen*	do/does not go	(non-past negative)
iki *mashita*	went	(past affirmative)
iki *masendeshita*	did not go	(past negative)

Exercise 1

Write the following verbs appropriately as in the example.

Example (went) *ikimashita*

1 (came)
3 (returned)
5 (do not come)

2 (did not go)
4 (will come)
6 (will go back)

Language points

Going places (2): direction marker e + go/come/return

The particle **e** is a direction marker and indicates which direction one moves towards. To say where someone goes, you use the following pattern:

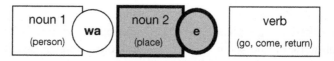

a. **Watashi wa shiyakusho e ikimasu.**   I will go to the city hall.
b. **Kimura-san wa uchi e kaerimashita.**   Mr Kimura went home.

To ask where someone goes, you use **doko** "where?" in the position of Noun 2.

c. Q: **Jonson-san wa doko e ikimashita ka.**
     Where has Mr Johnson gone?

A: **(Jonson-san wa) bijutsukan e ikimashita.**
     He has gone to the art gallery.

Note that the spelling for the particle **e** is 〜 (**he**).

わたしは　しやくしょ<u>〜</u>　いきます。　　I go to the city hall.

Time-related vocabulary

In Unit 2, you learned time-related vocabulary such as "day of the week", "month", "date", etc. Here is some new vocabulary:

Seasons and holidays

haru	spring	**fuyu**	winter
natsu	summer	**yasumi**	holiday
aki	autumn	**natsu-yasumi**	summer holiday

Words with **mai** (every)

mainichi	every day	**maishū**	every week
maiasa	every morning	**maitsuki**	every month
maiban	every evening	**maitoshi**	every year

Others

shūmatsu	(this/last) weekend	**saikin**	recently

Going places (3): when

The diagram below shows where to put the time-related information in a sentence:

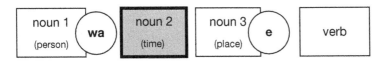

a. **Watashi wa <u>shūmatsu</u> dōbutsuen e ikimasu.**
   I go to the zoo at the <u>weekend</u>.

b. **Watashi wa <u>natsu-yasumi</u> yōroppa e ikimashita.**
   I went to Europe during <u>the summer holiday</u>.

To ask when one goes to a certain place, you use **itsu** "when" in the place of the time.

> c. Q: **Maiku-san wa <u>itsu</u> Kyōto e ikimashita <u>ka</u>.**
> <u>When</u> did you go to Kyoto, Mike?
>
> A: **(Watashi wa) <u>kinō</u> ikimashita.**
> I went there <u>yesterday</u>.

Exercise 2

Translate the following English sentences into Japanese.

1 I go to Japan every year.
2 My friend didn't come to my house yesterday.
3 Mr Suzuki will go to the museum this weekend.
4 Do you go to school every day, Miss Akita?

Exercise 3 (Audio 1:43)

Listen to the conversation and find out where and when Yoko and Mike are going.

1 Yoko   a) what city: _____   b) when: _____
2 Mike   a) what city: _____   b) when: _____

Dialogue 2

I went to the art gallery with my friend (Audio 1:44)

Mr Suzuki and Miss Walker are talking about what they did yesterday.

WŌKĀ	Suzuki-san wa kinō doko e ikimashita ka.
SUZUKI	Watashi wa kinō bijutsukan e ikimashita.
WŌKĀ	Dare to ikimashita ka.
SUZUKI	Tomodachi to ikimashita.
WŌKĀ	Nani de ikimashita ka.
SUZUKI	Densha de ikimashita.
WŌKĀ	Sō desu ka.

MISS WALKER	*Where did you go yesterday, Mr Suzuki?*
MR SUZUKI	*I went to the art gallery yesterday.*
MISS WALKER	*Who did you go there with?*
MR SUZUKI	*I went there with my friend.*
MISS WALKER	*How did you go there?*
MR SUZUKI	*I went there by train.*
MISS WALKER	*Really?*

Vocabulary

dare to	with whom?		**nani de**	by what? how?
to (particle)	with		**de** (particle)	by (means or tools)
tomodachi	friend(s)		**densha**	electric train

Language points

Going places (4): how

The particle which indicates the means of transportation or method
is **de**.

a. **Watashi wa <u>basu de</u> uchi e kaerimashita.**
   I went home <u>by bus</u>.

b. **Watashi wa mainichi <u>jitensha de</u> eki e ikimasu.**
   I go to the station <u>by bicycle</u> every day.

To ask the means of transportation or method, either **nani de** or **nan
de** is used.

c. Q: **Maiku-san wa <u>nani de</u> kaisha e ikimasu <u>ka</u>.**
      <u>How</u> do you commute to the company, Mike?

   A: **Watashi wa <u>densha de</u> kaisha e ikimasu.**
      I go there <u>by train</u>.

Note that "on foot" and "running" do not take **de** but are **aruite** and **hashitte** respectively.

>d. **Watashi wa <u>aruite</u> gakkō e ikimasu.**
>I go to school <u>on foot</u>.

Here is a list of words for means of transportation:

kuruma	car	**densha**	train
ōtobai	motorcycle	**basu**	bus
shinkansen	bullet train	**takushī**	taxi
hikōki	aeroplane	**jitensha**	bicycle

Going places (5): with whom

The particle **to** is equivalent to the English "with" and is used as below:

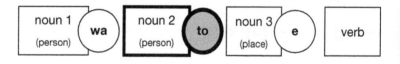

>a. **Watashi wa <u>Lī-san to</u> toshokan e ikimasu.**
>I go to the library with <u>Miss Lee</u>.

The interrogative to ask "who?" is **dare**. And "with whom?" is **dare to**.

>b. Q: **Maiku-san wa kinō <u>dare to</u> resutoran e ikimashita <u>ka</u>.**
> <u>With whom</u> did you go to the restaurant yesterday, Mike?

>A: **Watashi wa <u>tomodachi to</u> ikimashita.**
> I went there <u>with my friends</u>.

Note that **de** is used instead of **to** when indicating "with how many people".

>**hitori de**   alone   **futari de**   (as) two people

>c. Q: **Maiku-san wa <u>tomodachi to</u> sūpā e ikimasu ka.**
> Do you go to the supermarket <u>with your friends</u>, Mike?

>A: **Īe, (watashi wa) <u>hitori de</u> ikimasu.**
> No, I go there <u>on my own</u>.

Exercise 4

Answer the following questions, using the information about Mrs Imai's holiday plans for this year.

When	*How*	*With whom*	*Where*
Spring holiday	by train	with friends	London
Summer holiday	by aeroplane	with family	Italy

Example Imai-san wa haru-yasumi *doko e* ikimasu ka.
Rondon e ikimasu.

1 Imai-san wa haru-yasumi *nani de* Rondon e ikimasu ka.
2 Imai-san wa haru-yasumi *dare to* Rondon e ikimasu ka.
3 Imai-san wa *itsu* Itaria e ikimasu ka.
4 Imai-san wa *nani de* Itaria e ikimasu ka.
5 Imai-san wa *dare to* Itaria e ikimasu ka.

Exercise 5 (Audio 1:45)

Read out the following sentences and translate them into English.

1 わたしは きのう ひとりで あるいて ゆうびんきょくへ いきました。
2 たなかさんは まいにち ともだちと でんしゃで がっこうへ いきます。

Dialogue 3

How long does it take from London to Tokyo?
(Audio 1:46)

Mr Suzuki is asking Miss Walker about the distance between Japan and the UK.

SUZUKI	Wōkā-san no Igirisu no uchi wa doko desu ka.
WŌKĀ	Rondon desu.
SUZUKI	Rondon kara Tōkyō made hikōki de donokurai kakarimasu ka.
WŌKĀ	Sō desu ne. Rondon kara Tōkyō made 10-jikan gurai kakarimasu.
SUZUKI	Tōi desu ne.

MR SUZUKI	*Miss Walker, where is your home in the UK?*
MISS WALKER	*It is in London.*
MR SUZUKI	*How long does it take from London to Tokyo by plane?*
MISS WALKER	*Well, it takes around 10 hours.*
MR SUZUKI	*It is a long way, isn't it?*

 ## Vocabulary

Rondon	London	**kakarimasu**	to take (time/cost)
kara (particle)	from	**-jikan**	hours
made (particle)	to	**gurai** (or **kurai**)	about, around
donokurai	how long? (time)	**tōi** (i-adj.)	far

 # Language point

Going places (6): how long

"How long?" in Japanese is **donokurai**. To ask how long it is from X to Y, you say **X kara Y made donokurai desu ka**.

   a. Q: **Tōkyō kara Ōsaka made <u>donokurai</u> desu <u>ka</u>.**
      <u>How long</u> does it take from Tokyo to Osaka?

      A: **Shinkansen de <u>2-jikan han</u> desu.**
      It is <u>2.5 hours</u> by bullet train.

The answer could take various units of time, such as:

year	**-nen(kan)**	day	**-nichi (kan)**
month	**-kagetsu(kan)**	hour	**-jikan**
week	**-shū(kan)**	minute	**-fun/pun**

Gurai (or **kurai**) means "about, approximately" and comes after the unit of time. Although they are now used interchangeably, the general rule is that **gurai** follows nouns whereas **kurai** is used after pronouns such as **kono**, **sono**, or **ano**.

   b. **Shinkansen de <u>2-jikan han gurai</u> (or <u>kurai</u>) desu.**
      It is <u>about 2.5 hours</u> by bullet train.

Desu in the above pattern can be replaced by the verb **kakarimasu** "to take".

  c. **Tōkyō kara Ōsaka made shinkansen de 2-jikan han kurai kakarimasu.**
    It <u>takes</u> about 2.5 hours from Tokyo to Osaka by bullet train.

Exercise 6

Choose the appropriate interrogatives from the box below and write them in the spaces as shown in the example.

  Example Kono pasokon wa *dare no* desu ka.
               Yamamoto-san no desu.

1 Imai-san wa _____ e ikimasu ka.
    Shiyakusho e ikimasu.

2 _____ to ikimasu ka.
    Hitori de ikimasu.

3 Jonson-san wa _____ Kyōto e ikimashita ka.
    Shūmatsu ikimashita.

4 _____ de ikimashita ka.
    Densha de ikimashita.

5 Ōsaka kara Kyōto made _____ deshita ka.
    Densha de 15-fun kurai deshita.

nani	donokurai	~~dare no~~	doko	dare	itsu

Exercise 7

Put the appropriate word in the space as shown in the example. Write ✗ if nothing is required.

  Example Watashi wa shūmatsu sūpā *e* ikimashita.

1 Tanaka-san wa Jonson-san ____ uchi e kaerimashita.
2 Watashi wa basu ____ densha ____ kaisha e ikimasu.
3 Yōko-san wa hitori ____ gakkō e ikimasu.
4 Maiku-san wa mainichi aruite ____ kōen e ikimasu.
5 Watashi wa saikin kazoku ____ gaikoku ____ ikimashita.

Vocabulary

kōen   park

Hiragana of Unit 6

Long vowel sound

A vowel with the symbol ‾, pronounced longer than its counterpart without the symbol, is spelled out with two hiragana. The second hiragana is usually from the same vowel row as the first one, e.g. あ あ (**a a**) for **ā**, すう (**su u**) for **sū**.

Note that **ei** (えい) and **ou** (おう) spellings are pronounced as **ē** and **ō** respectively. Therefore a word which contains **ei** or **ou** is pronounced differently from how it is spelled. However, they use hiragana from different vowel rows to lengthen the vowel sounds.

			spelling	*pronunciation*
ā:	おかあさん	mother	o ka a sa n	o kā sa n
ī:	おいしいです	tasty	o i shi i de su	o i shī de su
ū:	ぎゅうにゅう	milk	gyu u nyu u	gyū nyū
ē:	ええ	yes	e e	ē
	がくせい	student	ga ku se i	ga ku sē
ō:	こおり	ice	ko o ri	kō ri
	たんじょうび	birthday	ta n jo u bi	ta n jō bi

Double consonant sound: っ

Two identical consonants such as **kk**, **tt** or **ss** mean that you insert a pause between the previous and the following sound. For instance, **kitte** has a short pause between **ki** and **te**. This pause is represented by small っ as below:

kitte	きって		**kite**	きて
a postage stamp	○●○		please come	○○
matte	まって		**mate**	まて
please wait	○●○		wait (command)	○○

Exercise 8

Circle the correct hiragana spelling for the transliterated Japanese words.

1 **gakkō** (school)　　　　　a. がこう　　　b. がっこう

2 **sumō** (*sumo* wrestling)　a. すもう　　　b. すうも

3 **tokē** (watch, clock)　　　a. とけ　　　　b. とうけい　　c. とけい

4 **yukkuri** (slowly)　　　　a. ゆくり　　　b. ゆっくり　　c. ゆうくり

5 **issai** (one year old)　　　a. いいさい　　b. いさい　　　c. いっさい

6 **motto** (more)　　　　　　a. もっと　　　b. もうと　　　c. もと

Unit Seven

Watashi wa yoku sūpā de hiru-gohan o kaimasu

I often buy lunch at the supermarket

In this unit you will learn about:

- describing one's daily activities (various verbs)
- describing when and where an action takes place
- saying "nothing", "no one" and "nowhere"
- how to ask the meaning of an unknown word
- terms of frequency
- katakana of Unit 7

アイウエオ　カキクケコ　サシスセソ　ガギグゲゴ　ザジズゼゾ

Dialogue 1

What time did you get up yesterday? **(Audio 1:47)**

Mr Ito and Mrs Parker are talking about what they did yesterday.

ITŌ	Pākā-san wa kinō nan-ji ni okimashita ka.
PĀKĀ	Watashi wa gozen 7-ji ni okimashita.
ITŌ	Sorekara nani o shimashita ka.
PĀKĀ	Shinbun o yomimashita. Soshite, asa-gohan o tabemashita.
ITŌ	Sō desu ka. Sorekara doko e ikimashita ka.
PĀKĀ	Doko(e)mo ikimasendeshita.

MR ITO	*Mrs Parker, what time did you get up yesterday?*
MRS PARKER	*I got up at 7 a.m.*
MR ITO	*And what did you do?*
MRS PARKER	*I read the newspaper. Then I ate breakfast.*
MR ITO	*Is that so? Where did you go after that?*
MRS PARKER	*I did not go anywhere.*

Vocabulary

ni (particle)	at, on, in [time marker]	**shinbun**	newspaper
sorekara	and then, also, after that	**yomimashita**	read (past tense)
		asa-gohan	breakfast
o (particle)	[object marker]	**tabemashita**	ate
shimashita	did (something)	**doko(e)mo**	nowhere

Language points

Verbs for daily activities

okimasu	to wake up, get up	**kikimasu**	to listen (to), hear
nemasu	to go to bed, sleep	**kakimasu**	to write
tabemasu	to eat	**yomimasu**	to read
nomimasu	to drink	**kaimasu**	to buy
mimasu	to see, watch, look	**shimasu**	to do

Some nouns can attach **shimasu** "do" to become a verb.

benkyō	study	**benkyō shimasu**	to study
ryōri	cooking	**ryōri shimasu**	to cook
shigoto	occupation, work	**shigoto shimasu**	to work
kaimono	shopping	**kaimono shimasu**	to do some shopping
unten	driving	**unten shimasu**	to drive

Particle o: object marker

The particle **o** marks the object of a sentence such as "an apple" in "I eat an apple." The object and its marker tend to come just before the verb.

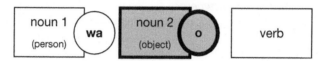

a. **Watashi wa maiasa <u>ringo o</u> tabemasu.**
I eat <u>an apple</u> every morning.

b. **Watashi no otōto wa <u>kuruma o</u> unten shimasen.**
My younger brother does not drive <u>a car</u>.

c. **Watashi wa kinō <u>Nihon no hon o</u> yomimashita.**
I read <u>a Japanese book</u> yesterday.

Note that the spelling for the particle **o** is を, not お.

わたしは　まいあさ　<u>りんごを</u>　たべます。
I eat <u>an apple</u> every morning.

To ask for information about the object, you use **nani** "what?" in the position of Noun 2.

d. Q: **Anata wa kinō <u>nani o</u> benkyō shimashita <u>ka</u>.**
<u>What</u> did you study yesterday?

A: **Watashi wa kinō <u>Nihon-go o</u> benkyō shimashita.**
I studied <u>Japanese language</u> yesterday.

The following is a list of new vocabulary that could be used as the object of the verbs introduced in this unit:

Food and drink

tabemono	food	**nomimono**	drink, beverage
gohan	meal, cooked rice	**(o)sake**	alcohol, Japanese *sake*
asa-gohan	breakfast	**bīru**	beer
hiru-gohan	lunch	**wain**	wine
ban-gohan	supper, dinner	**sūpu**	soup
okashi	confectionery	**(o)mizu**	water

Things

tegami	letter	**intānetto**	the Internet
mēru	email		

Exercise 1

Which verbs in the box below can be used for the following objects? Write them in the spaces. The numbers in the brackets indicate how many verbs you need to write.

Example   asa-gohan (breakfast) **o** *tabemasu/kaimasu*   (2)

1 tegami (letter) **o** _____ (2)
2 (o)sake (alcohol) **o** _____ (2)
3 mēru (email) **o** _____ (2)
4 rajio (radio) **o** _____ (2)
5 kuruma (car) **o** _____ (2)
6 Nihon-go (Japanese) **o** _____ (4)

> tabemasu   nomimasu   yomimasu   kikimasu   kakimasu
> okimasu   shimasu   kaimasu   unten shimasu   benkyō shimasu

Language point

Particle ni: time marker

The particle **ni** is attached to a time-related word to indicate a specific time.

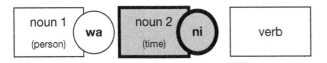

a. **Watashi wa maiasa <u>gozen 7-ji ni</u> okimasu.**
   I wake up <u>at 7 a.m.</u> every morning.

Ni is optional for some time-related words such as days of the week, holidays, etc.

b. **Watashi wa <u>do-yōbi (ni)</u> kaisha e ikimasen.**
I do not go to work (*lit.* the company) <u>on Saturdays</u>.

c. **Anata wa <u>natsu-yasumi (ni)</u> doko e ikimasu ka.**
Where do/will you go <u>during the summer holiday</u>?

Note that **ni** cannot follow words such as **kyō** "today", **senshū** "last week", **rainen** "next year", **mainichi** "every day".

d. **Watashi wa (✓ kyō   ✗ kyō <u>ni</u>) sūpā e ikimasu.**
I will go to the supermarket <u>today</u>.

Note: flexible word order

Japanese word order is flexible as long as the predicate of the sentence (such as a verb, adjective, etc.) is at the end of the sentence. Hence, the following three sentences are all correct for "I studied Japanese from 10 to 1 yesterday":

a. **Watashi wa kinō 10-ji kara 1-ji made Nihon-go o *benkyō shimashita*.**
b. **Kinō watashi wa 10-ji kara 1-ji made Nihon-go o *benkyō shimashita*.**
c. **Watashi wa kinō Nihon-go o 10-ji kara 1-ji made *benkyō shimashita*.**

Exercise 2

Write Miss Yamada's schedule for tomorrow in Japanese, based on the information below.

Example

wake up at 7.30 a.m.   *Yamada-san wa ashita gozen*
Yamada-san no ashita   *7-ji han ni okimasu.*

1 watch TV   1 _____.
2 work from 9 a.m. to 5 p.m.   2 _____.
3 eat lunch with friends   3 _____.
4 listen to music   4 _____.
5 go to bed at 10.30 p.m.   5 _____.

Language point

Interrogative word + mo

When **mo** is attached to an interrogative word such as **nani, doko** and **dare**, it adds a negative meaning as below (except for **itsumo**, which means "always"):

nani (a question word for things) + **mo** = **nanimo** (nothing)
doko (a question word for places) + **mo** = **dokomo** (nowhere)
dare (a question word for people) + **mo** = **daremo** (no one)

The object marker **o** is not used with these words (sentence a), whereas the direction marker **e** can be used (sentence b).

 a. **Watashi wa ashita <u>nanimo</u> shimasen.**
    I will <u>not</u> do <u>anything</u> tomorrow.

 b. **Watashi wa kinō <u>doko(e)mo</u> ikimasendeshita.**
    I did<u>n't</u> go <u>anywhere</u> yesterday.

Exercise 3 (Audio 1:48)

Taro and Maria are talking about what they did at the weekend. Listen and write a ✓ if the statement agrees with what they say. Write a ✗ if not.

1 ( ) Taro woke up at 9 a.m. last Saturday.
2 ( ) Taro ate sushi with his friend last Sunday.
3 ( ) Maria watched a Japanese film and drank Japanese <u>sake</u> last
     Saturday.

Dialogue 2

I eat sushi with my hands (Audio 1:49)

Mr Ito and Mrs Parker are talking about how they eat sushi.

ITŌ	Pākā-san wa donna tabemono ga suki desu ka.
PĀKĀ	Watashi wa Nihon no (o)sushi ga totemo suki desu.
ITŌ	Sō desu ka. Nani de (o)sushi o tabemasu ka.
PĀKĀ	Watashi wa (o)hashi de (o)sushi o tabemasu. Itō-san wa nani de (o)sushi o tabemasu ka.

ITŌ	Watashi wa te de (o)sushi o tabemasu.
PĀKĀ	Sō desu ka.

MR ITO	*Mrs Parker, what kind of food do you like?*
MRS PARKER	*I like Japanese sushi very much.*
MR ITO	*Really? How do you eat sushi?*
MRS PARKER	*I eat sushi with chopsticks. How do you eat sushi, Mr Ito?*
MR ITO	*I eat sushi with my hands.*
MRS PARKER	*Really?*

Vocabulary

(o)sushi	Japanese sushi	nani de	how to . . . , by what means, with what
(o)hashi	chopsticks	te	hand

Language point

Particle de (1): "using . . ." or "in"

In Unit 6 (page 73–74), you learned the particle **de** as the marker for the means of transportation (e.g. **basu de**). Here, you see more examples of **de**:

(tool) + **de**

a. **Watashi wa (o)hashi de gohan o tabemasu.**
   I eat meals <u>with (a pair of) chopsticks</u>.

b. Q: **Nani de (o)sushi o tabemasu ka.**
   <u>With what</u> do you eat sushi?

   A: **Watashi wa te de sushi o tabemasu.**
   I eat sushi <u>with my hands</u>.

naifu	knife	(o)hashi	(a pair of) chopsticks
fōku	fork	te	hand
supūn	spoon	enpitsu	pencil

(language) + **de**

When you want to know how to say a word or phrase in a certain language, the following pattern is used:

c. Q: **"Lunch" wa <u>Nihon-go de</u> nan desu ka.**
   What is "lunch" <u>in Japanese</u>?

A: **"Hiru-gohan" desu.**
   It is "hiru-gohan".

d. Q: **"Tabehōdai" wa <u>Ēgo de</u> nan desu ka.**
   What is "tabehōdai" <u>in English</u>?

A: **"Eat as much as you can" desu.**
   It is "Eat as much as you can."

Exercise 4

Answer the following questions in Japanese, using any information given in brackets.

1 Anata wa nani de rāmen o tabemasu ka. (a pair of chopsticks)
   Watashi wa (   ) de rāmen o tabemasu.

2 Anata wa nani de hanbāgā o tabemasu ka. (hands)
3 "Shinkansen" wa Ēgo de nan desu ka.
4 "Family" wa Nihon-go de nan desu ka.

Dialogue 3

Where did you read the book? (**Audio 1:50**)

Mr Ito is asking Mrs Parker what she did yesterday.

ITŌ	Pākā-san wa kinō nani o shimashita ka.
PĀKĀ	Watashi wa kinō hitori de hon o yomimashita.
ITŌ	Doko de hon o yomimashita ka.
PĀKĀ	Toshokan de hon o yomimashita.
ITŌ	Pākā-san wa yoku toshokan e ikimasu ka.
PĀKĀ	Īe, yoku ikimasen ga, tokidoki ikimasu.
ITŌ	Sō desu ka.

MR ITO	*Mrs Parker, what did you do yesterday?*
MRS PARKER	*I read a book (alone) yesterday.*
MR ITO	*Where did you read the book?*
MRS PARKER	*I read it at the library.*
MR ITO	*Do you often go to the library, Mrs Parker?*
MRS PARKER	*Not often, but sometimes.*
MR ITO	*Really?*

 Vocabulary

| **de** (particle) | at, in [place marker] | **yoku** | often |
| **doko de** | where?, at what place? | **tokidoki** | sometimes |

 Language point

Particle de **(2): place marker**

The particle **de** is attached to a place-related word to indicate the place where an action occurs.

a. **Watashi wa kyō <u>resutoran de</u> ban-gohan o tabemasu.**
   I will eat dinner <u>at a restaurant</u> today.

b. **Watashi wa kinō <u>toshokan de</u> Nihon-go o benkyō shimashita.**
   I studied Japanese <u>in the library</u> yesterday.

The question phrase for this is **doko de**.

c. Q: **Jon-san wa <u>doko de</u> kono jisho o kaimashita <u>ka</u>.**
      John, <u>where</u> did you buy this dictionary?

   A: **<u>Nihon de</u> kaimashita.**
      I bought it <u>in Japan</u>.

Do not confuse this particle with the direction marker **e** (Unit 6, page 70–71).

d. **Watashi wa <u>resutoran e</u> ikimasu.**   I go <u>to the restaurant</u>.

Exercise 5

Change the word order so that the sentences make sense.

1 watashi/de/kissaten/o/nomimasu/wa/kōhī
2 Pākā-san/terebi/uchi/mimasen/o/de/wa
3 ka/doko/kaimono shimasu/anata/de/wa

Language point

Frequency

Here is a list of words which indicate frequency. *Note that a sentence with **amari** or **zenzen** always ends with the negative form.

always	**itsumo**	occasionally	**tamani**
often	**yoku**	not very aften	**amari***
sometimes	**tokidoki**	never, not at all	**zenzen***

a. **Watashi wa <u>yoku</u> hon o yomimasu.**   I <u>often</u> read books.
b. **Watashi wa <u>zenzen</u> hon o yomi*masen*.**   I <u>never</u> read books.

Exercise 6

Put the appropriate particle or word in the brackets. Write ✗ if no particle is required.

Example   Watashi wa <u>supūn (*de*)</u> sūpu (*o*) nomimashita.

1 Watashi wa tokidoki <u>intānetto (   )</u> ongaku o kikimasu.
2 Watashi wa <u>mainichi (ᵃ   ) kuruma (ᵇ   )</u> unten shimasu.
3 Watashi wa kyonen <u>Nihon (   )</u> sushi o tabemashita.
4 Anata wa maiasa <u>nan-ji (   )</u> okimasu ka.
5 Watashi wa kinō <u>nani (   )</u> kaimasendeshita.

Exercise 7 (**Audio 1:51**)

Following is an extract from Maria's diary. Read out the text and complete the following English text accordingly.

Watashi wa sengetsu Nihon e ikimashita. Nihon de yoku rāmen o tabemashita. Rāmen wa totemo oishikatta desu. Sorekara, Tōkyō de kirēna ohashi o kaimashita. Soshite, Kyōto de ēga o mimashita. Nihon-go de mimashita. Muzukashikatta desu ga, omoshirokatta desu.

Maria went to Japan [1]_____. She often [2]_____. She found it very tasty. In Tokyo, she [3]_____. In Kyoto, she watched a film in [4]_____. She found it difficult but enjoyable.

Vocabulary

rāmen   Japanese ramen noodle soup

Katakana of Unit 7

Katakana is used to transcribe words which are originally foreign words. Katakana is also used for the names of some animals and plants. You will learn the basic 48 katakana characters plus combined sounds and special sounds from Unit 7 to Unit 10. To check the stroke order of each katakana and download an extra exercise sheet, go to www.routledge.com/cw/colloquials.

	1	2	3		1	2	3
a ア	ア	ア		sa サ	サ	サ
i イ	イ	イ		shi シ	シ	シ
u ウ	ウ	ウ		su ス	ス	ス
e エ	エ	エ		se セ	セ	セ
o オ	オ	オ		so ソ	ソ	ソ
ka カ	カ	カ		**Voiced sound**		
ki キ	キ	キ		K → G		S → Z, SH → J
ku ク	ク	ク		カ (ka) → ガ (ga)		サ (sa) → ザ (za)
				キ (ki) → ギ (gi)		シ (shi) → ジ (ji)
ke ケ	ケ	ケ		ク (ku) → グ (gu)		ス (su) → ズ (zu)
				ケ (ke) → ゲ (ge)		セ (se) → ゼ (ze)
ko コ	コ	コ		コ (ko) → ゴ (go)		ソ (so) → ゾ (zo)

Exercise 8

Read out the following Japanese words written in katakana and write how to read them in the brackets below.

1 アイス ice cream
(__ __ __)

2 コイ koi carp
(__ __)

3 カキ persimmon
(__ __)

4 スイカ watermelon
(__ __ __)

5 キウイ kiwi
(__ __ __)

6 クイズ quiz
(__ __ __)

7 アサガオ morning glory
(__ __ __ __)

8 ジグザグ zigzag
(__ __ __ __)

Unit Eight

Ōsaka ni yūmēna (o)shiro ga arimasu

There is a famous castle in Osaka

In this unit you will learn about:

- describing the existence of things and people using **arimasu** and **imasu**
- listing more than two nouns by using **ya** "and so on"
- counting objects or people: numerals (suffix counters)
- terms of location (on, below, in front of, behind, etc.)
- katakana of Unit 8

タチツテト　ナニヌネノ　ハヒフヘホ
ダヂヅデド　バビブベボ　パピプペポ

 Dialogue 1

 There is a castle in Osaka **(Audio 2:1)**

Mr Miller is a friend of Miss Ogawa from work. He told her that he has never visited Osaka, so she has taken him there.

MIRĀ	Ogawa-san. Ōsaka wa nigiyaka desu ne.
OGAWA	Hai. Ōsaka ni ī resutoran ya omoshiroi (o)mise ga takusan arimasu.
MIRĀ	Oshiro mo arimasu ka.
OGAWA	Hai, yūmēna (o)shiro ga arimasu. Itsumo (o)shiro ni kankōkyaku ga imasu.
MIRĀ	Jā, totemo nigiyaka desu ne.
OGAWA	Hai.

MR MILLER	*Miss Ogawa, Osaka is lively, isn't it?*
MISS OGAWA	*Yes, Osaka has many things such as good restaurants and interesting shops.*
MR MILLER	*Is there also a castle (in Osaka)?*
MISS OGAWA	*Yes, there is. There are always tourists there.*
MR MILLER	*Then, it (Osaka castle) is very lively, isn't it?*
MISS OGAWA	*Yes.*

Vocabulary

ni (particle)	in, at [location marker]	**ya** (particle)	and (among other things)
takusan	many, a lot	**(o)mise**	shop, store
arimasu	to be, there is (something)	**(o)shiro**	castle
		imasu	to be, there is (someone)

Language point

Existence of things and people (1): arimasu and imasu

The Japanese equivalents of the English "there is/are" are **arimasu** and **imasu**. The former is used for inanimate things (e.g. a chair, a book) or animate things which cannot move at will (e.g. plants), whereas the latter is used for animate things (e.g. a boy, a cat). Remember that there is no plural/singular distinction in Japanese, unlike English (see Introduction p. xii). The particle **ni** indicates the location of something or someone.

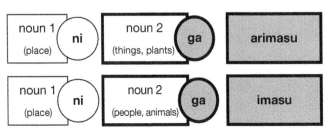

The question word for Noun 2 is either **nani** "what?" or **dare** "who?".

a. Q: **Tōkyō ni <u>nani</u> ga arimasu <u>ka</u>.**
   <u>What</u> is in Tokyo?

   A: **Tōkyō ni Tōkyō Sukai Tsurī ga arimasu.**
   Tokyo has Tokyo Sky Tree Tower.

b. Q: **Tōkyō ni <u>dare</u> ga imasu <u>ka</u>.**
   <u>Who</u> is in Tokyo?

   A: **Tōkyō ni watashi no kazoku ga imasu.**
   My family is in Tokyo.

Do you remember how to say "nothing" and "nobody"? (Unit 7)

| <u>Nani mo</u> **arimasen.** | There is <u>nothing</u>. |
| <u>Dare mo</u> **imasen.** | There is <u>nobody</u>. |

Vocabulary

Nouns used with **imasu**

People		*Animals*	
onna no hito	woman	**inu**	dog
otoko no hito	man	**neko**	cat
onna no ko	girl	**usagi**	rabbit
otoko no ko	boy		
kankōkyaku	tourist		

Nouns used with **arimasu**

In town/nature		*In the house*	
ēgakan	cinema	**heya**	room
(o)mise	store, shop	**niwa**	garden
-noriba	rank, stop	**ima**	living room
(takushī noriba)	(taxi rank)	**genkan**	entrance hall
chizu	map	**shinshitsu**	bedroom
(o)shiro	castle	**daidokoro**	kitchen
(o)tera	temple	**beddo**	bed
Fujisan	Mt. Fuji	**tsukue**	desk
hana	flower		

Exercise 1

Choose the appropriate verb and underline it as shown in the example.

Example Kono machi ni eki ga (a. imasu b. arimasu).

1 Kōen ni onna no ko ga (a. imasu   b. arimasu).
2 Asoko ni nani ga (a. imasu   b. arimasu) ka.
3 Ēgakan ni dare mo (a. imasen   b. arimasen).
4 Watashi no shinshitsu ni beddo to pasokon ga (a. imasu
  b. arimasu).

Exercise 2

Add the missing words and complete the sentences.

Example There is a cinema in my town.
     Watashi no machi *ni* ēgakan *ga* arimasu.

1 A man and a woman are in the restaurant.
  _____ ni otoko no hito to _____ ga _____.

2 There was a bicycle in the garden this morning.
  Kesa _____ ni jitensha _____ arimashita.

3 There is nobody in the kitchen.
  _____ ni _____ imasen.

4 What is in the entrance hall?
  _____ ni _____ ga arimasu _____.

Vocabulary

kesa this morning

Language point

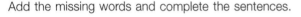

Listing more than two nouns by using ya "and so on"

The particle **ya** means "and so on" and implies that the nouns given
are a couple of examples.

a. **Watashi no heya ni beddo <u>to</u> tsukue ga arimasu.**
   There are a bed <u>and</u> a desk in my room.

b. **Watashi no heya ni beddo <u>ya</u> tsukue ga arimasu.**
   There are <u>several objects such as</u> a bed <u>and</u> a desk in my room.

 Dialogue 2

 I bought three apples and two bottles of wine
(**Audio 2:2**)

Mr Miller was on the way home when he saw Miss Ogawa outside
the supermarket. She had a big shopping bag which looked heavy.

MIRĀ	Konnichiwa, Ogawa-san. Takusan kaimono shimashita ne.
OGAWA	Hai, iroiro na mono o kaimashita.
MIRĀ	Sūpā de nani o kaimashita ka.
OGAWA	Ringo o mittsu to wain o ni-hon kaimashita. Sorekara, zasshi mo kaimashita.
MIRĀ	Wain wa ikura deshita ka.
OGAWA	Wain wa ip-pon 1000-en deshita.

MR MILLER	*Hello, Miss Ogawa. You bought a lot, didn't you?*
MISS OGAWA	*Yes, I bought various things.*
MR MILLER	*What did you buy at the supermarket?*
MISS OGAWA	*I bought three apples and two bottles of wine there. And I also bought a magazine.*
MR MILLER	*How much was the wine?*
MISS OGAWA	*It was 1000 yen per bottle.*

 Vocabulary

iroiro na	various
mono	thing(s)
-tsu (counter suffix)	counter for material things in general
-hon (counter suffix)	counter for long, slender things

Language point

Counting objects or people: numerals (suffix counters)

When you count objects or people, you need to use the appropriate counter for the item. Here are some of the counters (more can be found in the Grammar Summary):

Counter	Type of object	1–10	?
-ko	Small object (egg, apple, etc.)	**ikko/niko/sanko/yonko/goko rokko/nanako/hakko/kyūko/jukko**	**Nan-ko**
-hon (**pon**, **bon**)	Long, slender object (pen, bottle, umbrella, etc.)	**ippon/nihon/sanbon/yonhon/gohon roppon/nanahon/happon/kyūhon/juppon**	**Nan-bon**
-dai	Machinery (car, computer, etc.)	**ichidai/nidai/sandai/yondai/godai rokudai/nanadai/hachidai/kyūdai/jūdai**	**Nan-dai**
-mai	Thin, flat object (paper, CD, shirt, etc.)	**ichimai/nimai/sanmai/yonmai/gomai rokumai/nanamai/hachimai/kyūmai/jūmai**	**Nan-mai**
-nin	People	**hitori/futari/sannin/yonin/gonin rokunin/nananin/hachinin/kyūnin/jūnin**	**Nan-nin**
-kai	Time	**ikkai/nikai/sankai/yonkai/gokai rokkai/nanakai/hakkai/kyūkai/jukkai**	**Nan-kai**

Note that "one person" and "two persons" are "**hitori**" and "**futari**" respectively and do not use "**-nin**".

Another counter is **-tsu**. This counter covers material things in general. Note that the **-tsu** system is used only up to ten. Eleven and higher are counted by using the numbers introduced on page 24. The interrogative for this is **ikutsu**.

1	**hitotsu**	4	**yottsu**	7	**nanatsu**	10	**tō**
2	**futatsu**	5	**itsutsu**	8	**yattsu**		
3	**mittsu**	6	**muttsu**	9	**kokonotsu**	?	**ikutsu**

Exercise 3

Write the appropriate counter for the following items, using the number in the brackets. Avoid **-tsu**.

Example kuruma (3) *san-dai*

1 ringo (5) _____   2 otoko no ko (4) _____
3 kasa (1) _____   4 chizu (2) _____
5 kētai denwa (4) _____   6 enpitsu (7) _____

 Language point

Using counters in a sentence

Here are some examples of how to use a counter in a sentence. Note that a counter does not take any particle.

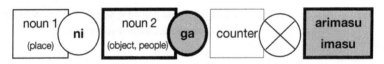

a. **Watashi no uchi ni terebi ga <u>2-dai</u> arimasu.**
There are <u>two</u> TVs in my house.

b. **Kōen ni hito ga <u>10-nin</u> imasu.**
There are <u>ten</u> people in the park.

c. **Otōto wa mainichi kono CD o <u>ik-kai</u> kikimasu.**
My younger brother listens to this CD <u>once</u> every day.

Kudasai is used when you request someone to give you something or when you have decided to purchase something.

d. **Kyōto no chizu o <u>1-mai kudasai</u>.**
<u>Please give me a</u> map of Kyoto.

Exercise 4

Translate the following sentences into Japanese.

Example I ate an apple yesterday.
Watashi wa kinō ringo o hitotsu tabemashita.

1 Please give me three Kyoto maps.
2 I study Japanese two hours every day.
3 There are three men in my house.

Exercise 5 (Audio 2:3)

How many of the following items are in Taro's house? Write the answers
with the appropriate counters.

   Example CD 20-*mai*

1 tokē   _____   2 hito _____
3 pasokon _____   4 kasa _____

Vocabulary

| zenbu de in total | minna de everyone |

Dialogue 3

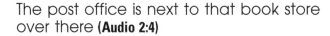

The post office is next to that book store over there (Audio 2:4)

Mr Miller is in Okinawa on vacation. He is looking for a post office
to send a postcard. When he left the hotel, the receptionist told
him that there was a post office around here.

MIRĀ	Sumimasen, yūbinkyoku wa doko ni arimasu ka.
TSŪKŌNIN	Yūbinkyoku desu ka. Asoko ni hon-ya ga arimasu ne.
MIRĀ	Hai.
TSŪKŌNIN	Yūbinkyoku wa ano hon-ya no tonari ni arimasu.
MIRĀ	Sō desu ka. Dōmo arigatō gozaimasu.
TSŪKŌNIN	Īe, dō itashimashite.

MR MILLER	*Excuse me but where is the post office?*
PASSER-BY	*Post office? You can see a book store over there, can't you?*
MR MILLER	*Yes.*

PASSER-BY *The post office is next to that book store.*
MR MILLER *Is it? Thank you very much.*
PASSER-BY *You are welcome.*

Vocabulary

tsūkōnin	passer-by	**-ya**	store, shop
hon-ya	book store	**dō itashimashite**	you are welcome

Language point

Location

The following words are used to indicate the location of an item or people.

ue	on, above	**shita**	under, below
hidari	left	**migi**	right
mae	in front of	**ushiro**	behind, back
naka	inside	**chikaku**	near
soto	outside	**tonari**	next to

a. *Tēburu no ue ni ringo ga arimasu.*
   There is an apple *on the table*.

b. *Hito no mae ni ringo ga arimasu.*
   There is an apple *in front of the person*.

c. *Kaban no naka ni ringo ga arimasu.*
   There is an apple *in the bag*.

Exercise 6

Translate the following sentences into Japanese. The first word is given.

1 There are two boys behind the person.
   Hito
2 There is one mobile phone in the bag.
   Kaban

3 There is a big house next to the building.

Biru _____

Vocabulary

biru building

Language point

Existence of things and people (2):
X wa Y ni arimasu/imasu

When you talk about something or someone and both you and the listener know about them, the item (or person) is taken up as the topic of the sentence and marked by **wa** instead of **ga**.

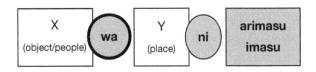

In the following dialogues, Speaker Q1 uses **wa** on the assumption that a) there must be a post office in the town and that Speaker A1 also assumes so, whereas Speaker Q2 uses **ga** because he or she does not know whether or not there is a post office nearby.

a. Q1: **Yūbinkyoku wa doko ni arimasu ka.**
   Where is the post office?

   A1: **Yūbinkyoku wa ano hon-ya no tonari ni arimasu.**
   It is next to that book store.

b. Q2: **Kono chikaku ni yūbinkyoku ga arimasu ka.**
   Is there a post office near here?

   A2: **Hai, asoko ni arimasu.**
   Yes, it is over there.

Exercise 7

Answer the following questions, using the information in the brackets.

Example
Yūbinkyoku wa doko ni arimasu ka. (opposite the station)
Eki no mae ni arimasu.

1 Anata wa doko ni imasu ka. (inside the station)
2 Hon-ya wa doko ni arimasu ka. (to the left of the bank)
3 Kōen wa doko ni arimasu ka. (between the convenience store
   and the hotel)
4 Takushī noriba wa doko desu ka. (near the library)

Vocabulary

X to Y no aida   between X and Y

Exercise 8 (Audio 2:5)

Read out the following text and write ✓ if the statement agrees with it.
Write ✗ if not.

わたしの　まちは　ちいさいですが、べんりな　まちです。まちのなかに
おみせが　たくさん　あります。えきの　まえに　ほんやが　あります。
わたしは　よく　そこで　ほんを　かいます。ほんやの　となりに　きっさてんが
あります。そこの　こうちゃは　とても　おいしいです。きっさてんの　うしろに
えいがかんが　あります。わたしは　そこで　ときどき　えいがを　みます。

Watashi no machi wa chīsai desu ga benrina machi desu. Machi
no naka ni omise ga takusan arimasu. Eki no mae ni hon-ya ga
arimasu. Watashi wa yoku soko de hon o kaimasu. Hon-ya no tonari
ni kissaten ga arimasu. Soko no kōcha wa totemo oishī desu. Kissaten
no ushiro ni ēgakan ga arimasu. Watashi wa soko de tokidoki ēga
o mimasu.

1 (   ) There are many shops in my town.
2 (   ) There is a library in front of the station.
3 (   ) There is a cinema behind the café.

Katakana of Unit 8

	1	2	3			1	2	3
ta タ	タ	タ	ha ハ		ハ	ハ
chi チ	チ	チ	hi ヒ		ヒ	ヒ
tsu ツ	ツ	ツ	fu フ		フ	フ
te テ	テ	テ	he ヘ		ヘ	ヘ
to ト	ト	ト	ho ホ		ホ	ホ
na ナ	ナ	ナ				
ni ニ	ニ	ニ				
nu ヌ	ヌ	ヌ				
ne ネ	ネ	ネ				
no ノ	ノ	ノ				

Voiced sounds

T→D, Ch→J, Ts→Z   H/F→B, H→P

タ (ta) → ダ (da)   ハ (ha) → バ (ba)
チ (chi) → ヂ (ji)   ヒ (hi) → ビ (bi)
ツ (tsu) → ヅ (zu)   フ (fu) → ブ (bu)
テ (te) → デ (de)   ヘ (he) → ベ (be)
ト (to) → ド (do)   ホ (ho) → ボ (bo)

パ (pa) ピ (pi) プ (pu) ペ (pe) ポ (po)

Exercise 9

Read out the following Japanese words written in katakana and write
how to read them in the brackets below.

1 イヌ dog
(__ __)

2 ネコ cat
(__ __)

3 ドイツ Germany
(__ __ __)

4 テニス tennis
(__ __ __)

5 ポテト potato
(__ __ __)

6 カナダ Canada
(__ __ __)

7 ネクタイ tie
(__ __ __ __)

8 ピアニスト pianist
(__ __ __ __ __)

Unit Nine

Nichi-yōbi issho ni ēga o mimasen ka

Won't you watch a film with me on Sunday?

In this unit you will learn about:

- talking about holidays and travel
- saying "Have you already...?" and "Not yet"
- how to express one's desire using [Verb-stem] + **tai**
- how to state the purpose of going to a certain place
- how to invite someone to do something
- katakana of Unit 9

マミムメモ　　ヤユヨ　　ラリルレロ　　ワヲン

Dialogue 1

I want to take a lot of photos **(Audio 2:6)**

Emma and Norio are members of the same tennis club. The club has an annual training trip to Nagano prefecture and they are in charge of the arrangements this year.

NORIO	Ema-san, mō densha no kippu o kaimashita ka.
EMA	Īe, mada desu. Kyō no gogo intānetto de kaimasu.
NORIO	Sō desu ka. Ema-san, Nagano wa hajimete desu ka.
EMA	Hai, hajimete desu.

NORIO Nagano de nani o shitai desu ka.

EMA Takusan shashin o toritai desu. Soshite onsen ni hairitai desu.

Vocabulary

mō	already	**ikitai desu**	want to go
kippu	ticket	**shashin**	photo
mada	not yet	**torimasu**	to take (a photo)
hajimete	(for) the first time	**onsen**	hot spring
(verb)-tai desu	want to (+ verb)	**hairimasu**	to enter

Dialogue 1 exercise

Write ✓ if the statement agrees with the dialogue. Write ✗ if not.

1 ( ) Emma has not bought the train tickets yet but will do so this afternoon.

2 ( ) Emma once went to Nagano prefecture and took a lot of photos.

Language points

Holidays and travel

Noun		Verb	
shashin	picture, photo	**torimasu**	to take (a
onsen	hot spring		picture)
sumō	*sumo* wrestling	**hairimasu**	to enter
kankō	tourist	**yasumimasu**	to rest
annaijo	information	**kaemasu**	to change
ryokan	Japanese style	**(ni) tomarimasu**	to stay
	hotel		overnight (at)
washitsu	Japanese style	**yoyaku shimasu**	to reserve
	room	**kyanseru**	to cancel
yōshitsu	Western style	**shimasu**	
	room	**chūmon**	to order
		shimasu	

Have you already...? Not yet.

Mō means "already" and is used to say that or ask whether someone has completed a certain action. Therefore, the sentence always takes the past tense ([V-**mashita**]).

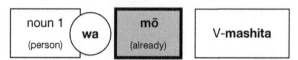

noun 1 (person) **wa**	**mō** (already)	V-**mashita**

    a. **Watashi wa mō densha no kippu o kaimashita.**
       I have already bought the train ticket.

    b. **Katō-san wa mō hoteru o yoyaku shimashita ka.**
       Have you already reserved a hotel, Mr/Ms Kato?

How to answer such a question positively and negatively:

    b1. **Hai, mō yoyaku shimashita.**
        Yes, I have already reserved it.

    b2. **Īe, mada desu.**
        No, not yet.

Note that **mada** "yet" takes either **desu** (as above) or [V-**te**] + **imasen**. How to make the **te**-form from the **masu**-form of the verb will be introduced in Unit 13 (pages 156–7).

Exercise 1

Write the answer as indicated in the brackets.

1 Anata wa mō kippu o kaimashita ka. (Yes)
2 Anata wa mō ryokan ni tomarimashita ka. (No)
3 Anata wa mō sumō o mimashita ka. (No)

Language point

Expressing one's desire (action): (Verb-stem) + tai

[Verb-stem] + **tai** expresses the speaker's desire to do something. The verb stem [V-stem] is what is left after removing **masu** from the verb. For instance, the verb stems of **tabemasu** and **mimasu** are **tabe** and **mi** respectively. the tense is indicated in the **tai** part and **tai** inflects as an **i**-adjective.

	ta i	desu	want to
Verb ~~masu~~ +	ta kunai	desu	do/does not want to
	ta katta	desu	wanted to
	ta kunakatta	desu	did not want to

The object in this structure can be followed by either **o** or **ga**.

a. **Watashi wa sushi o/ga tabetai desu.**
I want to eat sushi.

b. **Watashi wa kyō terebi o/ga mitakunai desu.**
I do not want to watch TV today.

Particles such as the direction marker (**e**) or location marker (**de**) remain unchanged. The person who you meet (**aimasu**) is marked by **ni**.

c. **Watashi wa *Nihon e* ikitakatta desu.**
I wanted to go *to* Japan.

d. **Watashi wa kyō *kissaten de* kōhī o/ga nomitai dsu.**
I want to drink coffee *at the café* today.

e. **Watashi wa *Tanaka-san ni* aitai desu.**
I want to see/meet *Mr Tanaka*.

Note that [V-stem] + **tai** can be made into a question by adding the question marker **ka**. However, asking a person (especially someone senior) what they wish to do using this structure is often considered impolite. A simple question is often used instead.

Sensē wa bīru o (✗ nomitai desu ka   ✓ nomimasu ka).
Teacher, would you have some beer?

Exercise 2

Fill in the blanks with the appropriate forms.

masu form	want to	do not want to	wanted to	did not want to
yasumimasu 1) (rest)	2)		**yasumitakatta** **desu** 3)	
4) (take a picture)	**toritai** **desu** 5)	6)		**toritakunakatta** **desu**
7) (enter)	8)	**hairitakunai** **desu**	9)	10)

Exercise 3

Translate the following sentences into Japanese.

> *Example* I want to read Japanese books.
> *Watashi wa Nihon no hon o (or ga)*
> *yomitai desu.*

1 I want to talk with my friend.
2 I want to see my family.
3 I want to exercise in the park.

Vocabulary

(to/ni) hanashimasu	to talk (with/to)
(ni) aimasu	to meet/see (someone)
undō shimasu	to exercise

Dialogue 2

I went to America to see my friend in New York **(Audio 2:7)**

Emma and Norio are talking about how their summer holidays were.

NORIO Ema-san wa natsu-yasumi ni doko e ikimashita ka.
EMA   Watashi wa natsu-yasumi ni Amerika e ikimashita.

NORIO	Nani o shi ni Amerika e ikimashita ka.
EMA	Nyūyōku no tomodachi ni ai ni ikimashita.
NORIO	Nyūyōku de nani o shimashita ka.
EMA	Tomodachi to Nyūyōku o kankō shimashita.

Vocabulary

Nyūyōku New York

kankō shimasu to go sightseeing

Dialogue 2 exercise

Write ✓ if the statement agrees with the dialogue. Write ✗ if not.

1 ( ) Emma went to New York with her friend last summer.
2 ( ) Emma and her friend went sightseeing in New York.

Language point

Indicating the purpose of "go", "come" and "return"

This pattern is used to give one's purpose of going (**ikimasu**), coming (**kimasu**) or returning (**kaerimasu**). The purpose is marked with the particle **ni**. Nouns which themselves entail an action (e.g. studying, cooking, travelling) can appear before **ni**.

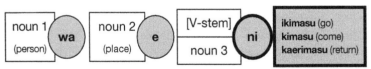

| noun 1 (person) | **wa** | noun 2 (place) | **e** | [V-stem] / noun 3 | **ni** | ikimasu (go) / kimasu (come) / kaerimasu (return) |

a. **Watashi wa ashita sūpā e <u>pan to yasai o kai ni</u> ikimasu.**
   I will go to the supermarket <u>to buy bread and vegetables</u> tomorrow.

b. **Watashi wa Nihon e <u>Nihon-go o benkyō shi ni</u> kimashita.**
   I came to Japan <u>to study Japanese</u>.

c. **Watashi wa Nihon e <u>Nihon-go no benkyō ni</u> kimashita.**
   I came to Japan <u>for the purpose of studying Japanese</u>.

Exercise 4

Write your plan for today in Japanese.

Example   (noon/café/eat lunch)
   *Watashi wa hiru kissaten e hiru-gohan
   o tabe ni ikimasu.*

1 (morning/library/read books)
2 (noon/park/run)
3 (evening/cinema/watch a film)

Vocabulary

hiru	noon		ban or yoru	evening
asa	morning		hashirimasu	to run

Dialogue 3

Won't you go to see sumo with me? (Audio 2:8)

It is Friday afternoon. Emma and Norio have played tennis together at the tennis club and are now talking in the club lounge.

NORIO   Ema-san wa Nihon de mō sumō o mimashita ka.
EMA   Īe, mada desu. Totemo mitai desu ga...
NORIO   Jā, konshūmatsu issho ni sumō o mi ni ikimasen ka.
EMA   Hontō desu ka. Ureshī desu. Demo sumō wa nan-yōbi
        desu ka.
NORIO   Nichi-yōbi desu. Ema-san wa nichi-yōbi isogashī desu ka.
EMA   Īe, hima desu.
NORIO   Watashi no tomodachi mo issho ni ikimasu ga, ī desu ka.
EMA   Mochiron desu.
NORIO   Jā, issho ni ikimashō.

Vocabulary

issho ni	together	**ureshī** (i-adj.)	happy
[V-stem] +	won't you...?,	**isogashī** (i-adj.)	busy
masen ka	would you like to...	**mochiron**	of course
ikimasen ka	won't you go?	**[V-stem] + mashō**	let's
hontō desu ka	really?	**ikimashō**	let's go

Dialogue 3 exercise

Write ✓ if the statement agrees with the dialogue. Write ✗ if not.

1 ( ) Emma has already watched sumo in Japan.
2 ( ) Emma and Norio are going to watch sumo together this Sunday.

Language point

Suggesting doing something together: (V-stem) + masen ka

[V-stem] + **masen ka** is used when one suggests doing something together with someone. **Issho ni** "together" is often used in this structure.

Issho ni	[V-stem] **masen ka**
(together)	(shall we?)

a. **Issho ni tenisu o shimasen ka.**
   Shall we/would you like to play tennis together?

b. **Issho ni Fujisan e ikimasen ka.**
   Won't you/would you like to go to Mt. Fuji with me?

c. **Issho ni resutoran e tabe ni ikimasen ka.**
   Won't you/would you like to go to the restaurant together [with me] to eat?

Exercise 5

Suggest to your friend Masako that you do the following activities in the brackets together.

Example (play basketball)
> *Masako-san, issho ni basukettobōru o shimasen ka.*

1 (watch a DVD at my house)
2 (go to a hot spring next month)
3 (run every morning)

Vocabulary

basukettobōru	basketball
DVD (pronounced as **dī bui dī**)	DVD

Language point

Accepting or rejecting suggestions: (V-stem) + mashō

To accept a suggestion, you add **mashō** after the verb stem ([V-stem] + **mashō**). This expression is equivalent to the English "let's".

a. Q: **Issho ni ban-gohan o tabemasen ka.**
   Won't you eat dinner with me?

   A: **Hai, (issho ni)** <u>tabemashō</u>.
   Yes, <u>let's eat</u> together.

b. Q: **Issho ni ēga o mi ni ikimasen ka.**
   Won't you go to the cinema together with me?

   A: **Ī desu ne. (Issho ni)** <u>ikimashō</u>.
   That sounds good. <u>Let's go</u>.

An unfinished sentence such as below is often used for rejecting the suggestion politely. **Chotto** means "a little" and it is a part of **chotto tsugō ga warui desu** "it is slightly inconvenient". Saying **chotto** with some hesitation will lead the listener to understand that you cannot accept their invitation.

  c. Q: **Issho ni tenisu o shimasen ka.**
      Won't you play tennis with me?

     A1: **Zannen desu ga, <u>chotto</u>...**   It is unfortunate <u>but</u>...
     A2: **Sumimasen ga, <u>chotto</u>...**   I am sorry <u>but</u>...

Useful expressions

chotto...	a little
tsugō ga warui desu	(the time/schedule) is unsuitable for me
zannen desu ga	It is regrettable/unfortunate but...

Exercise 6 (Audio 2:9)

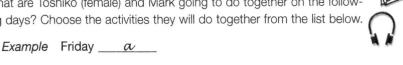

What are Toshiko (female) and Mark going to do together on the following days? Choose the activities they will do together from the list below.

   Example Friday   *a*

1 Saturday _____   2 Sunday _____

a. ~~play a game at Toshiko's house~~
b. watch tennis on TV
c. go to the park to run
d. watch a Japanese film at Toshiko's house
e. play tennis in the park

Vocabulary

  gēmu game

Exercise 7 (Audio 2:10)

Read out the following text and answer the questions in English.

わたしは　らいねん　2がつに　ほっかいどうへ　いきたいです。
ほっかいどうへ　「ゆきまつり」を　みに　いきたいです。「ゆきまつり」は、
ほっかいどうの　とても　ゆうめいな　おまつりです。ゆきの　ぞうが
たくさん　あります。わたしは　ゆきまつりの　しゃしんを　たくさん
とりたいです。そして、ほっかいどうで　おいしい　たべものを　たべたいです。

Watashi wa rainen 2-gatsu ni Hokkaidō e ikitai desu. Hokkaidō e "Yuki matsuri" o mi ni ikitai desu. "Yuki matsuri" wa, Hokkaidō no totemo yūmēna omatsuri desu. Yuki no zō ga takusan arimasu. Watashi wa "Yuki matsuri" no shashin o takusan toritai desu. Soshite, Hokkaidō de oishī tabemono o tabetai desu.

1 Why does this person want to go to Hokkaido?
2 What is Yuki matsuri?
3 What does this person want to do in Hokkaido? Give two
   activities.

Vocabulary

ほっかいどう	**Hokkaidō**	Hokkaido prefecture
ゆき	**yuki**	snow
（お）まつり	**(o)matsuri**	festival
ぞう	**zō**	statue

Katakana of Unit 9

	1	2	3			1	2	3
ma	マ	マ	マ		ra	ラ	ラ	ラ
mi	ミ	ミ	ミ		ri	リ	リ	リ
mu	ム	ム	ム		ru	ル	ル	ル
me	メ	メ	メ		re	レ	レ	レ
mo	モ	モ	モ		ro	ロ	ロ	ロ
ya	ヤ	ヤ	ヤ		wa	ワ	ワ	ワ
yu	ユ	ユ	ユ		o	ヲ	ヲ	ヲ
yo	ヨ	ヨ	ヨ		n/m	ン	ン	ン

Exercise 8

Read out the following Japanese words written in katakana and write how to read them in the brackets below.

1 ワイン wine
   (__ __ __)

2 メダル medal
   (__ __ __)

3 アメリカ America
   (__ __ __ __)

4 ロンドン London
   (__ __ __ __)

5 パソコン personal computer
   (__ __ __ __)

6 ライオン lion
   (__ __ __ __)

7 デジタルカメラ digital camera
   (__ __ __ __ __ __ __)

8 レストラン restaurant
   (__ __ __ __ __)

Unit Ten

Dōshite atarashī pasokon ga hoshī desu ka

Why do you want to have a new PC?

In this unit you will learn about:

- how to express one's desire to possess an object
- giving and asking reasons
- talking about one's illness
- stating what one owns, using **X wa Y ga arimasu**
- expressing one's gratitude
- giving and receiving things
- katakana of Unit 10: combined sounds

Dialogue 1

What do you want? (Audio 2:11)

Mr Clark and Miss Akita work at the same company. Tomorrow they will receive a bonus from the company.

KURĀKU	Akita-san, ashita wa bōnasu-bi desu ne. Akita-san wa bōnasu de nani ga hoshī desu ka.
AKITA	Watashi wa atarashī pasokon ga hoshī desu.
KURĀKU	Dōshite atarashī pasokon ga hoshī desu ka.
AKITA	Ima no pasokon wa mō furui desu kara. Soreni, ima no pasokon wa sukoshi osoi desu kara.
KURĀKU	Sō desu ka.

Vocabulary

bōnasu-bi	bonus day	**soreni**	besides
hoshī (i-adj.)	want (an object)	**osoi** (i-adj.)	slow, late
dōshite	why?	**sukoshi**	a little
kara	because		

Dialogue 1 exercise

Write ✓ if the statement agrees with the dialogue. Write ✗ if not.

1 (   ) Mr Clark is going to buy a new PC with the bonus.
2 (   ) Miss Akita's current PC is old and slow.

Language point

Expressing one's desire to possess
an object: hoshī

Hoshī is an adjective which expresses the speaker's desire to possess an object. It can also be used to ask what the listener wants. The object of this sentence is marked by **ga**. **Hoshī** is an i-adjective and inflects as below:

want	do not want	wanted	did not want
hoshi <u>i</u>	hoshi <u>kunai</u>	hoshi <u>katta</u>	hoshi <u>kunakatta</u>
desu	**desu**	**desu**	**desu**

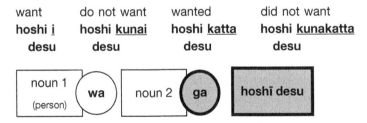

a. **Watashi wa tanjōbi purezento ni <u>hana ga hoshī desu</u>.**
   I <u>want flowers</u> for my birthday present.

b. **Kekkon iwai ni <u>nani ga hoshī desu ka</u>.**
   <u>What</u> do you <u>want</u> for your wedding gift?

Exercise 1

Answer the following questions, using the information given in the brackets.

1 Anata wa tanjōbi ni nani ga hoshī desu ka. (Japanese dictionary)
2 Anata wa donna kuruma ga hoshī desu ka. (fast car)
3 Anata wa kekkon iwai ni nani ga hoshī desu ka. (lovely photo frame)

Vocabulary

hayai (i-adj.)	fast, early	**kawaī** (i-adj.)	cute, lovely, pretty
kekkon iwai	wedding gift	**shashin tate**	photo frame

Language point

Giving and asking reasons (1): dōshite and ~ kara

The interrogative **dōshite** is used to ask for reasons. **Dōshite** can appear both in the middle of a sentence and at the beginning of a sentence.

    a. **Kurāku-san wa <u>dōshite</u> Nihon-go o benkyō shimasu <u>ka</u>.**
    <u>Why</u> do you study Japanese, Mr Clark?

    b. **<u>Dōshite</u> Fujita-san wa kinō isogashikatta desu <u>ka</u>.**
    <u>Why</u> were you busy yesterday, Mrs Fujita?

"Because" in Japanese is **kara**. Note that a statement which explains a reason comes before **kara**.

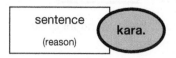

    c. Q: **Fujisan wa <u>dōshite</u> yūmē desu <u>ka</u>.**
    <u>Why</u> is Mt. Fuji famous?

      A: *(Fujisan wa) Nihon de ichi-ban takai yama desu <u>kara</u>.*
      <u>Because</u> it is the highest mountain in Japan.

Exercise 2

Answer the following questions, using the information given in the
brackets.

Example Anata wa dōshite Nihon-go o benkyō shimasu ka.
(I like Japanese books.)
*Watashi wa Nihon no hon ga suki desu
kara.*

1 Anata wa dōshite kinō pātī e kimasendeshita ka.
(I was ill last night. *lit.* I was illness last night.)
2 Anata wa dōshite Kyōto e ikitai desu ka.
(I want to see old temples.)
3 Anata wa dōshite yoku Rondon e ikimasu ka.
(My family are in London.)

Vocabulary

byōki illness, sickness

Dialogue 2

I am going home because I have a headache (Audio 2:12)

It is Friday. Mr Clark and Miss Akita have just finished the day's
work and are tidying up their desks.

KURĀKU	Akita-san, korekara tomodachi to karaoke ni ikimasu. Akita-san mo issho ni ikimasen ka.
AKITA	Ikitai desu ga, sukoshi atama ga itai desu kara, kyō wa uchi e kaerimasu.
KURĀKU	Sore wa ikemasen ne. Watashi wa kusuri ga arimasu ga, nomimasu ka.
AKITA	Arigatō gozaimasu. Jā, hitotsu kudasai.

Vocabulary

karaoke	karaoke
atama ga itai	to have a headache
atama	head
itai (i-adj.)	ache, painful
sore wa ikemasen	that is bad
kusuri	medicine, drug
arimasu	to have, own

Dialogue 2 exercise

Write ✓ if the statement agrees with the dialogue. Write ✗ if not.

1 ( ) Miss Akita will not go to karaoke with Mr Clark because she has a headache.
2 ( ) Miss Akita will take some medicine she has bought before.

Language points

Illness

Here are some illness-related expressions. Note that **itai** "painful" and **warui** "bad" are **i**-adjectives, whereas **arimasu** "to have" is a verb.

atama ga itai	have a headache
ha ga itai	have a toothache
kimochi ga warui	feel unwell, feel sick
netsu ga arimasu	have a fever
nodo ga itai	have a sore throat
onaka ga itai	have a stomachache

a. <u>**Atama ga itai desu.**</u> **Kusuri o kudasai.**
<u>I have a headache.</u> Please give me some medicine.

b. Q: **Kinō dōshite pātī e kimasendeshita ka.**
Why didn't you come to the party yesterday?

A: <u>**Onaka ga itakatta desu**</u> **kara.**
Because <u>I had a stomachache.</u>

Ownership: arimasu

In Unit 8, you learned **arimasu** as "there is/are" (pages 93–94). This **arimasu** is also used to express ownership.

a. **Watashi wa netsu ga <u>arimasu</u>.**
   I <u>have</u> a fever.

b. Q: **Kurāku-san wa Nihon no chizu ga <u>arimasu ka</u>.**
      Do you <u>have</u> a map of Japan, Mr Clark?

   A: **Īe, <u>arimasen</u>.**
      No, I <u>do not have</u> one.

Giving and asking reasons (2)

When two sentences are connected and one of them states the reason for the other, they are connected by **kara** "because, so, so that". Note that the reason appears in the first sentence, as shown below.

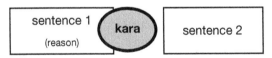

a. ***Fujisan wa kirē desu <u>kara</u>, yūmē desu.***
   Mt. Fuji is beautiful <u>so</u> it is famous.

b. ***Kimochi ga warui desu <u>kara</u>, nanimo tabetakunai desu.***
   I feel unwell <u>so</u> I do not want to eat anything.

Exercise 3

Connect the first and second parts of the sentence so that they make sense, using the phrases in the box below.

   Example Kyō wa yasumi desu **kara** (*b*)

1 Watashi wa Nihon no ēga ga suki desu **kara** (   )
2 Kinō netsu ga arimashita **kara** (   )

3 Watashi wa ryokō ga suki desu **kara** (   )
4 Jikan ga arimasen **kara** (   )

---

a. asa kara ban made uchi de nemashita.
~~b. kaisha e ikimasen.~~   c. isogimashō.
d. yoku uchi de mimasu.   e. yoku gaikoku e ikimasu.

Vocabulary

ryokō	travel, trip	**isogimasu**	to hurry
jikan	time		

Dialogue 3

A doctor gave me some medicine (Audio 2:13)

It is Monday morning. Miss Akita and Mr Clark have just arrived at work.

AKITA   Kurāku-san, senshū no kin-yōbi wa kusuri o arigatō gozaimashita.
KURĀKU   Dō itashimashite. Akita-san wa mō daijōbu desu ka.
AKITA   Hai, do-yōbi oisha-san ni kusuri o moraimashita kara.
KURĀKU   Sō desu ka. Sore wa yokatta desu.
AKITA   Tokorode, kin-yōbi no karaoke wa dō deshita ka.
KURĀKU   Totemo tanoshikatta desu. Kondo Akita-san mo issho ni ikimashō.
AKITA   Hai, zehi.

Vocabulary

daijōbu(na) (**na**-adj.)	all right, OK	**tokorode**	by the way
oisha-san	(medical) doctor	**kondo**	next time
moraimashita	received	**zehi**	by all means, definitely

Dialogue 3 exercise

Write ✓ if the statement agrees with the dialogue. Write ✗ if not.

1 (   ) Miss Akita went to see a doctor to receive some medicine last Saturday.

2 (   ) Mr Clark did not go to karaoke last Friday.

Language points

Expressing one's gratitude

Arigatō gozaimashita is an expression to show one's gratitude. It is different from **arigatō gozaimasu** in that **arigatō gozaimashita** is used when the action that you feel grateful for has been completed.

a. **Kinō wa <u>arigatō gozaimashita</u>.**
<u>Thank you</u> for yesterday.

b. **Kinō wa kusuri o <u>arigatō gozaimashita</u>.**
<u>Thank you</u> for giving me the medicine yesterday.

Giving and receiving

The verbs **agemasu** and **moraimasu** mean "to give" and "to receive". The recipient of the action is marked by **ni**.

a. **Kurāku-san wa Akita-san ni kusuri o <u>agemashita</u>.**
Mr Clark <u>gave</u> Miss Akita some medicine.

b. **Akita-san wa Kurāku-san ni kusuri o <u>moraimashita</u>.**
Miss Akita received some medicine from Mr Clark.

Note that when you are involved in this action as a giver or receiver, the action must be described from your viewpoint.

Exercise 4

Underline the right word as in the example.

> *Example*   Yamada-san wa Kurāku-san ni DVD o (<u>a. agemashita</u>
>   b. moraimashita).   (receiver: Kurāku-san)

1   Watashi wa Yamada-san ni Igirisu no omiyage o (a. agemashita
    b. moraimashita).   (receiver: Yamada-san)
2   Watashi wa Yamada-san ni hana o (a. agemashita
    b. moraimashita).   (receiver: I)
3   (a. Maria-san   b. Watashi) wa (c. Maria-san   d. watashi)
    ni Nihon no hon o agetai desu.   (giver: I)
4   Sensē wa maishū gakusē ni shukudai o (a. agemasu
    b. moraimasu).   (giver: sensē)

Vocabulary

omiyage souvenir, gift	**shukudai** homework

Exercise 5 (**Audio 2:14**)

Mariko has recently moved house. As house-warming presents, she received a lot of things from her friends but she also gave some of her belongings to them. Now another friend, Bob, has come to her house. Listen to their conversation and find out who gave what to whom.

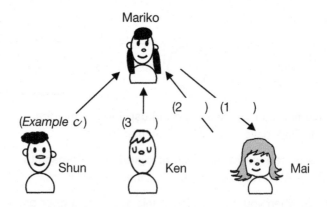

a. tokē	b. terebi	~~c. shashin-tate~~	d. denwa	e. hana

Exercise 6

Put the correct particle or word in the space. Write ✗ if nothing is needed.

1 Watashi wa ima (o)mizu _____ hoshī desu.
2 Atama ga itai desu _____, kusuri o nomimasu.
3 Watashi wa tomodachi _____ omoshiroi hon o moraimashita.
4 Watashi wa yoku toshokan _____ shukudai o shimasu.
5 Watashi wa kuruma ª_____ ichi-dai ᵇ_____ arimasu.

Exercise 7 (Audio 2:15)

Read out the following text and write ✓ if the statement agrees with the text and ✗ if not.

はるこさんは わたしの ともだちです。あしたは はるこさんの
たんじょうびです。はるこさんは はなが すきですから、わたしは
はるこさんに きれいな はなを あげます。そして、はるこさんは
かびんが ありませんから、かびんも あげます。

Haruko-san wa watashi no tomodachi desu. Ashita wa Haruko-san no tanjōbi desu. Haruko-san wa hana ga suki desu kara, watashi wa Haruko-san ni kirēna hana o agemasu. Soshite, Haruko-san wa kabin ga arimasen kara, kabin mo agemasu.

1 ( ) I will give Haruko some beautiful flowers because she likes flowers.
2 ( ) I will give her a vase as well because I found a really nice one.

Vocabulary

kabin vase

Katakana of Unit 10

As with hiragana, "ヤ" "ュ" and "ヨ" can be attached to another katakana to create a combined sound. "ヤ" "ュ" and "ヨ" are written one quarter of the usual size.

キャ(kya)	キュ(kyu)	キョ(kyo)	ギャ(gya)	ギュ(gyu)	ギョ(gyo)
シャ(sha)	シュ(shu)	ショ(sho)	ジャ(ja)	ジュ(ju)	ジョ(jo)
チャ(cha)	チュ(chu)	チョ(cho)	ヂャ(ja)	ヂュ(ju)	ヂョ(jo)
ニャ(nya)	ニュ(nyu)	ニョ(nyo)			
ヒャ(hya)	ヒュ(hyu)	ヒョ(hyo)	ビャ(bya)	ビュ(byu)	ビョ(byo)
ピャ(pya)	ピュ(pyu)	ピョ(pyo)			
ミャ(mya)	ミュ(myu)	ミョ(myo)			
リャ(rya)	リュ(ryu)	リョ(ryo)			

In addition, "ア", "イ", "エ" and "オ" can be used with other Katakana.

ウィ: [**ui**] in ウィキペディア Wikipedia
ウェ: [**ue**] in ウェンディ Wendy
ウォ: [**uo**] in ウォーカー Walker

シェ: [**she**] in ミシェル Michelle   ティ: [**ti**] in ティム Tim
ジェ: [**je**] in ジェニー Jennie   ディ: [**di**] in ジュディス Judith

ファ: [**fa**] in クリストファー Christopher
フィ: [**fi**] in フィリップ Philip
フェ: [**fe**] in フェスティバル festival
フォ: [**fo**] in フォックス fox

[**v**] sound is spelled as either [B] (バビブベボ) or [V] (ヴァヴィヴ ヴェヴォ).
[**tho**] sound is spelled out as ソ [so] or ト [to].   Thornton ソーントン
[**thu**] sound is spelled out as ス [su]   Southampton サウスハン プトン
[**tha/the**] sound is spelled out as サ [sa].   Catherine キャサリン
[**fa/fi/fu/fe/fo**] **and** [**pha/phi/phe/pho**] become ファ、フィ、フ、 フェ、フォ.
[**or/er/ar/ir/ur**] become long sounds (ー).   George ジョージ, Robert ロバート

Exercise 8

A. Which English names do the following names in katakana represent?

Example キャサリン (*d*)

1 エリザベス (　)　　　　2 ビビアン／ヴィヴィアン (　)
3 ジェームズ (　)　　　　4 ベンジャミン (　)
5 マシュー (　)

a. Vivian	b. Matthew	c. Benjamin
d. Catherine	e. Elizabeth	f. James

B. Which places do the following names in katakana represent?

1 カルフォルニア (　)　　　2 リオデジャネイロ (　)
3 バンクーバー (　)　　　　4 バーミンガム (　)
5 ニューデリー (　)

a. Vancouver	b. Birmingham	c. California
d. New Delhi	e. Rio de Janeiro	

Unit Eleven

Shinjuku Gyoen wa hirokute kirēna kōen desu

Shinjuku Gyoen is a spacious and beautiful park

In this unit you will learn about:

- more adjectives
- how to connect sentences which contain i-adjectives, **na**-adjectives and nouns
- talking about the weather
- how to express a change of state, using adjective + **narimasu**
- how to change adjectives into adverbs
- kanji of Unit 11

　一、二、三、四、五、六、七、八、九、十、百、千、万、円

Dialogue 1

Shinjuku Gyoen is a spacious and beautiful park
(Audio 2:16)

Mr Tanaka and Miss Smith are friends. They are discussing their plans for this weekend.

たなか	スミスさんは　きゅうじつ　よく　なにを　しますか。
スミス	わたしは　よく　こうえんへ　さんぽに　いきます。
たなか	そうですか。じゃあ、こんしゅうの　どようび　いっしょに しんじゅく　ぎょえんへ　いきませんか。
スミス	しんじゅくぎょえんは　なんですか。

たなか　しんじゅくぎょえんは　ひろくて　きれいな　こうえんです。
　　　　しんじゅくに　あります。
スミス　しんじゅくえきから　とおいですか。
たなか　いいえ、ちかいですよ。
　　　　しんじゅくえきから　あるいて　10ぷんぐらいです。
スミス　それは　べんりですね。
　　　　じゃあ、こんしゅうの　どようび　いっしょに　いきましょう。

TANAKA	Sumisu-san wa kyūjitsu yoku nani o shimasu ka.
SUMISU	Watashi wa yoku kōen e sanpo ni ikimasu.
TANAKA	Sō desu ka. Jā, konshū no do-yōbi, issho ni Shinjuku Gyoen e ikimasen ka.
SUMISU	Shinjuku Gyoen wa nan desu ka.
TANAKA	Shinjuku Gyoen wa hirokute kirēna kōen desu. Shinjuku ni arimasu.
SUMISU	Shinjuku eki kara tōi desu ka.
TANAKA	Īe, chikai desu yo. Shinjuku eki kara aruite 10-pun gurai desu.
SUMISU	Sore wa benri desu ne. Jā, konshū no do-yōbi, issho ni ikimashō.

Vocabulary

きゅうじつ	**kyūjitsu**	off-duty day, day off
さんぽ	**sanpo**	walk, stroll
(さんぽします)	**(sanpo shimasu)**	(to go for a walk)
しんじゅくぎょえん	**Shinjuku Gyoen**	one of the parks in Tokyo
ひろい (i-adj.)	**hiroi**	spacious
ちかい (i-adj.)	**chikai**	near, close

Dialogue 1 exercise

Write ✓ if the statement agrees with the dialogue. Write ✗ if not.

1 (　) Shinjuku Gyoen is a beautiful and spacious park.
2 (　) Shinjuku Gyoen is far from Shinjuku station.

Language point

Adjectives

As you learned in Unit 5, Japanese adjectives have two types: **i**-adjectives and **na**-adjectives (pages 56–57). All **i**-adjectives have い (**i**) at the end whereas **na**-adjectives end with various sounds.

i-adjectives

あまい	**amai**	sweet	あかるい	**akarui**	bright
からい	**karai**	hot, spicy	くらい	**kurai**	dark
やわらかい	**yawarakai**	soft	おおい	**ōi**	many
ひろい	**hiroi**	spacious	すくない	**sukunai**	few
せまい	**semai**	narrow	うるさい	**urusai**	noisy
おもい	**omoi**	heavy	こわい	**kowai**	scary
かるい	**karui**	light (weight)	うつくしい	**utsukushī**	beautiful

na-adjectives

けんこう(な)	**kenkō(na)**	healthy	あんぜん(な)	**anzen(na)**	safe
じゆう(な)	**jiyū(na)**	free			

Exercise 1

Circle the appropriate adjective which matches the English translation.

1 (a. せまい   b. はやい   c. おそい)   でんしゃ (a *fast* train)
2 (a. おもい   b. かるい   c. こわい)   かばん   (a *light-weight* bag)
3 (a. あかるい   b. うるさい   c. くらい)   へや   (a *dark* room)
4 (a. けんこうな b. あんぜんな c. じゆうな) じかん   (*free* time)
5 (a. あまい   b. からい   c. ちかい)   コーヒー (*sweet* coffee)

Language point

Connecting sentences which contain i-**adjectives**, na-**adjectives and nouns**

So far, you have learned how to connect nouns or sentences in the following ways: **to**, as in **hon *to* zasshi** "a book *and* a magazine" and

soshite/sorekara, as in **Kono kōen wa hiroi desu.** *Soshite*, **kirē desu** "This park is spacious. *And* it is beautiful". In this unit, you will learn how to join two or more sentences into one by using the **te**-form.

i-adjectives

When **i**-adjectives are followed by another predicate such as another adjective, "**i**" in the **i**-adjective (e.g. **atarashii**) becomes **kute** (**kunakute** for the negative form).

Examples

(i-adj.) ——→	(drop **i**) →	(add ***kute***)	(add ***kunakute*** for negative)
ōki*i* big	**ōki**	**ōki*kute***	**ōki*kunakute***
atarashi*i* new	**atarashi**	**atarashi*kute***	**atarashi*kunakute***

a. **Kono resutoran no tabemono wa *oishikute*, yasui desu.**
   The food at this restaurant is *delicious and* cheap.

b. **Watashi wa *amakute* oishī kōhī ga suki desu.**
   I like *sweet and* tasty coffee.

Note that **ii desu** "good" becomes **yokute** instead of **ikute**.

i*i* good   ***yokute*** good   ***yokunakute*** not good

na-adjectives and nouns

When **na**-adjectives or nouns are followed by another predicate, **desu** after the **na**-adjectives/nouns (e.g. **shizuka** desu, **gakusē** desu) becomes **de** (**dewanakute** for the negative form).

Examples

na-adjectives

(**na**-adj.) ——→	(drop **na**) →	(affirmative / negative)	
anzen*na* safe	**anzen**	**anzen *de***	**anzen *dewanakute***
benri*na* convenient	**benri**	**benri *de***	**benri *dewanakute***
shizuka*na* quiet	**shizuka**	**shizuka *de***	**shizuka *dewanakute***

Nouns

(noun) ——————→	(affirmative / negative)	
gakusē student	**gakusē *de***	**gakusē *dewanakute***
21-sai 21 years old	**21-sai *de***	**21-sai *dewanakute***

a. **Yamada-san wa** *shizuka* **de**, *shinsetsuna* **hito desu.**
   Mrs Yamada is *a quiet* *and* kind person.

b. **Kono machi wa** *anzen* **de** *benri* **desu.**
   This town is *safe* *and* convenient.

c. **Watashi no ane wa** *21-sai* **dewanakute**, *22-sai* **desu.**
   My elder sister *is not 21* *but* 22 years old.

Note that **ga** "but" is used when the connected sentences disagree with each other in terms of the positive/negative value.

Kono resutoran wa *kirē dewa arimasen* **ga** *oishī* **desu.**
This restaurant is *not clean* *but* its food is tasty.

Watashi no uchi wa *benri desu* **ga** *chotto semai* **desu.**
My house is *convenient* *but* short of space.

Exercise 2

Fill in the blanks with the appropriate forms.

		Connective form (affirmative)	Connective form (negative)
i-adj.	atsui **desu** (hot)	atsu**kute**	atsu**kunakute**
	chikai desu (near)	1)	2)
	ī desu (good)	3)	4)
na-adj.	daijōbu **desu** (all right)	daijōbu **de**	daijōbu **dewanakute**
	suki desu (like)	5)	6)
	kenkō desu (healthy)	7)	8)
Noun	gakusē **desu** (student)	gakusē **de**	gakusē **dewanakute**
	kaisha desu (company)	9)	10)

Exercise 3

Connect the following two sentences into one, using the appropriate connective form.

Example   Kono kōen wa (hiroi) *hirokute* kirē desu.
            (This park is spacious and beautiful.)

1 Nihon-go wa (omoshiroi)_____ tanoshī desu.
  (Japanese is interesting and enjoyable.)
2 Nihon no tabemono wa karada ni (ī)_____ oishī desu.
  (Japanese food is healthy and tasty.)
3 Kinō no pātī wa (nigiyaka)_____ tanoshikatta desu.
  (The party yesterday was lively and fun.)
4 Yamada-san wa sakkā ga (jōzu)_____, furansu-go ga wakarimasu.
  (Mr Yamada is good at football and understands French.)
5 Kore wa (watashi no tokē)_____, sore wa otōto no tokē desu.
  (This is my watch and that is my younger brother's watch.)

Vocabulary

karada ni ī	healthy (*lit.* "good for one's body")
sakkā	football

Dialogue 2

It became warmer in the afternoon (Audio 2:17)

Mr Tanaka and Miss Smith are talking about last weekend.

たなか	スミスさんは　せんしゅうの　しゅうまつ　なにを　しましたか。
スミス	ともだちと　ちかくの　やまへ　いきました。
たなか	そうですか。てんきは　どうでしたか。
スミス	よかったですよ。ごぜんは　すこし　くもりで、さむかったですが、ごごから　あたたかく　なりました。
たなか	やまの　ちょうじょうまで　いきましたか。
スミス	はい。あるいて　いきましたから　2じかん　かかりました。
たなか	それは　たいへんでしたね。
スミス	はい。でも、ちょうじょうからの　けしきは　ほんとうにうつくしかったです。
たなか	ちょうじょうは　ひとが　おおかったですか。
スミス	いいえ、すくなかったです。

TANAKA	Sumisu-san wa senshū no shūmatsu nani o shimashita ka.
SUMISU	Tomodachi to chikaku no yama e ikimashita.

TANAKA   Sō desu ka. Tenki wa dō deshita ka.
SUMISU   Yokatta desu yo. Gozen wa sukoshi kumori de, samukatta
         desu ga, gogo kara atatakaku narimashita.
TANAKA   Yama no chōjō made ikimashita ka.
SUMISU   Hai. Aruite ikimashita kara, 2-jikan kakarimashita.
TANAKA   Sore wa taihen deshita ne.
SUMISU   Hai. Demo, chōjō kara no keshiki wa hontō ni
         utsukushikatta desu.
TANAKA   Chōjō wa hito ga ōkatta desu ka.
SUMISU   Īe, sukunakatta desu.

 ## Vocabulary

やま	**yama**	mountain
くもり	**kumori**	cloudy
あたたかい (i-adj.)	**atatakai**	warm
なります	**narimasu**	to become
ちょうじょう	**chōjō**	top, summit
けしき	**keshiki**	view, scenery

 ## Dialogue 2 exercise

Write ✓ if the statement agrees with the dialogue. Write ✗ if not.

1 (   ) On the day when Miss Smith went to the nearby mountain, it
         was cold in the morning but became warm in the afternoon.
2 (   ) Miss Smith could not see any view from the top of the mountain
         because of the cloud.

 ## Language points

Vocabulary for weather

hare sunny   **kumori** cloudy   **kaze** wind   **ame** rain   **yuki** snow

a. **Kyō wa <u>hare</u> desu.**
It is <u>fine weather</u> today.

b. **Kinō wa <u>yuki</u> deshita kara, samukatta desu.**
Yesterday it <u>was snowy</u> so it was cold.

c. **Ashita no tenki wa, <u>kumori</u> tokidoki <u>ame</u> desu.**
As for tomorrow's weather, it will be <u>cloudy</u> with occasional <u>rain</u>.

Expressing a change of state: adjective + narimasu

Adjective + **narimasu** "become" is used to indicate a change of state of something, someone, or some place. The form before **narimasu** differs between **i**-adjectives and **na**-adjectives/nouns as below:

i-adjective + narimasu

When **i**-adjectives are in front of **narimasu**, you change **i** to **ku** as below:

a. **Gogo kara <u>atataka*ku*</u> narimasu.**
It will <u>become warm</u> from the afternoon.

b. **Saikin gogo 8-ji kara <u>kura*ku*</u> narimasu.**
It <u>has been getting dark</u> after 8 p.m. recently.

Note that **ī** "good" becomes **yoku** instead of "**iku**".

c. **Tenki ga <u>*yoku*</u> narimashita.**
The weather <u>has become better</u>.

na-adjective/noun + narimasu

When **na**-adjectives or nouns are in front of **narimasu**, you add **ni** as below:

d. **Kusuri o nomimashita kara, <u>genki*ni*</u> narimashita.**
I <u>have got better</u> (*lit.* become well), because I took some medicine.

e. **Watashi wa tenisu ga <u>jōzu*ni*</u> narimashita.**
I <u>became good</u> at playing tennis.

f. **Sengetsu 21-sai _ni_ narimashita.**
I <u>became 21 years old</u> last month.

g. **Watashi wa Ēgo no sensē _ni_ naritai desu.**
I <u>want to become an English teacher.</u>

Exercise 4

Change the words in the brackets appropriately as shown in the example.

Example Watashi no ane wa (isha) _isha nī_ narimashita.

1 Kinō kara (samui)_____ narimashita.
2 Watashi wa Nihon no ēga ga (suki)_____ narimashita.
3 Watashi wa raigetsu (25-sai)_____ narimasu.
4 Ashita kara kyūjitsu desu kara (hima)_____ narimasu.

Language point

Changing adjectives into adverbs

Adjectives can be changed into adverbs as shown below:

i-adjectives: change **i** to **ku**

> **karu_i_** light – **karu_ku_** lightly
> **yawaraka_i_** soft – **yawaraka_ku_** softly

a. **Ashita kara ryokō desu kara, watashi wa konban <u>hayaku</u> nemasu.**
Because I am going on a trip from tomorrow, I will go to bed <u>early</u> tonight.

b. **Watashi wa namae o ōki_ku_ kakimashita.**
I wrote my name <u>in large print</u>. (_lit._ "I wrote my name large".)

na-adjectives: change **na** to **ni**

shizuka(*na*) quiet – **shizuka*ni*** quietly
anzen(*na*) safe – **anzen*ni*** safely

c. **Kinō watashi wa toshokan de *shizuka<u>ni</u>* Nihon-go o benkyō shimashita.**
Yesterday, I studied Japanese <u>quietly</u> at the library.

d. **Ano hito wa *jōzu<u>ni</u>* te de sushi o tabemasu.**
That person eats sushi with his/her hands <u>well</u>.

Exercise 5

Change the following adjectives in the brackets into adverbs appropriately.

1 Watashi wa kesa <u>(hayai)</u>_____ okimashita.
   (I woke up early this morning.)
2 Buraun-san wa Nihon no uta o totemo <u>(jōzu)</u>_____ utaimasu.
   (Miss Brown sings a Japanese song very well.)
3 Watashi wa kinō <u>(osoi)</u>_____ nemashita.
   (I went to bed late yesterday.)
4 Kodomo ga <u>(jiyū)</u>_____ e o kakimasu.
   (A child draws a picture freely.)

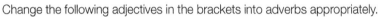

Vocabulary

uta	song
utaimasu	to sing
kodomo	child, children, kid

Exercise 6 (Audio 2:18)

Listen to the conversation between Mr Tanaka and Miss Smith and write
✓ if the statement agrees with it and ✗ if not.

1 ( ) It has become cold and dark.
2 ( ) Mr Tanaka and Miss Smith have decided to go to a coffee
    shop.

Kanji: Historical background and kun-yomi/on-yomi

Kanji, which is commonly used along with hiragana and katakana, was imported from China to Japan around 2,000 years ago by Japanese monks. At that time, the Japanese language did not have its own writing system. After importing kanji, the Japanese people developed hiragana and katakana by simplifying or taking a part of a kanji. Nowadays, Japanese pupils learn 2,136 kanji set by the Ministry of Education, Culture, Sports, Science and Technology in 2010 before completing their nine-year compulsory education. This book will introduce you to approximately 60 kanji.

One of the characteristics of kanji is that it carries both sound and meaning. For example, kanji 「私」 tells you that its sound is **watashi** and it means I. What makes learning kanji slightly difficult is that the majority of kanji characters have multiple sounds and meanings. Those whose sounds have come from Japanese pronunciation are called **kun-yomi** and those whose sounds have come from Chinese pronunciation are called **on-yomi**. This book gives both readings, as shown in the following table. Hiragana and katakana are used for kun-yomi and on-yomi respectively, as found in Japanese dictionaries. However, you use hiragana when you transcribe kanji in order to read it.

Kan-ji	Kun-yomi	On-yomi	Meaning
私 ノ ㄥ 千 千 禾 私 私	わたし	シ	I, private

As for when to use **kun/on-yomi**, the basic rule is that you use **kun-yomi** when the kanji is used either on its own or with hiragana but you use **on-yomi** when the kanji appears in conjunction with other kanji. For instance, you use **kun-yomi** for 私 when it appears on its own, whereas you use **on-yomi** for 私学 "private school" as it is used together with another kanji. Note, however, that a lot of exceptions exist so it is advisable that you remember the kanji as part of your vocabulary.

It is very important to follow the stroke order when you write kanji. The basic rules regarding stroke order include (a) draw from left to right (e.g. 「一」), (b) draw from top to bottom (e.g. 「人」) and (c) draw from left component (e.g. for 「休」, draw 「亻」 first) or top component (e.g. 「売」, draw 「土」 first).

Exercise 7

A. Write "K" when the underlined kanji uses kun-yomi and "O" when it uses on-yomi.

Example 富士山 (*O*) あの山 (*K*) 男子 (*O*) 男の子 (*K*)

1 この人 this person ( )
2 日本人 Japanese people ( )
3 休日 day off ( )
4 休みます to rest ( )
5 木 a tree ( )
6 木曜日 Thursday ( )
7 強いです strong ( )
8 勉強します to study ( )

B. Draw 私 in the boxes below, according to the stroke order. Note that the right half of the character 「ム」 consists of only two strokes.

Extra kanji exercise sheets for Units 11–16 are free to download at: www.routledge.com/cw/colloquials.

Kanji of Unit 11: Kanji for numbers

Kanji	Kun-yomi	On-yomi	Meaning	Kanji	Kun-yomi	On-yomi	Meaning
一 一	ひと(つ)	イチ	one	八 ノ 八	やっ(つ)	ハチ	eight
二 ー 二	ふた(つ)	ニ	two	九 ノ 九	ここの(つ)	キュウ/ク	nine
三 ー ニ 三	みっ(つ)	サン	three	十 ー 十	とお	ジュウ	ten
四 丨 冂 冈 四 四	よっ(つ)	ヨン/シ	four	百 ー 丆 一 丆 百 百		ヒャク/ ビャク/ピャク	hundred
五 ー 丁 五 五	いつ(つ)	ゴ	five	千 ノ 乙 千	ち	セン/ゼン	thousand
六 丶 一 亠 六	むっ(つ)	ロク	six	万 ー 丂 万		マン	ten thousand
七 ー 七	なな(つ)	ナナ/シチ	seven	円 丨 冂 冂 円		エン	Yen, circle

Exercise 8

Write how to read the following numbers in hiragana as the example shows. Japanese is read right to left when written vertically.

Example　ななじゅうきゅうえん　七十九円

十	九	八	七	六	五	四	三	二	一
八 つ	二 つ	一 つ	六 百 二 十 円	二 十 万 円	一 万 八 千 円	十 七 さい	三 千 四 百 五 十 円	三 十 九 さい	百 円

Unit Twelve

Musuko-san wa se ga takai desu ne

Your son is tall, isn't he?

In this unit you will learn about:

- how to describe one's physical features, using the **X wa Y ga** + adjective structure
- comparative and superlative expressions
- terms for body parts and colours
- kanji of Unit 12

人、山、川、女、子、口、上、下、大、小

Dialogue 1

He is tall (Audio 2:19)

Mrs Kato is showing a picture of her son to her friend, Mr Jones.

かとう	ジョーンズさん、これは むすこの しゃしんです。
ジョーンズ	かとうさんに そっくりですね。いま なんさいですか。
かとう	せんげつ 16さいに なりました。
ジョーンズ	むすこさんは あしが ながいですね。そして せが たかいですね。
かとう	はい、かぞくのなかで いちばん せが たかいです。
ジョーンズ	いま、なんセンチぐらい ですか。
かとう	たぶん 185センチぐらい です。

KATŌ	Jōnzu-san, kore wa musuko no shashin desu.
JŌNZU	Katō-san ni sokkuri desu ne. Ima nan-sai desu ka.
KATŌ	Sengetsu 16-sai ni narimashita.
JŌNZU	Musuko-san wa ashi ga nagai desu ne. Soshite se ga takai desu ne.
KATŌ	Hai, kazoku no naka de ichi-ban se ga takai desu.
JŌNZU	Ima, nan-senchi gurai desu ka.
KATŌ	Tabun 185-senchi gurai desu.

Vocabulary

むすこ	**musuko**	son
そっくり (な) (**na**-adj.)	**sokkuri(na)**	to closely resemble someone
あし	**ashi**	leg, foot
ながい (**i**-adj.)	**nagai**	long
せが たかい	**se ga takai**	tall
せ	**se**	stature, height
〜のなかで	**...no naka de**	among
いちばん	**ichi-ban**	first, best, top, most
センチ	**senchi**	centimetre
たぶん	**tabun**	probably, maybe

Dialogue 1 exercise

Write ✓ if the statement agrees with the dialogue. Write ✗ if not.

1 ( ) Mrs Kato's son has long legs.
2 ( ) Mrs Kato's son is smallest in the family.

Language points

Body parts

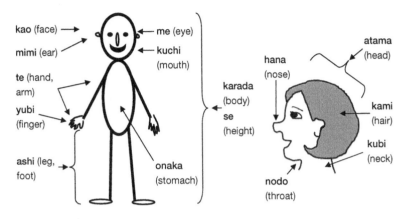

Describing things with the X wa Y ga + adjective structure

In the **X wa Y ga** + adjective structure, X takes the main topic of the sentence and Y takes what is related to X, followed by the adjective which describes Y. For instance, you want to talk about Japan, particularly about its fish, which you find tasty. In this case, **Nihon** "Japan" is the main topic of the sentence (X) and **sakana** "fish" the related topic (Y) as in **Nihon wa sakana ga oishī desu**.

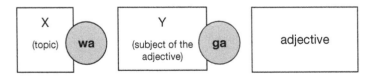

a. **Nihon <u>wa</u> sakana <u>ga</u> oishī desu.**
Talking about Japan, its fish is tasty.

b. **Yamamoto-san <u>wa</u> kami <u>ga</u> kirē desu.**
Miss Yamada has beautiful hair.

c. **Kimura-san <u>wa</u> me <u>ga</u> ōkī desu.**
Mrs Kimura has big eyes.

Exercise 1

Write the appropriate body parts in the brackets and adjectives on the line according to the English meaning.

Example Tokiko-san wa (*se*) ga *takai desu*. (Tokiko is tall.)

1 Tokiko-san wa (   ) ga _____ (Tokiko has long hair.)
2 Tokiko-san wa (   ) ga _____ (Tokiko has black eyes.)
3 Tokiko-san wa (   ) ga _____ (Tokiko has small hands.)
4 Tokiko-san wa (   ) ga _____ (Tokiko is clever. [*lit.* "Tokiko's head/brain is good"])

Vocabulary

kuroi (**i**-adj.)   black

Exercise 2

Answer the following questions, using the cue in the brackets. For question 4, write your own answer.

Example Nihon wa nani ga benri desu ka. (bullet train)
Nihon wa shinkansen ga benri desu.

1 Nihon wa nani ga yūmē desu ka. (Mt. Fuji)
2 Kyōto wa nani ga ōi desu ka. (old temples)
3 Nihon no tabemono wa nani ga oishī desu ka. (sushi)
4 Anata no kuni wa nani ga yūmē desu ka.

Language point

Superlative expressions: ichi-ban + adjective

When you want to say "the most + adjective", you use **ichi-ban** "the best, the most" before the adjective. For instance, "I like tennis the most" in Japanese is **Watashi wa tenisu ga <u>ichi-ban</u> suki desu**. To specify what items are compared, **. . . no naka de** "among . . ." is used in two ways: 1) listing all the items (**X to Y to Z no naka de**) or 2) stating the category which X, Y and Z belong to (**[Category] no naka de**).

a. *Tenisu <u>to</u> sakkā <u>to</u> basukettobōru <u>no naka de</u>*
   (watashi wa) *tenisu <u>ga</u> ichi-ban* **suki desu.**
   I like *tennis* <u>the best among</u> *tennis, football and basketball.*

b. *Supōtsu <u>no naka de</u>* **(watashi wa)** *tenisu <u>ga</u> ichi-ban*
   suki desu.
   I like *tennis* <u>the most among</u> *sports.*

To ask a question with this structure, you put an interrogative word in the position of Y as shown above, followed by the verbal question marker **ka** at the end of the sentence. The interrogative word is determined by what is being asked (time, place, person, etc.).

c. Q: **Hiragana to katakana to kanji no naka de <u>dore</u> ga ichi-ban muzukashī desu ka.**
   <u>Which</u> do you find most difficult, Hiragana, Katakana or Kanji?

   A: **<u>Kanji</u> ga ichi-ban muzukashī desu.**
   <u>Kanji</u> is most difficult.

d. Q: **Kuni no naka de <u>doko</u> ga ichi-ban ōkī desu ka.**
   <u>Which country/where</u> is the biggest country?

   A: **<u>Roshia</u> ga ichi-ban ōkī desu.**
   <u>Russia</u> is the biggest.

Note that when the **~wa ~ga** + adjective structure is used in this pattern, **ga** will appear twice.

e. Q: **Kazoku no naka de, dare <u>*ga*</u> ichi-ban <u>se *ga* takai</u> desu ka.**
   Who is the tallest of the family?

   A: **Watashi <u>*ga*</u> ichi-ban <u>se *ga* takai</u> desu.**
   I am the tallest.

f. Q: **Tomodachi no naka de dare <u>*ga*</u> ichi-ban <u>ashi *ga* hayai</u> desu ka.**
   Who is the fastest among your friends?

   A: **Shinji-san <u>*ga*</u> ichi-ban <u>ashi *ga* hayai</u> desu.**
   Shinji is the fastest.

Exercise 3

Translate the following English sentences into Japanese.

Example I like "な" the most among all the Hiragana.
Watashi wa hiragana no naka de「な」
ga ichiban suki desu.

1 August is the hottest [month] of the year.
2 Wednesday is the busiest [day] of the week.
3 Of Spanish, Japanese and French, I am best at French.

Vocabulary

ichi-nen	a year	「 」	Japanese quotation marks
is-shūkan	a week		equivalent to English " "

Dialogue 2

I prefer the brighter coloured one (Audio 2:20)

Mr Jones is buying a new pair of glasses and Mrs Kato is helping him to choose them.

ジョーンズ	かとうさん、このめがねやは　おきゃくさんが　おおいですね。
かとう	ここは　やすくて　にんきが　ありますから。
ジョーンズ	いろいろな　めがねが　ありますね。
かとう	そうですね。ジョーンズさんは　あかるい　いろと　くらい いろと　どちらのほうが　すきですか。
ジョーンズ	あかるい　いろ　のほうが　すきです。
かとう	じゃあ、この　あかい　めがねは　どうですか。
ジョーンズ	ちょっと　はでですね。
かとう	じゃあ、この　ちゃいろい　めがねは　どうですか。
ジョーンズ	すてきですね。それに　します。

JŌNZU	Katō-san, kono megane-ya wa okyakusan ga ōi desu ne.
KATŌ	Koko wa yasukute ninki ga arimasu kara.
JŌNZU	Iroiro na megane ga arimasu ne.

KATŌ	Sō desu ne. Jōnzu-san wa akarui iro to kurai iro to dochira no hō ga suki desu ka.
JŌNZU	Akarui iro no hō ga suki desu.
KATŌ	Jā, kono akai megane wa dō desu ka.
JŌNZU	Chotto hade desu ne.
KATŌ	Jā, kono chairoi megane wa dō desu ka.
JŌNZU	Suteki desu ne. Sore ni shimasu.

Vocabulary

おきゃくさん	**okyakusan**	visitor, customer
にんき	**ninki**	popularity
いろ	**iro**	colour
どちら	**dochira**	which one of the two
のほうが〜より + adj.	**...no hō ga...yori** + adj.	be more (adj.) than ...
あかい (i-adj.)	**akai**	red
はで (な) (na-adj.)	**hade(na)**	showy, gaudy
ちゃいろい (i-adj.)	**chairoi**	brown
すてき (な) (na-adj.)	**suteki(na)**	wonderful
〜にします	**...ni shimasu**	I will take..., an expression for stating one's own choice

Dialogue 2 exercise

Write ✓ if the statement agrees with the dialogue. Write ✗ if not.

1 (   ) Mr Jones prefers bright colours to dark colours.
2 (   ) Mr Jones has decided to buy a red pair of glasses.

Language points

Colours

The majority of colour terms are i-adjectives but there are some which are nouns. When "i" is dropped from the i-adjective colour term, it becomes a colour noun.

i-adjective			Noun	
akai	red	→	**aka**	red
aoi	blue	→	**ao**	blue
kuroi	black	→	**kuro**	black
shiroi	white	→	**shiro**	white
kīroi	yellow	→	**kīro**	yellow
chairoi	brown	→	**chairo**	brown
			midori	green
			pinku	pink

Comparing two things: X wa Y yori **+ adjective**

A sentence which compares two items (X and Y) takes the **X wa Y yori** + adjective structure. **Yori** is equivalent to the English "than" and is attached to the noun (Y) which is less [adjective]. Therefore, X is more [adjective] than Y.

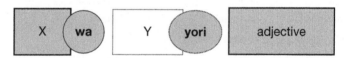

a. **Nihon <u>wa</u> Igirisu <u>yori</u> ōkī desu.**
   Japan is bigger <u>than</u> the UK.

b. **Kyō <u>wa</u> kinō <u>yori</u> samui desu.**
   Today is colder <u>than</u> yesterday.

The interrogative for this pattern is **dochira (no hō)**, meaning "which one of the two". The sentence pattern for questioning is **X to Y to dochira (no hō) ga** + adjective **ka**, whereas the pattern for replying is **X no hō ga** + adjective. **No hō** can be omitted in the question sentence, but not in the reply.

c. Q: **Akarui iro to kurai iro to <u>*dochira (no hō)*</u> ga suki desu <u>ka</u>.**
   <u>Which</u> do you prefer, bright colours or dark colours?

   A: **<u>*Akarui iro <u>no hō</u>*</u> ga suki desu.**
   I prefer bright colours.

To answer "both of them", you say **dochira mo**. Note that you do not use **ga** after **dochira mo**.

d. Q: **Shinkansen to hikōki to _dochira (no hō)_ ga benri deshita ka.**
   Which was more convenient, the bullet train or aeroplane?

   A: **_Dochira mo_ benri deshita.**
   Both were convenient.

Exercise 4 (Audio 2:21)

Read out the following sentences and answer the questions by indicating either a) or b) as shown in the example.

Example このほんは　あのほんより　おもいです。
Which is heavier, this book or that book over there?
a. このほん　b. あのほん

1 ひのでスーパーは　あさひスーパーより　たかいです。
Which supermarket is more expensive?
a. ひのでスーパー　b. あさひスーパー

2 でんしゃは　バスより　はやいです。
Which is faster, train or bus?　a. でんしゃ　b. バス

3 ほんださんは　もりさんより　かみが　ながいです。
Who has shorter hair, Miss Honda or Miss Mori?
a. ほんださん　b. もりさん

4 きのうは　きょうより　あたたかかったです。
Which was colder, today or yesterday?　a. きょう　b. きのう

Exercise 5

Answer the following questions in Japanese.

Example Basu to densha to dochira no hō ga suki desu ka.
(densha)
Densha no hō ga suki desu.

1 Getsu-yōbi to ka-yōbi to dochira no hō ga hima desu ka.
(getsu-yōbi)
2 Hiragana to katakana to dochira no hō ga muzukashī desu ka.
(katakana)
3 Umi to yama to dochira no hō ga suki desu ka. (both, like)

Vocabulary

umi   sea, ocean

Exercise 6 (Audio 2:22)

Listen to a series of conversations between Kelley and Kenji and answer the following questions.

1 Who is tallest in Kenji's family?
   a. Kenji's father   b. Kenji's elder sister   c. Kenji
2 Which guitar does Kenji use most often?
   a. the new white guitar   b. the old white guitar
   c. the big new guitar
3 What month does Kelley like most?
   a. April   b. July   c. December

Vocabulary

wakai (i-adj.) young	**gitā** guitar
tsukaimasu to use	

Exercise 7

Put the appropriate word in the space from the box below. The same word can be used more than once.

Example   Tanaka-san wa me _ga_ kire desu.

1 Supōtsu no naka ᵃ_____ tenisu ᵇ_____ ichi-ban suki desu.
2 Ashita wa kyō _____ atatakai desu.
3 Nihon ᵃ_____ yama ᵇ_____ ōi desu.
4 Q: Akai megane ᵃ_____ chairoi megane ᵇ_____ dochira no hō
      ᶜ_____ ī desu ka.
   A: Chairoi megane no hō ᵈ_____ ī desu.
5 Q: Bīru ᵃ_____ wain ᵇ_____ dochira no hō ᶜ_____ suki desu ka.
   A: Dochira ᵈ_____ suki dewa arimasen.

ga	mo	wa	o
yori	no	de	to

Kanji of Unit 12: Kanji with two or three strokes

Kanji	Kun-yomi	On-yomi	Meaning	Kanji	Kun-yomi	On-yomi	Meaning
人 ノ 人	ひと	ジン／ニン	person	口 l ⼝ 口	くち	コウ	mouth
山 l 凵 山	やま	サン／ザン	mountain	上 l ⼘ 上	うえ	ジョウ	above, on, up
川 ノ 川 川	かわ／がわ	セン	river	下 ー ⼘ 下	した	ゲ	below, under
女 く ⼥ 女	おんな	ジョ	woman female	大 ー ナ 大	おお(きい)	ダイ	big
子 ⁊ ⼦ 子	こ	シ	child	小 ⼘ ⼩ 小	ちい(さい)	ショウ	small

Exercise 8

Write how to read the underlined kanji in hiragana.

1 あの<u>女</u>の<u>人</u>は　デパートで　<u>口</u>べに(lipstick)を　買^かいます。

2 富士^{ふじ}<u>山</u>*は　日本^{にほん}の<u>山</u>です。　*Mt. Fuji

3 あかちゃん (baby) は　手^てが　<u>小</u>さいです。

4 このエレベーターは　<u>上</u>に　行^いきますか。<u>下</u>に　行^いきますか。

5 あの<u>人</u>は　イギリス<u>人</u>ですか。アメリカ<u>人</u>ですか。

6 昨日^{きのう}、　<u>一人</u>*で　<u>大</u>きいケーキを　食^たべました。　*alone

7 私は　昨日^{きのう}　<u>川</u>で　遊^{あそ}びました。

Unit Thirteen
Koko ni suwatte mo ī desu ka
May I sit down here?

In this unit you will learn about:

- verb grouping: Group 1, Group 2, Group 3
- how to make the **te**-form of a verb ([V-**te**]) from the **masu**-form ([V-**masu**])
- how to make a polite request using [V-**te**] + **kudasai**
- saying "how to . . ."
- how to ask, grant and deny permission
- kanji of Unit 13

日、月、火、水、木、土、今、友、少、分

Dialogue 1

Please tell me how to read this kanji **(Audio 2:23)**

Mr Holmes is at a Japanese noodle bar (**udon-ya**), examining a menu written in Japanese.

ホームズ	あのう、すみませんが、このかんじの よみかたを おしえてください。
てんいん	ああ、そのかんじは 「てんぷら」です。
ホームズ	そうですか。じゃあ、「てんぷらうどん」を ください。
てんいん	はい、かしこまりました。
ホームズ	それから、「てんぷらうどん」といっしょに ビールも いっぽん もってきてください。
てんいん	はい、かしこまりました。

HŌMUZU	Anō sumimasen ga, kono kanji no yomikata o oshiete kudasai.
TEN'IN	Ā, sono kanji wa "tenpura" desu.
HŌMUZU	Sō desu ka. Jā, "tenpura udon" o kudasai.
TEN'IN	Hai, kashikomarimashita.
HŌMUZU	Sorekara, "tenpura udon" to issho ni bīru mo ippon motte kite kudasai.
TEN'IN	Hai, kashikomarimashita.

Vocabulary

よみかた	yomikata	how to read
[V-stem] かた	[V-stem] + **kata**	how to . . .
おしえてください	oshiete kudasai	please tell me
[V-て] ください	[V-**te**] + **kudasai**	please (do)
てんぷら	tenpura	*tempura* (a Japanese dish)
うどん	udon	Japanese noodles made of wheat flour
もってきてください	motte kite kudasai	please bring (something)
もってきます	motte kimasu	to bring (something to somewhere)
かしこまりました	kashikomarimashita	certainly

Dialogue 1 exercise

Write ✓ if the statement agrees with the dialogue. Write ✗ if not.

1 (   ) Mr Holmes asked the waitress how to cook "tenpura udon".
2 (   ) Mr Holmes asked the waitress to bring both "tenpura udon" and beer together.

Language point

Verb grouping

Just as there are two types of adjective (**i**-adjectives and **na**-adjectives), there are three groups of Japanese verbs: Group 1, Group 2 and Group 3. This grouping is very important when it comes to making various forms such as the <u>te-form</u> (which you will learn in this unit), the <u>ta-form</u> (Unit 15) and the <u>dictionary form</u> (Unit 16). Below is a list of the new verbs in this unit. The numbers 1, 2 and 3 indicate which group each verb belongs to. Can you find any rule for each group?

Vocabulary

はらいます	**haraimasu**	1	to pay
おきます	**okimasu**	1	to put (something)
おくります	**okurimasu**	1	to send (e.g. an email)
もっていきます	**motte ikimasu**	1	to take (something to somewhere)
つれていきます	**tsurete ikimasu**	1	to take (someone to somewhere)
おもいだします	**omoidashimasu**	1	to remember, recall
がんばります	**ganbarimasu**	1	to hang on, work hard to do, try one's best
よびます	**yobimasu**	1	to call (a taxi)
きをつけます	**ki o tsukemasu**	2	to be careful
とめます	**tomemasu**	2	to pull up (a car), stop
たすけます	**tasukemasu**	2	to help, rescue
みせます	**misemasu**	2	to show
おぼえます	**oboemasu**	2	to remember, memorize
とどけます	**todokemasu**	2	to deliver
おしえます	**oshiemasu**	2	to teach, tell
つれてきます	**tsurete kimasu**	3	to bring (someone to somewhere)
クリックします	**kurikku shimasu**	3	to click

The following shows how to tell which group each verb belongs to from its **masu**-form.

Group 1 verbs

Verbs that end with the "**i**" sound before **masu**:

い<u>き</u>ます go   よ<u>み</u>ます read   あ<u>い</u>ます meet
ik<u>i</u> masu   **yom<u>i</u> masu**   **a<u>i</u> masu**

Note that some verbs such as those below belong to Group 2, though they end with the "**i**" sound before **masu.**

おきます get up   かります borrow   おります get off
oki masu   **kari masu**   **ori masu**

Group 2 verbs

Verbs with only *one Hiragana syllable* before **masu:**

みます see, watch   います be, exist   ねます sleep
mi masu   **i masu**   **ne masu**

Verbs that end with the "**e**" sound before **masu:**

たべます eat   あげます give   かけます make a call
tabe masu   **age masu**   **kake masu**

Group 3 verbs (irregular)

There are only two irregular verbs plus verbs with **shimasu** (e.g. **benkyō shimasu**).

きます come   します do
ki masu   **shi masu**

You can find a full list of verbs with groupings and various conjugations in the Appendix.

Exercise 1

Indicate which group the following verbs belong to.

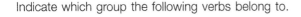

Example   motte ikimasu   (take something to somewhere)   [*1*]

1 oboemasu   (to remember)   [   ]
2 okimasu   (to put)   [   ]
3 okurimasu   (to send)   [   ]
4 kurikku shimasu   (to click)   [   ]
5 haraimasu   (to pay)   [   ]
6 kimasu   (to come)   [   ]
7 shimasu   (to do)   [   ]
8 misemasu   (to show)   [   ]

Language point

Verb te-form (1): how to make the "te-form"

So far, you have learned four types of **masu**-form conjugation.

non-past affirmative	non-past negative	past affirmative	past negative
たべます	たべません	たべました	たべませんでした
tabemasu	**tabemasen**	**tabemashita**	**tabemasendeshita**

In this unit, you will learn a new form, the **te**-form. The **te**-form ([V-**te**]) is very useful because with it, you can express more, such as a polite request (e.g. "Please tell me . . ."), asking permission (e.g. "May I use . . . ?"), action in progress ("I am writing . . ."), etc.

How to make the **te**-form from the **masu**-form is determined by which group the verb belongs to.

Group 1 verbs

In order to make the **te**-form from a group 1 verb, find the sound before **masu** and change it according to the rules below:

い (i)、ち (chi)、り (ri)	→	って (tte)
あいます a<u>i</u>masu meet	→	あ<u>って</u> a<u>tte</u>
まちます ma<u>chi</u>masu wait	→	ま<u>って</u> ma<u>tte</u>
*いきます i<u>ki</u>masu go	→	い<u>って</u> i<u>tte</u>
び (bi)、み (mi)、に (ni)	→	んで (nde)
あそびます aso<u>bi</u>masu play	→	あそ<u>んで</u> aso<u>nde</u>
のみます no<u>mi</u>masu drink	→	の<u>んで</u> no<u>nde</u>
き (ki)、ぎ (gi)	→	いて (ite)、いで (ide)
かきます ka<u>ki</u>masu write	→	か<u>いて</u> ka<u>ite</u>
いそぎます iso<u>gi</u>masu hurry	→	いそ<u>いで</u> iso<u>ide</u>
し (shi)	→	して (shite)
はなします hana<u>shi</u>masu talk	→	はな<u>して</u> hana<u>shite</u>

Note that the **te**-form of いきます **ikimasu** "go" is いって **itte**, not いきて ikite.

Group 2 and 3 verbs

In order to make the **te**-form from group 2 and 3 verbs, you delete **masu** and add **te** as below:

ます (masu)			→	て (te)	
2	たべます	tabe<u>masu</u> eat	→	たべて	tabe<u>te</u>
2	みます	mi<u>masu</u> see	→	みて	mi<u>te</u>
2	ねます	ne<u>masu</u> sleep	→	ねて	ne<u>te</u>
3	きます	ki<u>masu</u> come	→	きて	ki<u>te</u>
3	します	shi<u>masu</u> do	→	して	shi<u>te</u>

Exercise 2

Change the following verbs into the **te**-form. For Group 1, look at the sound before **masu**.

1 あそびます	2 つれてきます
3 いきます	4 がんばります
5 おぼえます	6 みせます
7 もっていきます	8 いそぎます
9 おくります	10 クリックします

Language point

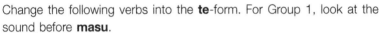

Verb te-form (2): polite requests using (V-te) + kudasai

[V-te] + **kudasai** is an expression used to make a polite request.

verb-te	kudasai

a. **Sono shashin o <u>misete kudasai</u>.**
   <u>Please show</u> me that photo.

b. **Kasa o <u>motte kite kudasai</u>.**
   <u>Please bring</u> an umbrella with you.

c. **<u>Sumimasen ga</u> kono kanji no kakikata o <u>oshiete kudasai</u>.**
   <u>Excuse me but please tell</u> me how to write this kanji.

Omitting **kudasai** makes the request sound very casual, which is suitable only among those in a close relationship, such as friends.

    d. **Sono shashin o <u>misete</u>.**   <u>Show</u> me that photo.

Exercise 3

Connect the following verbs and **kudasai** appropriately and write the English meaning in the brackets.

    Example misemasu + kudasai = *misete kudasai*
                (please show (me))

1 kakimasu   + kudasai = _____
  (   )
2 kyanseru shimasu + kudasai = _____
  (   )
3 ki o tsukemasu   + kudasai = _____
  (   )
4 oshiemasu   + kudasai = _____
  (   )
5 okimasu   + kudasai = _____
  (please wake up)
6 okimasu   + kudasai = _____
  (please put (something))

Exercise 4 (**Audio 2:24**)

Listen to the conversation between a male speaker and a female speaker and underline what the male speaker has agreed to do.

    Example a. takushī o yobimasu   <u>b. takushī o tomemasu</u>

1 a. shashin o misemasu   b. shashin o torimasu
2 a. chizu o okurimasu   b. chizu o kakimasu

Language point

How to . . .

To say "how to . . .", simply take away **masu** from the verb and add **kata** to form a noun.

yomi~~masu~~ + **kata** = **yomikata**   how to read
oboe~~masu~~ + **kata** = **oboekata**   how to remember

Note that the object of the verb is marked by **no**, not o.

a. **<u>Kono kanji *no* yomikata</u> o oshiete kudasai.**
   Please tell me <u>how to read this kanji</u>.

Exercise 5

Suppose you are in the following situation. Make a polite request in Japanese.

1 You are in a restaurant. You want the restaurant staff to tell you how to use chopsticks.
2 You want to know how to go to the Fuji Hotel. Ask a passer-by politely.

Dialogue 2

You must not wear the slippers in the room (Audio 2:25)

Mr Holmes has just arrived at a Japanese inn (**ryokan**) with his colleagues. This is his first time staying at a Japanese inn. Now he is asking a couple of questions of his colleague and friend, Mrs Nagano, who has taken him to his room.

ながの	ホームズさんのへやは　ここです。
ホームズ	ここですか。ひろいですね。あれ、へやのなかに　げんかんが　ありますね。どうしてですか。
ながの	へやのなかで　くつを　はいてはいけませんから。
ホームズ	そうですか。あれ、げんかんに　スリッパが　ありますね。へやのなかで　スリッパを　はきますか。
ながの	いいえ、へやのなかで　はいてはいけません。へやのそとで　はいてください。
ホームズ	わかりました。ところで、へやのなかで　たばこを　すってもいいですか。
ながの	いいえ、ホームズさんのへやは　きんえんですから、たばこを　すっては　いけません。でも、りょかんの　ロビーで　すってもいいですよ。

NAGANO   Hōmuzu-san no heya wa koko desu.

HŌMUZU   Koko desu ka. Hiroi desu ne. Are, heya no naka ni genkan ga arimasu ne. Dōshite desu ka.

NAGANO   Heya no naka de kutsu o haitewa ikemasen kara.

HŌMUZU   Sō desu ka. Are, genkan ni surippa ga arimasu ne. Heya no naka de surippa o hakimasu ka.

NAGANO   Īe, heya no naka de haitewa ikemasen. Heya no soto de haite kudasai.

HŌMUZU   Wakarimashita. Tokorode, heya no naka de, tabako o sutte mo ī desu ka.

NAGANO   Īe, Hōmuzu-san no heya wa kin'en desu kara, tabako o suttewa ikemasen. Demo, ryokan no robī de sutte mo ī desu yo.

Vocabulary

あれ	**are**	Look!, Oh no!
はきます	**hakimasu**	to wear (shoes, trousers, etc.)
はいてもいいです	**haite mo ī desu**	(one) may wear
[V-て]もいいです	**[V-te] + mo ī desu**	(you) may do
はいてはいけません	**haitewa ikemasen**	(one) must not wear
[V-て]はいけません	**[V-te] + wa ikemasen**	must not
たばこ	**tabako**	tobacco, cigarette
すいます	**suimasu**	to smoke
スリッパ	**surippa**	(a pair of) slippers
きんえん	**kin'en**	non-smoking
ロビー	**robī**	lobby

Dialogue 2 exercise

Write ✓ if the statement agrees with the dialogue. Write ✗ if not.

1 (   ) The slippers in the entrance room are for Mr Holmes to use inside the room.

2 (   ) A smoking area can be found in the lobby of the inn.

Language point

Verb te-form (3): asking, granting and denying permission

[V-**te**] + **mo ī desu** is used to grant permission. To ask permission, simply add **ka** at the end as [V-**te**] + **mo ī desu ka**.

verb-**te**	**mo ī desu** (may)

a. Q: **Pātī ni tomodachi o *tsurete kite mo ī desu ka*.**
   May I bring my friends to the party?

    A1: **Hai, *(tsurete kite mo) ī desu* yo.**   Yes, you <u>can</u>.
    A2: **Hai, dōzo.**   Yes, please do.

b. Q: **Koko ni kuruma o *tomete mo ī desu ka*.**
      May I <u>park</u> a car here?

    A: **Sumimasen ga chotto . . .**
      I am afraid that it is slightly [problematic].

[V-**te**] + **wa ikemasen** is used to deny permission. This expression is a strong denial (prohibition) and its usage is usually restricted to cases such as stating the law, regulations, etc.

verb-**te**	**wa ikemasen** (must not)

c. **Kono tatemono no naka de tabako o *suttewa ikemasen*.**
   <u>No</u> smoking <u>is permitted</u> in this building.

Exercise 6

Translate the following English sentences into Japanese.

Example   May I read books here?
      Koko de hon o yonde mo ī desu ka.

1 May I pay by credit card?
2 May I use this pen?
3 You must not drink alcohol here.

Vocabulary

kādo de   by (credit) card

Exercise 7

Connect the first and second parts of the sentence appropriately using the phrases in the box below. The first part is the reason why one is asking for permission.

Example   Atama ga itai desu kara (*c*)

1   Kono kaban wa omoi desu kara (   )
2   Kono kotoba ga wakarimasen kara (   )
3   Sukoshi samui desu kara (   )

a. koko ni oite mo ī desu ka.	b. mado o shimete mo ī desu ka.
c. kaette mo ī desu ka.	d. jisho o mite mo ī desu ka.

Vocabulary

kotoba   word
mado   window
shimemasu   to close, shut

Exercise 8 (Audio 2:26)

The following text describes a certain place. Read out the text and guess where it is.

ここは　ばしょです。とても　ひろい　ばしょです。たくさん　いすが　あります。ここで　ほんを　よんでもいいです。ビールや　ワインを　のんでもいいです。そして、えいがを　みながら、ごはんを　たべてもいいです。しかし、たばこを　すってはいけません。それから、けいたいでんわで　はなしてはいけません。まどを　あけてもいけません。あぶないですから、このなかで　はしってはいけません。このなかには　たくさん　ひとが　いますから、うるさくしてはいけません。

ここは　どこですか。

Vocabulary

ばしょ	**basho**	place
いす	**isu**	chair
しかし	**shikashi**	but
あぶない (i-adj.)	**abunai**	dangerous
みながら	**minagara**	while watching, while seeing
〜ながら	**-nagara**	while doing . . .
あけます	**akemasu**	to open
うるさくします	**urusaku shimasu**	to make a noise

Kanji of Unit 13: Kanji with 3 or 4 strokes

Kanji	Kun-yomi	On-yomi	Meaning	Kanji	Kun-yomi	On-yomi	Meaning
日	ひ/び/か	ニチ/ニ/ジツ	day, sun	土	つち	ド	ground, soil
一 冂 冃 日				一 十 土			
月	つき	ゲツ/ガツ	month, moon	今	いま	コン	now
丿 几 月 月				丿 人 𠆢 今			
火	ひ	カ	fire	友	とも	ユウ	friend
丶 丷 少 火				一 ナ 方 友			
水	みず	スイ	water	少	すく (ない) すこ (し)	ショウ	little, few
丿 가 가 水				丿 小 小 少			
木	き	モク	tree	分	わ (ける)	フン/ブン	divide, minute
一 十 才 木				丿 八 分 分			

Exercise 9

Write how to read the underlined kanji in hiragana.

1 <u>今日</u>*は<u>火</u>曜<u>日</u>**です。<u>昨日</u>は<u>月</u>曜<u>日</u>**でした。*今日, meaning
  "today" is read irregularly and does not use either on-yomi or
  kun-yomi. **日 in this case uses **kun-yomi**.

2 <u>私</u>は　<u>少</u>し　<u>水</u>が　<u>飲</u>みたいです。

3 あの<u>木</u>の<u>下</u>に　<u>私</u>の<u>友達</u>*が　います。*友 in this case uses
  kun-yomi.

4 <u>明日</u>は　<u>土曜日</u>です。

5 この<u>漢字</u>の<u>読み方</u>が　<u>分</u>かりません。

6 <u>日本</u>は　<u>今</u>、3<u>時</u>15<u>分</u>です。

7 「<u>今月</u>」は<u>英語</u>で this month です。

Unit Fourteen

Kinō no yoru 8-ji goro ēga o mite imashita

I was watching a film at around 8 p.m. yesterday

> In this unit you will learn about:
>
> - stating a sequence of actions, using [V-te] and [V-te] + **kara**
> - describing an action in progress: [V-te] + **imasu**
> - describing a present state: [V-te] + **imasu**
> - describing habitual actions: [V-te] + **imasu**
> - kanji of Unit 14
>
>   手、中、外、左、右、文、父、母、田、目

Dialogue 1

Please get on the bus and then get off at the stop "In front of Sakura Hospital" **(Audio 2:27)**

Mr Enokida is giving his colleague, Ms Kim, directions to his house because she is visiting his place this Saturday for the first time.

えのきだ　キムさんは　どようび　なにで　わたしのうちへ　きますか。
キム　　　でんしゃで　いきます。
えのきだ　じゃあ、「さくらえき」で　でんしゃを　おりて、みなみぐちから
　　　　　でてください。みなみぐちの　まえに　バスていが　ありますから、
　　　　　そこで　73ばんの　バスに　のって　「さくらびょういんまえ」で
　　　　　おりてください。

キム　　「さくらびょういんまえ」は　いくつめの　バスてい　ですか。
えのきだ　4つめの　バスていです。

ENOKIDA   Kimu-san wa do-yōbi nani de watashi no uchi e kimasu
          ka.
KIMU   Densha de ikimasu.
ENOKIDA   Jā, "Sakura eki" de densha o orite, minami-guchi kara
          dete kudasai. Minami-guchi no mae ni basutē ga arimasu
          kara, soko de 73-ban no basu ni notte "Sakura Byōin
          Mae" de orite kudasai.
KIMU   "Sakura Byōin Mae" wa ikutsu-me no basutē desu ka.
ENOKIDA   Yottsu-me no basutē desu.

Vocabulary

おります	orimasu	to get off
みなみぐち	minami-guchi	south exit
みなみ	minami	south
～ぐち	-guchi	exit
バスてい	basutē	bus stop
でます	demasu	to leave, get out
のります	norimasu	to get on, ride
いくつめ	ikutsu-me	how many
～め	-me	order in numbers

Dialogue 1 exercise

Write ✓ if the statement agrees with the dialogue. Write ✗ if not.

1 (　) Mr Enokida lives in front of Sakura station.
2 (　) Ms Kim will have to take a train and then catch a bus to get
      to Mr Enokida's house.

Language point

Giving directions

Here is some vocabulary related to directions. Check with the pictures below which particle is used with which movement.

Vocabulary

みち	michi	street, road
かど	kado	corner
はし	hashi	bridge
こうさてん	kōsaten	crossroads
しんごう	shingō	traffic lights
つぎ	tsugi	next
のります	norimasu	to get on
おります	orimasu	to get off
のりかえます	norikaemasu	to change (means of transportation)
わたります	watarimasu	to cross
まがります	magarimasu	to turn

basu ni norimasu

basu o orimasu

A kara B ni norikaemasu

michi o watarimasu

hashi o watarimasu

kado o (migi ni) magarimasu

-me is used to indicate the order with numbers.

hitotsu-me/futatsu-me/mittsu-me (no kado)
first/second/third (corner)

Exercise 1 (Audio 2:28)

Which buildings are the
following hotels?

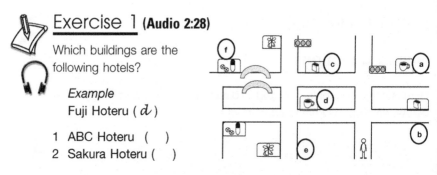

Example
Fuji Hoteru (*d*)

1 ABC Hoteru (   )
2 Sakura Hoteru (   )

Vocabulary

massugu   straight on, ahead

Language point

Verb te-**form (4): actions in succession**

The **te**-form of a verb is used when a sentence has more than one verb
and the actions in the sentence happen (or happened) in succession.
For example, "I wake up, eat and go" are **okite, tabete, ikimasu.**
The tense of the sentence is indicated by the last verb.

verb-**te**	verb-**te**	V-**masu/mashita** V-**tai desu** (want to) [V-**te**] + **mo ī desu** (may) [V-**te**] + **kudasai** (please), etc.
(action 1)	(action 2)	

a. **Ane wa ashita machi e <u>itte</u>, Nihon-go no jisho o kaimasu.**
   My elder sister <u>will go</u> into town and <u>buy</u> a Japanese
   dictionary tomorrow.

b. **Watashi wa kinō gohan o <u>tabete</u>, shawā o <u>abite</u>,
   nemashita.**
   I <u>ate</u> supper, <u>took</u> a shower and <u>went</u> to bed yesterday.

c. **Watashi wa itsuka Nihon ni <u>itte</u>, Nihon no kaisha de
   <u>hatarakitai desu</u>.**
   I <u>want to go to</u> Japan and <u>work</u> for a Japanese company
   some day.

d. **Basu ni <u>notte</u>, yottsu-me no basutē de <u>orite kudasai</u>.**
<u>Please catch</u> a bus and <u>get off</u> at the fourth stop.

Vocabulary

shawā	shower	**sumimasu**	to live
abimasu	to take (a shower)	**hatarakimasu**	to work

Exercise 2

Make a sentence using the information in the brackets as shown in the example. All sentences start with **watashi**.

Example (ashita/tomodachi ni aimasu/sushi o tabemasu)
Watashi wa ashita tomodachi ni atte,
sushi o tabemasu.

1 (kinō/toshokan e ikimashita/hon o karimashita)
2 (kyō/7-ji ni okimashita/shawā o abimashita/terebi o mimashita)
3 (rainen/Nihon e ikitai desu/Fujisan ni noboritai desu)

Vocabulary

noborimasu to climb

Language point

Verb te-**form (5): after doing . . .**

When **kara** follows the **te**-form of a verb, it emphasizes the completion of the action.

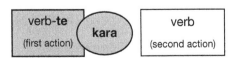

a. **Watashi wa itsumo ha o <u>migaite *kara*</u> nemasu.**
I always <u>brush my teeth *and then*</u> go to bed.

b. Q: **Uchi ni <u>kaette *kara*</u> nani o shimasu ka.**
What do you do <u>*after* returning</u> home?

A: **30-pun kurai yasumimasu.**
I take a rest for about 30 minutes.

 Vocabulary

ha	teeth	**migakimasu**	to brush

 Exercise 3

Make a sentence using the information in the brackets as shown in the example. All sentences start with **watashi**.

Example (wash clothes → watch DVD)
Watashi wa sentaku shite kara DVD o mimasu.

1 (have a meal → take a shower)
2 (cleaned my room → had a rest)
3 (arrived in Japan → phoned Mr Mori)

 Vocabulary

sentaku shimasu	to wash clothes
shokuji shimasu	to have a meal
sōji shimasu	to clean (a room, house, park, etc.)
(ni) tsukimasu	to arrive (at)

 Dialogue 2

 I was watching a Korean film at home **(Audio 2:29)**

Mr Enokida and Ms Kim are talking in the company office.

えのきだ　　キムさん、こんにちは。
キム　　　　あ、えのきださん、こんにちは。

えのきだ　キムさんは　きのうのよる　8じごろ　なにを　していましたか。

キム　　きのうは　あめが　ふっていましたから　うちで　かんこくの
　　　　えいがを　みていました。

えのきだ　おもしろかったですか。

キム　　はい、とても　おもしろかったです。わたしは　DVDを
　　　　もっていますから、いつか　えのきださんも　みてください。

ENOKIDA　Kimu-san, konnichiwa.

KIMU　　A, Enokida-san, konnichiwa.

ENOKIDA　Kimu-san wa kinō no yoru 8-ji goro nani o shite imashita
　　　　ka.

KIMU　　Kinō wa ame ga futte imashita kara, uchi de Kankoku no
　　　　ēga o mite imashita.

ENOKIDA　Omoshirokatta desu ka.

KIMU　　Hai, totemo omoshirokatta desu. Watashi wa DVD
　　　　o motte imasu kara, itsuka Enokida-san mo mite
　　　　kudasai.

Vocabulary

していました	shite imashita	was/were doing
[V-て]います	[V-**te**] + **imasu**	be [verb]-ing (present progressive action)
もっています	**motte imasu**	to own, possess
もちます	**mochimasu**	to hold, have, own
[V-て]います	[V-**te**] + **imasu**	describing a state of someone or something
いつか	**itsuka**	one day, some day

Dialogue 2 exercise

Write ✓ if the statement agrees with the dialogue. Write ✗ if not.

1 (　) Ms Kim was watching a Korean film at 8 p.m. last night.
2 (　) It was Mr Enokida who recommended that film to Ms Kim.

Language point

Verb te-form (6): describing an action in progress

[Verb-te] + imasu is used to describe an action in progress.

a. **Watashi wa ima kōhī o <u>nonde imasu</u>.**
   I <u>am drinking</u> a cup of coffee now.

b. **Watashi wa kyonen no ima goro Nihon o <u>ryokō shite</u>**
   <u>**imashita**</u>.
   I <u>was travelling</u> in Japan this time last year.

 Exercise 4

Complete the following sentences, using the information in brackets.

Example   Ai-san wa ima (sing a song)
            uta o utatte imasu.

1 Yōko-san wa ima (brush her teeth)
2 Lī-san wa ima (write an email)
3 Tōmasu-san wa kinō no 6-ji goro (work)
4 Kenji-san wa kinō no 10-ji goro (take a shower)

 Language point

Verb te-form (7): describing a state

[V-te] + imasu is also used to describe a state of someone or some-thing. Verbs such as **suwarimasu** "sit down", **tachimasu** "stand up", **kekkon shimasu** "marry" and **sumimasu** "live" are often used with this pattern.

a. **Otoko no hito ga asoko ni <u>suwatte imasu</u>.**
   A man <u>is seated</u> over there.

b. **Watashi wa <u>kekkon shite imasen</u>.**
   I <u>am not married</u>.

Vocabulary

	Action		State
mochimasu	to hold	**motte imasu**	to own, possess
sumimasu	to live	**sunde imasu**	to live
shirimasu	to get to know	**shitte imasu**	to know
tachimasu	to stand up	**tatte imasu**	to be standing
suwarimasu	to sit down	**suwatte imasu**	to be seated
iremasu	to put (something) in	**irete imasu**	to have (something) in
kekkon shimasu	to marry	**kekkon shite imasu**	to be married

The following examples show the difference between **sumimasu/ sunde imasu** "live" and **mochimasu/motte imasu** "have":

c1. **Watashi no ani wa ima Nihon ni <u>sunde imasu</u>.**
My elder brother currently <u>lives</u> in Japan.

c2. **Watashi wa rainen kara Nihon ni <u>sumimasu</u>.**
I will <u>live</u> in Japan from next year.

d1. **Watashi wa Nihon-go no jisho o <u>motte imasu</u>.**
I <u>own</u> a Japanese dictionary.

d2. **Yamada-san, kaban o <u>mochimashō ka</u>.**
<u>Shall I carry</u> your bag, Mrs Yamada?

Note that the negative form of **shitte imasu** "know" is **shirimasen**, instead of "**shitte imasen**".

e. Q: **Yamada-san o <u>shitte imasu ka</u>.**
Do you <u>know</u> Mrs Yamada?

A: **Īe, <u>shirimasen</u>.**
No, I <u>do not know</u> her.

Exercise 5

Translate the following into Japanese.

1 Mr Mori is seated in a car.
2 Mrs Okada owns two PCs.
3 Mr Takeda is married.
4 I do not know this song but I know that song.

Dialogue 3

I eat vegetables every day (Audio 2:30)

Mr Enokida and Ms Kim are talking about how they keep fit.

キム	えのきださんは けんこうのために なにを していますか。
えのきだ	わたしは まいにち やさいを たべています。それから ジョギングも しています。キムさんは。
キム	わたしは まいしゅうまつ ちかくの プールで およいでいます。
えのきだ	どのくらい およいでいますか。
キム	1じかんぐらい およいでいます。
えのきだ	すごいですね。

KIMU	Enokida-san wa kenkō no tame ni nani o shite imasu ka.
ENOKIDA	Watashi wa mainichi yasai o tabete imasu. Sorekara jogingu mo shite imasu. Kimu-san wa.
KIMU	Watashi wa maishūmatsu chikaku no pūru de oyoide imasu.
ENOKIDA	Donokurai oyoide imasu ka.
KIMU	1-jikan gurai oyoide imasu.
ENOKIDA	Sugoi desu ne.

Vocabulary

[noun] のために	[noun] **no tame ni**	for the benefit of [noun]
ジョギングをします	**jogingu o shimasu**	to jog
まいしゅうまつ	**maishūmatsu**	every weekend
ちかくの	**chikaku no**	nearby
すごい (i-adj.)	**sugoi**	great

Dialogue 3 exercise

Write ✓ if the statement agrees with the dialogue. Write ✗ if not.

1 (   ) Mr Enokida keeps fit by eating vegetables and jogging every day.

2 (   ) Ms Kim has decided to swim from the coming weekend.

Language point

Verb te-form (8): habitual action (V-te) + imasu

An activity which is done regularly or habitually is also expressed by [V-**te**] + **imasu**.

   a. **Watashi wa Nihon no kaisha de <u>hataraite imasu</u>.**
      I <u>work</u> for a Japanese company.

   b. **Watashi no tomodachi wa daigaku de Ēgo o <u>oshiete imasu</u>.**
      (My friend <u>teaches</u> English at university.

   c. **Kono kaisha wa kuruma o <u>tsukutte imasu</u>.**
      This company <u>manufactures</u> cars.

Exercise 6

What does Ms Kim do every day to improve her Japanese? Write what she does, using the information in the brackets.

   Example (write Kanji 10 times)
        Kimu-san wa mainichi kanji o 10-kai kaite imasu.

1 (listen to Japanese music)
2 (memorize words)
3 (watch Japanese TV)
4 (sing her favourite Japanese songs)

Kanji of Unit 14: Kanji with 4 or 5 strokes

Kanji	Kun-yomi	On-yomi	Meaning	Kanji	Kun-yomi	On-yomi	Meaning
手	て	シュ	hand	文		ブン/モン	letter, sentence
ノ ニ ニ 手				、 一 ナ 文			
中	なか	チュウ	middle, inside	父	ちち	フ	father
丨 口 口 中				ノ ハ グ 父			
外	そと	ゲ/ガイ	out, other, foreign	母	はは	ボ	mother
ノ ク タ タ 外				㇄ 口 모 모 母			
左	ひだり	サ	left	田	た/だ	デン	rice field
一 ナ ナ 左 左				丨 冂 冂 田 田			
右	みぎ	ウ/ユウ	right	目	め	モク	eye
ノ ナ オ 右 右				丨 冂 月 月 目			

Exercise 7

Write how to read the underlined kanji in hiragana.

1 私の<u>父</u>と<u>母</u>は　今　<u>外国</u>*に　います。*abroad

2 <u>山田</u>*さんは　<u>目</u>が　とても　きれいです。*Japanese name uses Kun-yomi.

3 <u>田中</u>*さんのお<u>父</u>さんは　レストランの<u>中</u>に　います。

4 マリアさんは　テニスが　<u>上手</u>*です。*be good at

5 私は　<u>手</u>で　すしを　食べます。

6 この<u>文</u>を　読んでください。

7 あのコンビニの<u>右</u>に　郵便局が　あります。コンビニの<u>左</u>に　おいしいレストランが　あります。

Unit Fifteen

Pūru de oyoidari, toshokan de hon o karitari shimasu

I do various things such as swimming in the pool and borrowing books from the library

In this unit you will learn about:

- Vocabulary for clothes and accessories
- how to make the **ta**-form of a verb: [V-**ta**]
- how to link verb sentences using the [V-**ta**] + **ri** [V-**ta**] + **ri** . . . pattern
- saying "after . . ." using [V-**ta**] + **ato de**
- talking about one's experiences in the past
- kanji of Unit 15

  本、先、生、学、好、何、字、年、車、毎

Dialogue 1

I want to do various things such as swimming in the pool, borrowing books from the library, etc.
(Audio 2:31)

Miss Inoue is Mr Hancock's friend. They are now talking about their plans for this weekend.

ハンコック	いのうえさんは、こんしゅうまつ　なにを　したいですか。
いのうえ	そうですね。プールで　およいだり、としょかんで　ほんを　かりたり　したいです。ハンコックさんは。

ハンコック　わたしは　まちへ　ふくを　かいに　いきたいです。
いのうえ　　なにを　かいたいですか。
ハンコック　あたらしい　ズボンや　セーターを　かいたいです。
いのうえ　　そうですか。

HANKOKKU	Inoue-san wa konshūmatsu nani o shitai desu ka.
INOUE	Sō desu ne. Pūru de oyoidari, toshokan de hon o karitari shitai desu. Hankokku-san wa?
HANKOKKU	Watashi wa machi e fuku o kai ni ikitai desu.
INOUE	Nani o kaitai desu ka.
HANKOKKU	Atarashī zubon ya sētā o kaitai desu.
INOUE	Sō desu ka.

Vocabulary

およぎます	**oyogimasu**	to swim
[V-た]り、[V-た]り	**[V-ta] + ri, [V-ta] + ri**	verb, verb, etc.
ふく	**fuku**	clothes
ズボン	**zubon**	trousers
セーター	**sētā**	sweater

Dialogue 1 exercise

Write ✓ if the statement agrees with the dialogue. Write ✗ if not.

1　(　) Miss Inoue does not want to swim this weekend.
2　(　) Mr Hancock wants to buy some clothes this weekend.

Language points

Vocabulary for clothes and accessories

ふく **fuku** is a generic term for clothes. There are several verbs for "wear, put on" in Japanese: きます **kimasu**, はきます **hakimasu**, かぶります **kaburimasu**, かけます **kakemasu** and します **shimasu**. The type of the clothes or accessories determines which verb should be used.

Vocabulary

Items used with **kimasu**

> **sētā** sweater, **shatsu** shirt, **kōto** coat, **sūtsu** suit, **shitagi**
> underwear, **kimono** Japanese clothes, kimono

Items used with **hakimasu**

> **zubon** trousers, **sukāto** skirt, **kutsu** shoes, **kutsushita** socks

Items used with **kaburimasu**

> **bōshi** cap, hat

Items used with **kakemasu**

> **megane** glasses

Items used with **shimasu**

> **nekutai** tie, **nekkuresu** necklace, **tokē** watch

The [V-**te**] + **imasu** pattern is used to describe what one wears (state).

> a. **Yamada-san wa akai sētā o <u>kite imasu</u>.**
>   Mr Yamada <u>wears</u> a red sweater.

> b. **Jonson-san wa megane o <u>kakete imasu</u>.**
>   Miss Johnson <u>wears</u> a pair of glasses.

How to make the verb た-**form**

Like the **te**-form, you use the **ta**-form ([V-**ta**]) to make various expressions such as talking about one's experience, listing representative activities, etc. To form the **ta**-form from the **masu**-form, you apply the **te**-form rule (Unit 13, pages 156–7) but change **te** or **de** to **ta** or **da** respectively, as shown below:

Group 1 verbs

Change the sound before **masu** according to the rules below:

a. い (i)、ち (chi)、り (ri) → った (**tta**)

meet	あ<u>い</u>ます	a<u>i</u>masu	→	あ<u>った</u>	atta
wait	ま<u>ち</u>ます	ma<u>chi</u>masu	→	ま<u>った</u>	ma<u>tta</u>
go	い<u>き</u>ます	i<u>ki</u>masu	→	い<u>った</u>	<u>itta</u>

b. び (bi)、み (mi)、に (ni) → んだ (**nda**)

| play | あそ**び**ます | **aso<u>b</u>imasu** | → | あそ<u>んだ</u> | **aso<u>nda</u>** |
| drink | の**み**ます | **no<u>m</u>imasu** | → | の<u>んだ</u> | **no<u>nda</u>** |

c. き (ki) → いた (ita)、ぎ (gi) → いだ (ida)

| write | か**き**ます | **ka<u>k</u>imasu** | → | か<u>いた</u> | **ka<u>ita</u>** |
| hurry | いそ**ぎ**ます | **iso<u>g</u>imasu** | → | いそ<u>いだ</u> | **iso<u>ida</u>** |

d. し (shi) → した (**shita**)

| talk | はな<u>し</u>ます | **hana<u>shi</u>masu** | → | はな<u>した</u> | **hana<u>shita</u>** |

Note that the **ta**-form of いきます **ikimasu** "go" is いった **itta**, not いきた "**ikita**".

Group 2 and 3 verbs

Simply change **masu** to **ta** as below:

Group 2

eat	たべ**ます**	**tabe<u>masu</u>**	→	たべ<u>た</u>	**tabe<u>ta</u>**
watch	み**ます**	**mi<u>masu</u>**	→	み<u>た</u>	**mi<u>ta</u>**
sleep	ね**ます**	**ne<u>masu</u>**	→	ね<u>た</u>	**ne<u>ta</u>**

Group 3

| come | き**ます** | **ki<u>masu</u>** | → | き<u>た</u> | **ki<u>ta</u>** |
| do | し**ます** | **shi<u>masu</u>** | → | し<u>た</u> | **shi<u>ta</u>** |

Exercise 1

Change the following verbs from the **masu**-form to the **ta**-form. The number in the brackets indicates which verb group they belong to.

Example たべます (2) **たべた**

1	きます (2)	2	きます (3)
	*to wear		*to come
3	します (3)	4	かけます (2)
5	はなします (1)	6	いきます (1)
7	およぎます (1)	8	かります (2)
9	はきます(1)	10	かぶります (1)

Language point

Verb ta-form (1): linking verb sentences

In Unit 14 (pages 168–9), you learned how to link verbs with the verb te-form ([V-**te**]). In this unit, you will learn another way of linking verbs with the verb ta-form: [V-**ta**] + **ri**, [V-**ta**] + **ri**. . . . This [V-**ta**] + **ri** [V-**ta**] + **ri** . . . pattern implies that the activities mentioned are merely an example of what the agent of the action does (or did, etc.), whereas the [V-**te**], [V-**te**] . . . pattern does not have such an implication, as shown below:

a. **Watashi wa kinō terebi o _mitari_, hon o _yondari_ shimashita.**
   Yesterday, I did various activities such as watching TV, reading a book.

b. **Watashi wa kinō terebi o _mite_, hon o yomimashita.**
   Yesterday, I watched TV and then read a book.

Note that this pattern requires **shimasu** and its variations at the end.

c. **Koko de tabako o _suttari_ shashin o _tottari_ shi_tewa ikemasen_.**
   You must not smoke, take photos, and so on.

d. **Watashi wa ashita ēga o _mitari_, pūru de _oyoidari_ shi_tai desu_.**
   I want to do various things tomorrow such as watching a film, swimming in the pool.

Exercise 2

Change the verb in the brackets appropriately.

Example   Konban tomodachi to denwa de (hanashimasu) *hanashita* ri, tegami o (kakimasu) *kaita* ri shitai desu.

1 Kinō wa heya o (sōji shimasu) [a)] _____, (sentaku shimasu)
   [b)] _____ ri shimashita.
2 Ashita gyūnyū o (kaimasu) [a)] _____ ri, toshokan de hon o
   (karimasu) [b)] _____ ri shimasu.

3 Watashi wa shūmatsu yoku machi e kaimono ni (ikimasu)
   a) _____ ri, naitokurabu de (odorimasu) b) _____ ri
shimasu.

4 Kinō mēru o (chekku shimasu) a) _____ ri, tomodachi ni
denwa o (kakemasu) b) _____ ri shimashita.

Vocabulary

gyūnyū	milk	**denwa o**	to make a
naitokurabu	nightclub	**kakemasu**	phone call
odorimasu	to dance		

Exercise 3 (Audio 2:32)

Kenji is talking to Mariko about what he did last weekend. Listen to their conversation and put a ✗ for the activities which Kenji did over the weekend.

a. watch a DVD (   )   b. buy a hat (   )
c. study English (   )   d. swim (   )
e. eat at a restaurant (   )   f. rest (   )

Dialogue 2

What did you do after graduating? (Audio 2:33)

Mr Hancock is asking Miss Inoue about her university.

ハンコック	いのうえさんは　いつ　だいがくを　そつぎょうしましたか。
いのうえ	わたしは　おととし　そつぎょうしました。
ハンコック	そつぎょうしたあと（で）、なにを　しましたか。
いのうえ	いろいろな　くにを　りょこうしました。
ハンコック	そうですか。いいですね。

HANKOKKU	Inoue-san wa itsu daigaku o sotsugyō shimashita ka.
INOUE	Watashi wa ototoshi sotsugyō shimashita.
HANKOKKU	Sotsugyō shita ato (de), nani o shimashita ka.
INOUE	Iroiro na kuni o ryokō shimashita.
HANKOKKU	Sō desu ka. Ī desu ne.

Vocabulary

そつぎょうします	**sotsugyō shimasu**	to graduate
そつぎょうしたあとで	**sotsugyō shita ato de**	after graduating
～あとで	**. . . ato de**	after . . .

Dialogue 2 exercise

Write ✓ if the statement agrees with the dialogue. Write ✗ if not.

1 (   ) Miss Inoue graduated from university two years ago.
2 (   ) Miss Inoue went back to Japan after her graduation.

Language point

Verb ta-form (2): after ~

"After" in Japanese is **ato de**. This can be used with nouns and verbs as below:

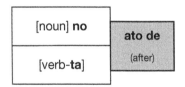

a. **Daigaku o <u>sotsugyō shita *ato de*</u> nani o shitai desu ka.**
   What do you want to do *after graduating* from university?

b. Q: **Itsu shukudai o shimasu ka.**
   When do you do your homework?

   A1: **<u>Gohan no *ato de*</u> shimasu.**
       I do it *after the meal*.

   A2: **Gohan o <u>tabeta *ato de*</u> shimasu.**
       I do it *after eating* the meal.

Note that **de** in **ato de** is often omitted in informal speech.

Exercise 4

Describe Miss Inoue's daily morning routine, using the information in brackets.

> *Example*   (jog for 30 minutes → rest)
>
>   *Inoue-san wa asa 30-pun jogingu o shita*
>   *ato de, yasumimasu.*

1 (rest → take a shower)
2 (drink tea → cook breakfast)
3 (eat breakfast → brush her teeth)
4 (brush her teeth → put on her clothes)

Vocabulary

tsukurimasu   to make, cook

Dialogue 3

Have you ever borrowed a book from this library? (Audio 2:34)

Miss Inoue has taken Mr Hancock to a local library.

いのうえ	ハンコックさんは、このとしょかんで ほんを かりたことが ありますか。
ハンコック	いいえ、ありません。としょかんカードが ありませんから。
いのうえ	じゃあ、きょう カードを つくりましょう。
ハンコック	むずかしくないですか。
いのうえ	いいえ、かんたんですよ。

INOUE	Hankokku-san wa kono toshokan de hon o karita koto ga arimasu ka.
HANKOKKU	Īe, arimasen. Toshokan kādo ga arimasen kara.
INOUE	Jā, kyō kādo o tsukurimashō.
HANKOKKU	Muzukashikunai desu ka.
INOUE	Īe, kantan desu yo.

Vocabulary

かりたことがあります	**karita koto ga arimasu**	have borrowed
[V-**ta**] ことがあります	[V-**ta**] + **koto ga arimasu**	have (done)
(としょかん) カード	**(toshokan) kādo**	(library) card
かんたん (な) (na-adj.)	**kantan(na)**	easy

Dialogue 3 exercise

Write ✓ if the statement agrees with the dialogue. Write ✗ if not.

1 ( ) Mr Hancock has never borrowed books from the library
where he is now.
2 ( ) Miss Inoue is going to make Mr Hancock's library card
today.

Language point

Verb tα-**form (3): talking about one's experiences in the past**

[V-**ta**] + **koto ga arimasu** is an expression used to describe one's experiences. To negate this sentence pattern, you simply change **arimasu** to **arimasen**.

verb-**ta**　　koto (ga)　　**arimasu**

a. **Watashi wa kimono o kita *koto ga arimasu*.**
I *have* worn Kimono in the past. (*lit.* "I have an experience
of wearing Kimono".)

b. Q: **Jon-san wa Fujisan ni nobotta *koto ga arimasu ka*.**
Have you *ever climbed* Mt. Fuji, John?

A1: **Hai, (nobotta koto ga) arimasu.**
Yes, I *have*.

A2: **Īe, (nobotta koto ga) arimasen.**
No, I *have not*.

[V-**ta**] + **koto ga arimasu** and [V-**mashita**] differ in that the former focuses on whether or not one has had a certain experience but the latter simply indicates that a certain action took place in the past.

   c. **Watashi wa kimono o <u>kita koto ga arimasu</u>.**
     I <u>have an experience of wearing</u> kimono.

   d. **Watashi wa kyonen kimono o <u>kimashita</u>.**
     I <u>wore</u> Kimono last year.

Exercise 5

Translate the following sentences into Japanese, using [V-**ta**] + **koto ga arimasu/arimasen**.

   Example I have been to Japan.
               Watashi wa Nihon e itta koto ga arimasu.

1 I have climbed Mt. Fuji.
2 My younger sister has not worn kimono.
3 Have you ever eaten sushi, Mr Hancock?
4 I have made sushi.

Exercise 6 (Audio 2:35)

Read out the following text and write ✓ for the activities Mrs Lee has done before and ✗ for what she has not done yet.

わたしは　リーです。きょねんまで　にほんに　すんでいました。にほんの
せいかつは　とても　たのしかったです。わたしは　にほんで　ふじさんに
のぼったり、かぶきを　みたり　しました。そして　ともだちと　すしを
つくったり　てんぷらを　たべたり　しました。でも、わたしは　まだ　おんせんに
はいったことが　ありません。そして、にほんの　おまつりを　みたことも
ありません。ですから、ことしの　なつ　また　にほんへ　いきたいです。

1 climbing Mt. Fuji   ( )
2 eating tempura   ( )
3 seeing Japanese festivals ( )
4 watching kabuki   ( )
5 going to a hot spring   ( )
6 making sushi   ( )

Vocabulary

かぶき **kabuki** a Japanese theatrical play

Kanji of Unit 15: Kanji with more than 5 strokes

Kanji	Kun-yomi	On-yomi	Meaning	Kanji	Kun-yomi	On-yomi	Meaning
本	もと	ホン	book, origin	何	なに/なん		what
一 十 才 木 本				ノ イ 仁 仃 何 何 何			
先	さき	セン	previous	字		ジ	letter, character
ノ 丶 牛 生 先 先				丶 ' 宀 宀 字 字			
生	い(きる)/う(まれる)	セイ	birth, live	年	とし	ネン	year, age
ノ 一 牛 牛 生				ノ 一 匕 牛 乍 年			
学	まな(ぶ)	ガク/ガッ	study	車	くるま	シャ	car
丶 ' ツ ツ 艸 学 学 学				一 厂 戸 戸 百 亘 車			
好	す(き)	コウ	like	毎		マイ	every
く 夂 女 女' 好 好				ノ 一 仁 勾 每 每 毎			

Exercise 7

Write how to read the underlined Kanji in Hiragana.

1　あの女の人は　私の　日本語の　先生です。
2　日本語の学生は　漢字を　勉強しています。
3　かばんの中に　何が　ありますか。
4　私は　一年(間)、日本に　住んでいました。
5　私は　日本人の友達に　この本を　もらいました。
6　私の友達は　日本の車が　好きです。
7　あなたは　毎日　電車に　乗りますか。

Unit Sixteen

Sukoshi dake Supein-go o hanasu koto ga dekimasu

I can speak a little bit of Spanish

In this unit you will learn about:

- talking about one's hobbies and leisure activities
- how to make the dictionary form of a verb ([V-dic.])
- how to change a verb into a noun, using [V-dic.] + **koto**
- describing one's ability or possibility: [V-dic.] + **koto ga dekimasu**
- kanji of Unit 16

  姉、妹、兄、弟、男、前、後、金、週、曜

Dialogue 1

My hobby is collecting guitars (**Audio 2:36**)

Mr Yanagi and Miss White are talking about their hobbies.

ホワイト	やなぎさんは　たくさん　ギターを　もっていますね。
やなぎ	はい。わたしのしゅみは　ギターを　あつめることですから。
	ホワイトさんのしゅみは　なんですか。
ホワイト	わたしのしゅみは　ピアノを　ひくことです。
やなぎ	そうですか。じゃあ　いつか　いっしょに　ピアノのコンサートへ
	いきませんか。
ホワイト	いいですね。ぜひ　いきましょう。

HOWAITO	Yanagi-san wa takusan gitā o motte imasu ne.
YANAGI	Hai, watashi no shumi wa gitā o atsumeru koto desu kara. Howaito-san no shumi wa nan desu ka.

HOWAITO   Watashi no shumi wa piano o hiku koto desu.
YANAGI   Sō desu ka. Jā, itsuka issho ni piano no konsāto e
          ikimasen ka.
HOWAITO   Ī desu ne. Zehi ikimashō.

Vocabulary

しゅみ	**shumi**	hobby
あつめること	**atsumeru koto**	collecting
あつめます	**atsumemasu**	to collect
ひくこと	**hiku koto**	playing
ひきます	**hikimasu**	to play (a keyboard or stringed instrument)
コンサート	**konsāto**	concert

Dialogue 1 exercise

Write ✓ if the statement agrees with the dialogue. Write ✗ if not.

1 (   ) Mr Yanagi's hobby is playing the guitar.
2 (   ) Miss White's hobby is playing the piano.

Language points

Hobbies and leisure activities

Shumi means "hobby". Below is some vocabulary relating to hobbies and leisure activities:

Exercise-related activities		*Indoor activities*	
suiē	swimming	**piano**	piano
sukī	skiing	**gitā**	guitar
sukēto	skating	**dokusho**	reading
karate	karate	**ikebana**	flower arrangement
jūdō	judo	**sadō**	tea ceremony
gorufu	golf	**shodō**	calligraphy

a. **Watashi no shumi wa dokusho desu.**
   My hobby is reading.

b. Q: **Kitamura-san no shumi wa nan desu ka.**
   What is your hobby, Mr Kitamura?

   A: **Watashi no shumi wa suiē desu.**
   My hobby is swimming.

The dictionary form of a verb

The dictionary form of a verb, referred to as the verb dictionary form ([V-dic.]), is the basic form of the verb. This form is called "dictionary form" because the Japanese dictionary uses this form. Like the **te**-form (Unit 13, pages 156–7), and the **ta**-form (Unit 15, pages 179–80), the verb dictionary form is used along with other expressions to make various meanings.

The following shows how to make the dictionary form from the **masu**-form.

Group 1 verbs: Replacing **-imasu** with the **-u** sound

masu-form	⟶	replace *-imasu* with *-u*	⟶	dictionary form

kaerimasu go back	**kaer** + **u**		**kaeru**
kakimasu write	**kak** + **u**		**kaku**
nomimasu drink	**nom** + **u**		**nomu**

Group 2 verbs: Replacing **-masu** with the **-ru** sound

masu-form	⟶	replace *-masu* with *-ru*	⟶	dictionary form

tabemasu eat	**tabe** + **ru**		**taberu**
misemasu show	**mise** + **ru**		**miseru**
nemasu sleep	**ne** + **ru**		**neru**

Group 3 verbs: They follow an irregular pattern

masu-form   *dictionary form*

shimasu do   ⟶   **suru**
kimasu come   **kuru**

Exercise 1

Change the following verbs from the **masu**-form to the dictionary form. The number in the brackets indicates which verb group they belong to.

1 よみます (1)   2 します (3)
3 いきます (1)   4 ひきます (1)
5 もってきます (3)   6 しらべます (2)

Vocabulary

しらべます   **shirabemasu**   to investigate, examine, check, study

Language point

Verb dictionary form (1): (V-dic.) + koto as a noun

As "-ing" is added to an English verb to change it from a verb to a noun (e.g. playing, watching), **koto** "thing" is added to a Japanese verb to turn it into an action or noun. Note that the form of the verb needs to be the dictionary form as in [V-dic.] + **koto**.

kikimasu	listen	→	**kiku *koto***	listening
mimasu	watch	→	**miru *koto***	watching
benkyō shimasu	study	→	**benkyō suru *koto***	studying
tegami o kakimasu	write a letter	→	**tegami o kaku *koto***	writing a letter

Exercise 2

Change the following verbs to nouns, using [V-dic.] + **koto** and then write their English meaning.

Example (a) かきます <u>かくこと writing</u>
(b) てがみを かきます <u>てがみを かくこと</u>
<u>writing a letter</u>

1 ひきます _____ _____
2 およぎます _____ _____
3 します _____ _____
4 テレビを みます _____ _____
5 しゃしんを とります _____ _____
6 ほんを よみます _____ _____
7 きってを あつめます _____ _____

Language point

Verb dictionary form (2): X wa **(V-dic.)** + koto desu

[V-dic.] + **koto** can appear in Y in the **X wa Y desu** structure.

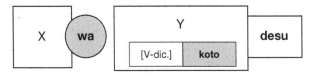

a. **Watashi no shumi wa *sakkā* desu.**
   My hobby is *football*.

b. **Watashi no shumi wa *sakkā o <u>suru koto</u>* desu.**
   My hobby is <u>*playing*</u> *football*.

c. **Watashi no yume wa *kashu ni <u>naru koto</u>* desu.**
   My dream is <u>*becoming*</u> *a singer*.

Exercise 3

What are their hobbies/dreams? Write an appropriate sentence as shown in the example. For 5, write your own hobbies or dreams.

> *Example* Mr Yoshida/playing the piano
>   *Yoshida-san no shumi wa piano o hiku koto desu.*

1 Mr Honda/hobby/cooking
2 Miss White/dream/making films
3 My friend/hobby/taking photos
4 My younger brother/dream/becoming a baseball player
5

Vocabulary

yume dream	**yakyū senshu** a baseball player

Exercise 4 (Audio 2:37)

Listen to the dialogue and choose the male speaker's hobby.

1 Yamamoto-san: a. playing golf   b. skiing
2 Morita-san: a. going to concerts   b. going to plays at the theatre
3 Hōmuzu-san: a. creating music   b. listening to music

Vocabulary

geki theatre play	**kashu** singer

Language point

Verb dictionary form (3): X wa **(V-dic.)** + koto ga + **adjective**

The nominalized verb [V-dic.] + **koto** can appear in Y in the **X wa Y ga** + adjective structure as well. Adjectives in this pattern are **suki** "like", **kirai** "dislike", **jōzu** "good at" and **heta** "poor at".

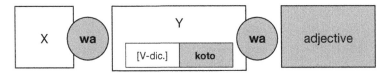

a. **Watashi wa** *Nihon no ongaku o* <u>kiku koto</u> **ga suki desu.**
   I <u>like *listening*</u> to Japanese music.

b. **Watashi wa** *sakkā o* <u>suru koto</u> **ga amari jōzu dewa arimasen.**
   I <u>am not so good at *playing*</u> football.

Exercise 5

Translate the following sentences into Japanese.

1 I like watching Japanese films.
2 My friend is good at playing the guitar.
3 I do not like driving a car so much.
4 My younger sister is good at drawing pictures.

Dialogue 2

Can you speak Spanish? (**Audio 2:38**)

Mr Yanagi is asking Miss White about her past before coming
to Japan.

やなぎ　　ホワイトさんは　にほんへ　くるまえに　どこに　すんでいましたか。
ホワイト　わたしは　メキシコに　すんでいました。
やなぎ　　じゃあ、スペインごを　はなすことが　できますか。
ホワイト　はい、すこしだけ　はなすことが　できます。
やなぎ　　すごいですね。

YANAGI　Howaito-san wa Nihon e kuru mae ni doko ni sunde
　　　　imashita ka.
HOWAITO　Watashi wa Mekishiko ni sunde imashita.
YANAGI　Jā, Supein-go o hanasu koto ga dekimasu ka.
HOWAITO　Hai, sukoshi dake hanasu koto ga dekimasu.
YANAGI　Sugoi desu ne.

Vocabulary

くるまえに	**kuru mae ni**	before coming
[V-dic.] まえに	**[V-dic.] mae ni**	before [+ verb]
だけ	**dake**	only
はなすことができます	**hanasu koto ga dekimasu**	can speak
できます	**dekimasu**	can

Dialogue 2 exercise

Write ✓ if the statement agrees with the dialogue. Write ✗ if not.

1 (   ) Miss White lived in Mexico before coming to Japan.
2 (   ) Miss White cannot speak Spanish at all.

Language point

Verb dictionary form (4): before . . .

Mae ni means "before". Like **ato de** "after", which you learned in Unit 15 (page 183), it can be used with nouns and verbs. Note that while **ato de** takes the verb **ta**-form before it ([V-**ta**] + **ato de**), **mae ni** takes the dictionary form ([V-dic.] + **mae ni**).

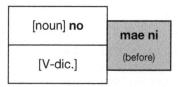

a. **Gohan no _mae ni_ shukudai o shimasu.**
   I do my homework _before_ the meal.

b. **Gohan o taberu _mae ni_ te o aratte kudasai.**
   Please wash your hands _before eating the meal_.

Note that the numeric counter such as **-nen** "year" and **-jikan** "hour" does not take **no** when it is used with this expression.

c. **Howaito-san wa <u>san-nen</u> _mae ni_ Nihon e kimashita.**
   Miss White came to Japan _three years ago_.

d. **Watashi wa <u>ni-jikan</u> *mae ni* gohan o tabemashita.**
I ate the meal <u>two hours ago</u>.

Exercise 6

Complete the following sentences according to the English meaning in the brackets.

Example   Watashi wa *taberu mae ni* te o araimasu.
(I wash my hands before eating.)

1 Kimura-san wa _____ uchi o tatemashita.
  (Mr Kimura built a house before marrying.)
2 Watashi wa hon o _____ denki o tsukemasu.
  (I switch on the light before reading a book.)
3 Watashi wa kami o _____ kami o araimasu.
  (I have my hair washed before it is cut (lit. "cutting").)
4 Watashi wa _____ nikki o kakimasu.
  (I write my diary before going to bed.)
5 Howaito-san wa _____ Nihon e kimashita.
  (Miss White came to Japan five years ago.)

Vocabulary

araimasu	to wash	tsukemasu	to turn on
tatemasu	to build	kirimasu	to cut
denki	light, electricity	nikki	diary

Language point

Verb dictionary form (5): describing ability or possibility

Dekimasu is a verb meaning "can do". The **X wa Y ga dekimasu** pattern is used to describe one's ability. Y takes either a noun or a nominalized verb ([V-dic.] + **koto**).

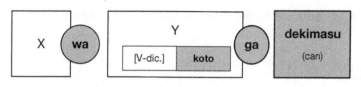

a. **Kimura-san wa <u>gitā ga dekimasu</u>.**
   Mr Kimura <u>can play the guitar</u>.

b. **Kimura-san wa <u>piano o hiku koto ga dekimasen</u>.**
   Mr Kimura <u>cannot play the piano</u>.

c. Q: **Kimu-san wa <u>oyogu koto ga dekimasu ka</u>.**
      <u>Can</u> you <u>swim</u>, Miss Kim?

   A-1: **Hai, (watashi wa oyogu koto ga) <u>dekimasu</u>.**
        Yes, I <u>can</u>.

   A-2: **Īe, (watashi wa oyogu koto ga) <u>dekimasen</u>.**
        No, I <u>cannot</u>.

This pattern is also used to express whether or not something is possible/allowed.

d. Q: **Koko de <u>oyogu koto ga dekimasu ka</u>.**
      <u>Is swimming allowed</u> here?

   A: **Īe, <u>dekimasen</u>.**
      No, it is <u>not allowed</u>.

 ## Exercise 7

Complete the following dialogues appropriately as shown in the example.

Example

MICHIKO *Tomu-san wa piano o hiku koto ga*
         dekimasu ka. (play the piano)
TOMU   Hai, dekimasu.

1 MICHIKO _____ (speak French)
   TOMU   Īe, dekimasen.
2 MICHIKO _____ (sing a Japanese song)
   TOMU   Hai, dekimasu.
3 MICHIKO _____ (skiing)
   TOMU   Hai, dekimasu.

4 MICHIKO _____ (write Kanji)

   TOMU   Hai, sukoshi dekimasu.

Exercise 8 **(Audio 2:39)**

Michiko is talking with her Chinese friend, Mr Chen. He recently bought
a new mobile phone. Listen to their conversation and write ✓ for the
functions the mobile phone has.

1 ( ) play golf   2 ( ) play tennis   3 ( ) create music
4 ( ) write Chinese   5 ( ) read Chinese   6 ( ) watch TV
7 ( ) check Kanji pronunciation

Exercise 9 **(Audio 2:40)**

Mr Brown, who is currently on holiday, wrote a postcard to his friend
Miss Machida. Read the card aloud first and write ✓ if the statements
below agree with it, and ✗ if not.

まちださん

げんきですか。わたしは　とても　げんきです。いま　おきなわに　います。
うみのまえの　ホテルに　とまっています。とても　すてきな　ホテルです。
ホテルから　うみまで　あるいて　いくことが　できますから、わたしは
まいにち　うみへ　いきます。でも、まだ　すこし　さむいですから　うみで
およぐことが　できません。ざんねんですね。

らいしゅう　とうきょうへ　かえります。とうきょうへ　かえるまえに、たくさん
おみやげを　かいます。まちださんの　おみやげも　かいますから
たのしみに　してくださいね。

じゃあ、また。

ブラウンより

Vocabulary

たのしみにします   **tanoshimini shimasu**   to look forward to

1 ( ) Mr Brown is staying at a hotel from where he can walk to the beach.
2 ( ) Mr Brown enjoys swimming in Okinawa every day.
3 ( ) Mr Brown has not bought a souvenir for Miss Machida yet.

Kanji of Unit 16: Kanji with more than 5 strokes

Kanji	Kun-yomi	On-yomi	Meaning	Kanji	Kun-yomi	On-yomi	Meaning
姉	あね	シ	elder sister	前	まえ	ゼン	front, before
妹	いもうと	マイ	younger sister	後	あと/ うし(ろ)	ゴ	behind, after
兄	あに	キョウ/ ケイ	elder brother	金	かね	キン	money, gold
弟	おとうと	ダイ	younger brother	週		シュウ	week
男	おとこ	ダン/ナン	man, male	曜		ヨウ	day of the week

Exercise 10

Write how to read the underlined kanji in hiragana.

1　私の<u>妹</u>は　<u>駅</u>の<u>前</u>に　<u>立</u>っています。

2　私は　<u>弟</u>が　二人います。

3　あなたは　<u>毎週</u>　<u>金曜日</u>　何を　しますか。

4　あの木の下の<u>男</u>の人は　私の<u>兄</u>です。

5　私のポケットの中に　お<u>金</u>が　<u>入</u>っています。

6　テストの<u>後</u>、一<u>緒</u>に　<u>遊</u>びに　行きましょう。

7　<u>兄弟</u> (brothers) と<u>姉妹</u> (sisters)

Translations of dialogues

This section contains translations of dialogues in Units 9 to 16. Translations of earlier dialogues can be found in the units.

Unit 9

Dialogue 1

NORIO *Emma, have you already bought the train tickets?*
EMMA *No, not yet. I am going to buy them online this afternoon.*
NORIO *Really? Is this your first time going to Nagano, Emma?*
EMMA *Yes, this is my first time.*
NORIO *What do you want to do in Nagano?*
EMMA *I want to take a lot of photos. And I want to try the hot spring.*

Dialogue 2

NORIO *Where did you go over the summer holiday, Emma?*
EMMA *I went to America in the summer holiday.*
NORIO *Why did you go there?*
EMMA *I went there to see my friend in New York.*
NORIO *What did you do in New York?*
EMMA *I went sightseeing in New York with my friend.*

Dialogue 3

NORIO *Emma, have you ever watched sumo before?*
EMMA *No, not yet. I would love to watch it.*

NORIO	*Then why don't you go to watch sumo with me this weekend?*
EMMA	*Really? I would be delighted to. But what day of the week is it?*
NORIO	*It is Sunday. Are you busy this Sunday, Emma?*
EMMA	*No, I am free.*
NORIO	*My friend is also coming but is that OK for you?*
EMMA	*Of course.*
NORIO	*Then let's go together.*

Unit 10

Dialogue 1

MR CLARK	*Miss Akita, tomorrow is bonus day, isn't it?*
	What do you want with that bonus?
MISS AKITA	*I want a new computer.*
MR CLARK	*Why do you want a new computer?*
MISS AKITA	*Because my current computer is already old. Besides, the current one is slightly slow.*
MR CLARK	*Is that so?*

Dialogue 2

MR CLARK	*I am going to go to karaoke with the others. Won't you come with us as well, Miss Akita?*
MISS AKITA	*I want to go but I will go home today because I have a headache.*
MR CLARK	*That is bad. I have some medicine. Would you like to take it?*
MISS AKITA	*Thank you. (Then,) please give me some.*

Dialogue 3

MISS AKITA	*Mr Clark, thank you for giving me the medicine last Friday.*
MR CLARK	*You're welcome. Are you all right now?*

MISS AKITA	*Yes, I received some medicine from a doctor last Saturday.*
MR CLARK	*Really? That was good.*
MISS AKITA	*By the way, how was karaoke last Friday?*
MR CLARK	*It was very enjoyable. Let's go (to karaoke) together next time.*
MISS AKITA	*Yes, by all means.*

Unit 11

Dialogue 1

MR TANAKA	*Miss Smith, what do you usually do on your days off?*
MISS SMITH	*I often go to the park for a walk.*
MR TANAKA	*Really? Then, shall we go to* Shinjuku Gyoen *together this Saturday?*
MISS SMITH	*What is* Shinjuku Gyoen?
MR TANAKA	*It is a spacious and beautiful park. It is in Shinjuku ward.*
MISS SMITH	*Is it far from Shinjuku station?*
MR TANAKA	*No, it is nearby. It is about a ten-minute walk from Shinjuku station.*
MISS SMITH	*That is handy. Then, let's go (there) together this Saturday.*

Dialogue 2

MR TANAKA	*Miss Smith, what did you do last weekend?*
MISS SMITH	*I went to a mountain nearby with my friend.*
MR TANAKA	*Really? How was the weather?*
MISS SMITH	*It was good. It was slightly cloudy and cold in the morning, but it became warm in the afternoon.*
MR TANAKA	*Did you go to the top of the mountain?*
MISS SMITH	*Yes. It took two hours because we walked.*
MR TANAKA	*That must be tough.*
MISS SMITH	*Yes. But the view from the top was really beautiful.*
MR TANAKA	*Were there a lot of people there?*
MISS SMITH	*No, there were not many (lit. few) people.*

Unit 12

Dialogue 1

MRS KATO	*Mr Jones, this is a photo of my son.*
MR JONES	*He looks very like you. How old is he now?*
MRS KATO	*He became 16 years old last month.*
MR JONES	*Really? He has long legs. And he is tall.*
MRS KATO	*Yes, he is the tallest in the family.*
MR JONES	*How tall is he?*
MRS KATO	*He is probably around 185cm.*

Dialogue 2

MR JONES	*Mrs Kato, this optician has many customers hasn't it.*
MRS KATO	*It is because this place is cheap and popular.*
MR JONES	*There are glasses with various colours.*
MRS KATO	*Indeed. Which colour do you prefer, a bright colour or a dark colour?*
MR JONES	*I prefer bright colours.*
MRS KATO	*Then, how about this red pair of glasses?*
MR JONES	*It is a little gaudy.*
MRS KATO	*Then, how about this brown pair of glasses?*
MR JONES	*They are lovely. I will take them.*

Unit 13

Dialogue 1

MR HOLMES	*Excuse me but please tell me how to read this kanji.*
A WAITRESS	*Ah, that kanji is "tenpura".*
MR HOLMES	*Really? Then, I will have "tenpura udon".*
A WAITRESS	*Certainly.*
MR HOLMES	*And please bring a bottle of beer with it.*
A WAITRESS	*Certainly.*

Dialogue 2

MRS NAGANO	*Mr Holmes, this is your room.*
MR HOLMES	*Is this it? It is spacious. Oh, there is an entrance hall in the room. Why?*
MRS NAGANO	*It is because you must not wear shoes inside the room.*
MR HOLMES	*Really? Oh, there are slippers in the entrance hall. Do I wear slippers inside the room?*
MRS NAGANO	*No, you must not wear slippers inside the room. Please use them outside the room.*
MR HOLMES	*I see. By the way, may I smoke in the room?*
MRS NAGANO	*No, you must not smoke because your room is "non-smoking". But you can smoke in the lobby.*

Unit 14

Dialogue 1

MR ENOKIDA	*Ms Kim, how are you coming to my place this Saturday?*
MS KIM	*I am going by train.*
MR ENOKIDA	*Then, please get off at Sakura station and go out of the south exit. A bus stop is in front of the south exit so please take a 73 bus and get off at the bus stop called "In front of Sakura Hospital".*
MS KIM	*How many stops do I have before arriving at "In front of Sakura Hospital"?*
MR ENOKIDA	*It is the fourth stop.*

Dialogue 2

MR ENOKIDA	*Hello, Ms Kim.*
MS KIM	*Oh hello, Mr Enokida.*
MR ENOKIDA	*Ms Kim, what were you doing at 8 p.m. in the evening yesterday?*
MS KIM	*I was watching a Korean film at home because it was raining yesterday.*

| MR ENOKIDA | *Was it enjoyable?* |
| MS KIM | *Yes, it was very enjoyable. I have the DVD of that film so please watch it some day.* |

Dialogue 3

MS KIM	*Mr Enokida, what do you do for your health?*
MR ENOKIDA	*I eat vegetables every day. And I also go jogging every weekend. How about you, Ms Kim?*
MS KIM	*I swim at the pool nearby.*
MR ENOKIDA	*How long do you swim?*
MS KIM	*I swim for about one hour.*
MR ENOKIDA	*That is great.*

Unit 15

Dialogue 1

MR HANCOCK	*Miss Inoue, what do you want to do this weekend?*
MISS INOUE	*Well, I want to do various things such as swimming in the pool, borrowing some books from the library. How about you, Mr Hancock?*
MR HANCOCK	*I want to go to the city centre to buy some clothes.*
MISS INOUE	*What do you want to buy?*
MR HANCOCK	*I want to buy clothes such as a new pair of trousers and a sweater.*
MISS INOUE	*Really?*

Dialogue 2

MR HANCOCK	*Miss Inoue, when did you graduate from university?*
MISS INOUE	*I graduated from university the year before last.*
MR HANCOCK	*What did you do after graduating?*

MISS INOUE   *I travelled in various countries.*
MR HANCOCK   *Really. That sounds nice.*

Dialogue 3

MISS INOUE   *Mr Hancock, have you ever borrowed a book from this library?*
MR HANCOCK   *No, I have not. (It is) because I do not have a library card.*
MISS INOUE   *Then, let's create one today.*
MR HANCOCK   *Isn't it difficult?*
MISS INOUE   *No, it is easy.*

Unit 16

Dialogue 1

MISS WHITE   *Mr Yanagi, you have many guitars, haven't you?*
MR YANAGI   *Yes. That is because my hobby is collecting guitars. What about your hobby, Miss White?*
MISS WHITE   *My hobby is playing the piano.*
MR YANAGI   *Really? Then, shall we go to a piano concert some day?*
MISS WHITE   *That is great. Definitely.*

Dialogue 2

MR YANAGI   *Where did you live before coming to Japan?*
MISS WHITE   *I lived in Mexico.*
MR YANAGI   *Then, can you speak Spanish?*
MISS WHITE   *Yes, I can speak it only a little.*
MR YANAGI   *That is great.*

Grammar summary

1 Topic marker **wa**

Unlike English, Japanese word order is very flexible (for example, "I study Japanese at the library every day" could be [I/every day/at the library/Japanese/study], [I/at the library/Japanese/every day/study], [every day/at the library/I/Japanese/study], or [Japanese/every day/ at the library/study]). Hence, the word order does not specify the function of the word in the sentence but the particles do (a full list of the particles can be found in section 7). One of the most important particles is the topic marker **wa**. The word followed by **wa** indicates what the sentence is talking about. For example, when you are talking about yourself (**watashi**) or the Japanese language (**Nihon-go**), you start the sentence with **Watashi wa** or **Nihon-go wa**, respectively. What follows the topic marker **wa** is the comment about the topic.

2 Sentence pattern

Although word order is flexible in Japanese, a Japanese sentence always ends in either a verb, an adjective, or a copula. The following shows how they conjugate (or inflect).

Noun + copula (desu)

I am/am not/was/was not Japanese.

Topic		Comment		
		Noun	*Copula*	
Watashi	**wa**	**Nihon-jin**	**desu**	(non-past affirmative)
			dewa/ja arimasen	(non-past negative)
			deshita	(past affirmative)
			dewa/ja arimasendeshita	(past negative)

i-adjectives and na-**adjectives**

Japanese has two types of adjective: **i**-adjectives and **na**-adjectives. They inflect differently as shown below:

i-adjectives

Japan is/is not/was/was not small.

Topic		Comment	
		i-adjective	
Nihon	**wa**	**chīsai <u>desu</u>**	(non-past affirmative)
		chīsa<u>kunai desu</u>	(non-past negative)
		chīsa<u>katta desu</u>	(past affirmative)
		chīsa<u>kunakatta desu</u>	(past negative)

na-adjectives

Japan is/is not/was/was not beautiful/clean.

Topic		Comment	
		na-adjective	
Nihon	wa	kirē <u>desu</u>	(non-past affirmative)
		kirē <u>dewa/ja arimasen</u>	(non-past negative)
		kirē <u>deshita</u>	(past affirmative)
		kirē <u>dewa/ja arimasendeshita</u>	(past negative)

When adjectives precede nouns, **i**-adjectives (e.g. **ī desu** "good") drop **desu** whereas **na**-adjectives (e.g. **yūmē desu** "famous") drop **desu** but take **na** as shown below:

i/na-adjective + noun

This is a good/famous book.

Topic		adjective	noun	copula	
Kore	wa	ī	hon	desu	(non-past affirmative)
				dewa/ja arimasen	(non-past negative)
		yūmē<u>na</u>		deshita	(past affirmative)
				dewa/ja arimasendeshita	(past negative)

Verbs

Japanese verbs, which conjugate as follows: **-masu**, **-masen**, **-mashita** and **-masendeshita**, appear at the end of the sentence. The object of the verb usually appears between the topic and the verb and it is marked by the object marker **o**.

I eat/do not eat/ate/did not eat an apple.

Topic		Comment		
		Object	Verb	
Watashi	wa	ringo	o	tabe<u>masu</u> (non-past affirmative) tabe<u>masen</u> (non-past negative) tabe<u>mashita</u> (past affirmative) tabe<u>masendeshita</u> (past negative)

3 Asking questions

To change a sentence into a question, the word order remains the same but **ka** is added at the end of the sentence.

a. **Yamada-san wa Nihon-jin desu.**
   Mr Yamada is Japanese.

b. **Yamada-san wa Nihon-jin desu <u>ka</u>.**
   Is Mr Yamada Japanese<u>?</u>

For a non-yes/no-question, the appropriate interrogative is used in the place of the missing information in addition to **ka** at the end of the sentence.

a. **Yamada-san wa Nihon-jin desu.**
   Mr Yamada is Japanese.

b. **Yamada-san wa <u>nani-jin</u> desu <u>ka</u>.**
   <u>What nationality</u> is Mr Yamada<u>?</u>

A full list of interrogative words can be found in section 8.

4 Plain style form

While the **desu/masu** form (shown in section 2) is a polite form which can be used in a formal situation, there is a plain style form counterpart. Plain style form is often used in conversation in a close relationship such as between friends or family members. If you want to learn more about this form, visit the website www.routledge.com/cw/colloquials.

5 Other expressions

Japanese verbs take more forms such as:

Verb stem ([V-stem]): **tabe** (the remaining part of the verb
   without **masu**)
Verb **te**-form ([V-**te**]): **tabete** (Units 13, 14)
Verb **ta**-form ([V-**ta**]): **tabeta** (Unit 15)
Verb dictionary form ([V-dic.]): **taberu** (Unit 16)

Along with other expressions, they make a variety of meanings, as
shown below:

(V-stem) +

[V-stem] + **masen ka**	Won't you [V]?	**Nichi-yōbi issho ni ēga o mimasen ka.**	9
[V-stem] + **mashō**	Let's [V]	**Hai, (issho ni) tabemashō.**	9
[V-stem] + **mashō ka**	Shall I [V]?	**Yamada-san, kaban o mochimashō ka.**	14
[V-stem] + **ni ikimasu**	The purpose of going/coming/ returning	**Watashi wa sūpā e pan o kai ni ikimasu.**	9
[V-stem] + **tai desu**	I want to [V]	**Watashi wa sushi o/ga tabetai desu.**	9

(V-te) +

[V-**te**] + **imasu**	be [V]-ing	**Ai-san wa ima Nihon-go o benkyō shite imasu.**	14
[V-**te**] + **imasu**	continuing state	**Watashi wa kekkon shite imasen.**	14
[V-**te**] + **imasu**	habitual action	**Watashi wa Nihon no kaisha de hataraite imasu.**	14
[V-**te**] + **kara** . . .	After [V1], do [V2]	**Watashi wa itsumo ha o migaite kara nemasu.**	14

[V-**te**] + kudasai	Please [V]	Sono shashin o <u>misete kudasai</u>.	13
[V-**te**] + **mo** ī desu	(You) may [V]	Koko ni <u>suwatte mo ī desu ka</u>.	13
[V-**te**], [V-**te**], . . .	to connect verb sentences	Watashi wa kinō gohan o <u>tabete</u>, shawā o <u>abite</u>, nemashita.	14
[V-**te**] + **wa** ikemasen	(You) must not [V]	Kutsu o <u>haitewa ikemasen</u>.	13

(V-ta) +

[V-**ta**] + **koto ga arimasu**	have experience of [V]-ing	Watashi wa kimono o <u>kita koto ga arimasu</u>. Jon-san wa Fujisan ni <u>nobotta koto ga arimasu ka</u>.	15
[V-**ta**] + **ri**, [V-**ta**] + **ri**	[V] and [V] and etc.	Watashi wa kinō terebi o <u>mitari</u>, hon o <u>yondari</u> shimashita.	15
[V-**ta**] + **ato de** . . .	after [V]	Sotsugyō <u>shita ato de</u> nani o shimashita ka.	15

(V-dic.) +

[V-dic.] + **koto ga dekimasu**	can [V]	Sukoshi dake Supein-go o <u>hanasu koto ga dekimasu</u>.	16
[V-dic.] + **koto**	changing verbs into nouns	Watashi no shumi wa piano o <u>hiku koto</u> desu.	16
[V-dic.] + **mae ni** . . .	before [V]	Gohan o <u>taberu mae ni</u> te o aratte kudasai.	16

6 **ko, so, a, do**

	Thing	Place	Place and direction (polite expression)	People	Demonstrative (*ko-so-a-do* + *noun*)
ko	**kore** this	**koko** here	**kochira** here/this way	**kochira** this person	**kono hon** this book
so	**sore** that	**soko** there	**sochira** there/that way	**sochira** that person	**sono hon** that book
a	**are** that one over there	**asoko** that place over there	**achira** that place/way over there	**achira** that person over there	**ano hon** that book over there
do	**dore** which one	**doko** where	**dochira** where	**donata** who	**dono hon** which book

7 Particles

Particle		Meaning and example	Unit
wa	は	sentence topic marker **Watashi <u>wa</u> Nihon-jin desu**	1
mo	も	also, to, as well as, even **Tanaka-san wa 29-sai desu. Watashi <u>mo</u> 29-sai desu.**	2
kara	から	from (beginning point in time or place, origin) **Ginkō wa gozen 10-ji <u>kara</u> desu.**	3
made	まで	until (up to and including) **Ginkō wa gogo 4-ji <u>made</u> desu.**	3
no	の	1) of **Anata <u>no</u> shigoto wa nan desu ka.** **Sore wa terebi <u>no</u> rimokon desu.**	1 4
		2) possessive marker **Sono kasa wa watashi <u>no</u> desu.**	4

Particle		Meaning and example	Unit
de	で	1) means, method (by, with)	
		Watashi wa basu <u>de</u> uchi e kaerimashita.	6
		Watashi wa te <u>de</u> sushi o tabemasu.	7
		2) in, at (location in/at which the action occurs or is done)	
		Watashi wa yoku sūpā <u>de</u> hirugohan o kaimasu.	7
o	を	direct object marker (thing acted upon)	
		Watashi wa yoku sūpā de hiru-gohan <u>o</u> kaimasu.	7
ni	に	1) indirect object ("receiver" of the action)	
		Watashi wa Akita-san <u>ni</u> purezento o agemasu.	10
		2) location in/at which something exists, resides, etc.	
		Ōsaka <u>ni</u> yūmē na oshiro ga arimasu.	8
		Watashi no ani wa ima Nihon <u>ni</u> sunde imasu.	14
		3) time (at, in)	
		Watashi wa maiasa gozen 7-ji <u>ni</u> okimasu.	7
		4) purpose (to)	
		Watashi wa ashita sūpā e pan o kai <u>ni</u> ikimasu.	9
		5) with	
		Nichi-yōbi issho <u>ni</u> ēga o mimasen ka?	9
ga	が	subject marker	
		Ōsaka ni yūmē na oshiro <u>ga</u> arimasu.	8
		Donna ongaku <u>ga</u> suki desu ka.	5
		Musuko-san wa se <u>ga</u> takai desu ne.	12
		Dōshite atarashī pasokon <u>ga</u> hoshī desu ka.	10
e	へ	direction (to, towards)	
		Watashi wa rainen Nihon <u>e</u> ikimasu.	6
ya	や	. . . , . . . , etc.	
		Watashi no heya ni beddo <u>ya</u> tsukue ga arimasu.	8

Particle		Meaning and example	Unit
to	と	1) . . . and . . . (for nouns) **hon <u>to</u> zasshi**	11
		2) together with **Watashi wa tomodachi <u>to</u> ikimasu.**	6
yo	よ	emphasis **Īe, chikai desu <u>yo</u>.** **Yo** is used for assertion. Some English equivalents are "I tell you", "you know", "believe me" and "I'd say".	11
ne	ね	tag question marker **Musuko-san wa se ga takai desu <u>ne</u>.**	12
yori	より	than, more . . . than . . . **Nihon wa Igirisu <u>yori</u> ōkī desu.**	12
dake	だけ	only **Sukoshi <u>dake</u> Supein-go o hanasu koto ga dekimasu.**	16

Other grammatical markers (conjunctions, etc)

Marker		Meaning and example	Unit
ga	が	but (conjunctive usage) **Nihon-go wa omoshiroi desu <u>ga</u>, muzukashī desu.**	5
demo	でも	however, but **Nihon-go wa omoshiroi desu. <u>Demo</u> muzukashī desu.**	5
soshite	そして	and, and then **Totemo oishī desu. <u>Soshite</u> totemo yasui desu.**	5
sorekara	それから	after that, and then **<u>Sorekara</u> nani o shimashita ka.**	7

Marker		Meaning and example	Unit
mae ni	まえに	1) in front of **Hito no <u>mae</u> ni ringo ga arimasu.**	8
		2) before **Gohan no <u>mae ni</u> shukudai o shimasu.**	16
kara	から	1) because Q: **Fujisan wa dōshite yūmē desu ka.** A: **(Fujisan wa) Nihon de ichi-ban takai yama desu <u>kara</u>.**	10
		Fujisan wa kirē desu <u>kara</u>, yūmē desu.	10
		2) after **Uchi ni kaette<u>kara</u> nani o shimasu ka.**	14
soreni	それに	besides, moreover <u>**Soreni**</u>**, ima no konpyūta wa sukoshi osoi desu kara.**	10
shikashi	しかし	however, but **Ēga o minagara gohan o tabetemo ī desu.**	13
		<u>**Shikashi**</u> **tabako o suttewa ikemasen.**	
goro	ごろ	about, around **Kinō no yoru 8-ji <u>goro</u> ēga o mite imashita.**	14

8 Interrogatives

Interrogative		English	Example	Unit
dare	だれ	who	**Ano hito wa <u>dare (donata)</u> desu ka.**	4
dare ga	だれが	who (subject)	**(O)shiro ni <u>dare ga</u> imasu ka.**	8
dare ni	だれに	to whom	<u>**Dare ni**</u> **hon o agemashita ka.**	10
dare no	だれの	whose	**Kono kasa wa <u>dare no</u> kasa desu ka.**	4
dare to	だれと	with whom	**Imai-san wa <u>dare to</u> Itaria e ikimasu ka.**	6

Interrogative		English	Example	Unit
dō	どう	how	Nihon no sēkatsu wa <u>dō</u> desu ka.	5
doko	どこ	where	(O)tearai wa <u>doko</u> desu ka.	3
doko de	どこで	(at/in/on) where	<u>Doko de</u> hon o yomimashita ka.	7
doko ni	どこに	(in) where	Biggu Ben wa <u>doko ni</u> arimasu ka.	8
doko no	どこの	from where	Sore wa <u>doko no</u> ongaku desu ka.	5
donna	どんな	what kind of	<u>Donna</u> ongaku ga suki desu ka.	5
dono	どの	which	Yamada-san wa <u>dono</u> tokē o kaimashita ka.	4
donokurai	どのくらい	how much/ how long/ how far	Rondon kara Tōkyō made hikōki de <u>donokurai</u> kakarimasu ka.	6
			<u>Donokurai</u> oyoide imasu ka.	14
dore	どれ	which (one)	Terebi no rimokon wa <u>dore</u> desu ka.	4
dōshite	どうして	why	Fujisan wa <u>dōshite</u> yūmē desu ka.	10
ikura	いくら	how much	Ano kamera wa <u>ikura</u> desu ka.	4
ikutsu	いくつ	how many	Ringo ga <u>ikutsu</u> arimasu ka.	8
itsu	いつ	when	Tanjōbi wa <u>itsu</u> desu ka.	2
nan	なん	what	Anata no onamae wa <u>nan</u> desu ka.	1
nan/ nani de	なん/なにで	how, by what means	<u>Nani de</u> bijutsukan e ikimashita ka.	6
nan-ban	なんばん	what number	Anata no denwa bangō wa <u>nan-ban</u> desu ka.	1
nan-gatsu	なんがつ	what month	Kinō wa <u>nan-gatsu</u> nan-nichi deshita ka.	2
nani ga	なにが	what (subject)	Tōkyō ni <u>nani ga</u> arimasu ka.	8
			Kekkon iwai ni <u>nani ga</u> hoshī desu ka.	10
nani o	なにを	what (object)	Sorekara <u>nani o</u> shimashita ka.	7
			Sūpā de <u>nani o</u> kaimashita ka.	8

Interrogative		English	Example	Unit
nan-ji	なんじ	what time	Ima <u>nan-ji</u> desu ka.	3
nan-nichi	なんにち	what day of the month	Kinō wa nan-gatsu <u>nan-nichi</u> deshita ka.	2
nan-sai	なんさい	how old	Sumisu-san wa <u>nan-sai</u> desu ka.	2
nan-yōbi	なんようび	what day of the week	Kyō wa <u>nan-yōbi</u> desu ka.	2

9 Adverbs and adverbial expressions

Degree

totemo	とても	very (much)	Kappu-rāmen wa <u>totemo</u> oishī desu.	5
chotto	ちょっと	slightly, a little	Kono machi wa <u>chotto</u> ōkī desu.	5
amari	あまり	not so much	Kono machi wa <u>amari</u> <u>ōkikunai desu</u>.	5
zenzen	ぜんぜん	not at all	Kono machi wa <u>zenzen</u> <u>ōkikunai desu</u>.	5

Quantity

takusan	たくさん	a lot, many	Machi ni omise ga <u>takusan</u> arimasu.	8
sukoshi	すこし	a few, a little	Machi ni omise ga <u>sukoshi</u> arimasu.	10
amari	あまり	not much, not many	Machi ni omise ga <u>amari arimasen</u>.	5
zenzen	ぜんぜん	none at all	Machi ni omise ga <u>zenzen arimasen</u>.	5

Frequency

itsumo	いつも	always	Watashi wa <u>itsumo</u> kissaten e ikimasu.	7
yoku	よく	often	Watashi wa <u>yoku</u> kissaten e ikimasu.	7
tokidoki	ときどき	sometimes	Watashi wa <u>tokidoki</u> kissaten e ikimasu.	7
tamani	たまに	occasionally	Watashi wa <u>tamani</u> kissaten e ikimasu.	7
amari	あまり	not very often	Watashi wa <u>amari</u> kissaten e <u>ikimasen</u>.	7
zenzen	ぜんぜん	never	Watashi wa <u>zenzen</u> kissaten e <u>ikimasen</u>.	7

Other adverbs and adverbial expressions

ichi-ban	いちばん	first, best most	Watashi wa gitā ga <u>ichi-ban</u> suki desu.	12
mada	まだ	not yet	Īe, <u>mada</u> desu.	9
mata	また	again	Jā <u>mata</u>, ashita.	5
mō	もう	already	<u>Mō</u> hoteru o yoyaku shimashita ka.	9
mochiron	もちろん	of course	Hai, <u>mochiron</u> ī desu yo.	9
mō ichido	もういちど	once more	<u>Mō ichido</u> yukkuri onegai shimasu.	3
motto	もっと	more	<u>Motto</u> yukkuri onegaishimasu.	6
tabun	たぶん	probably, maybe	<u>Tabun</u> 185-senchi kurai desu.	12
yukkuri	ゆっくり	slowly	Mō ichido <u>yukkuri</u> onegai shimasu.	3
zehi	ぜひ	by all means, definitely	Ī desu ne. <u>Zehi</u> ikimashō.	16
zenbu de	ぜんぶで	in total	<u>Zenbu de</u> ikutsu heya ga arimasu ka.	8

10 Numbers

	Roman letters	Hiragana	Kanji		Roman letters	Hiragana	Kanji
1	ichi	いち	一	50	gojū	ごじゅう	五十
2	ni	に	二	60	rokujū	ろくじゅう	六十
3	san	さん	三	70	nanajū	ななじゅう	七十
4	yon/shi	よん/し	四	80	hachijū	はちじゅう	八十
5	go	ご	五	90	kyūjū	きゅうじゅう	九十
6	roku	ろく	六	99	kyūjū kyū	きゅうじゅうきゅう	九十九
7	nana/shichi	なな/しち	七	100	hyaku	ひゃく	百
8	hachi	はち	八	200	nihyaku	にひゃく	二百
9	kyū/ku	きゅう/く	九	300	sanbyaku	さんびゃく	三百
10	jū	じゅう	十	400	yonhyaku	よんひゃく	四百
11	jū ichi	じゅういち	十一	500	gohyaku	ごひゃく	五百
12	jū ni	じゅうに	十二	600	roppyaku	ろっぴゃく	六百
13	jū san	じゅうさん	十三	700	nanahyaku	ななひゃく	七百
14	jū yon	じゅうよん	十四	800	happyaku	はっぴゃく	八百
	jū shi	じゅうし		900	kyūhyaku	きゅうひゃく	九百
15	jū go	じゅうご	十五				
16	jū roku	じゅうろく	十六	1,000	sen	せん	千
17	jū nana	じゅうなな	十七	2,000	nisen	にせん	二千
	jū shichi	じゅうしち		3,000	sanzen	さんぜん	三千
18	jū hachi	じゅうはち	十八	4,000	yonsen	よんせん	四千
19	jū kyū	じゅうきゅう	十九	5,000	gosen	ごせん	五千
	jū ku	じゅうく		6,000	rokusen	ろくせん	六千
20	nijū	にじゅう	二十	7,000	nanasen	ななせん	七千
30	sanjū	さんじゅう	三十	8,000	hassen	はっせん	八千
40	yonjū	よんじゅう	四十	9,000	kyūsen	きゅうせん	九千

	Roman letters	Hiragana	Kanji
10,000	ichiman	いちまん	一万
100,000	jūman	じゅうまん	十万
1,000,000	hyakuman	ひゃくまん	百万
10,000,000	issenman	いっせんまん	一千万
100,000,000	ichioku	いちおく	一億

11 Counters

tsu-system (general things)			**Thin, flat objects** (paper, stamps, shirts, CDs, DVDs, etc.)		
-tsu/～つ			**-mai/～まい/～枚**		
Q	**ikutsu**	いくつ	幾つ		
1	**hitotsu**	ひとつ	一つ		
2	**futatsu**	ふたつ	二つ		
3	**mittsu**	みっつ	三つ		
4	**yottsu**	よっつ	四つ		
5	**itsutsu**	いつつ	五つ		
6	**muttsu**	むっつ	六つ		
7	**nanatsu**	ななつ	七つ		
8	**yattsu**	やっつ	八つ		
9	**kokonotsu**	ここのつ	九つ		
10	**tō**	とお	十		
11	**jūichi**	じゅういち	十一		
12	**jūni**	じゅうに	十二		

Q	**nan-mai**	なんまい	何枚
1	**ichi-mai**	いちまい	一枚
2	**ni-mai**	にまい	二枚
3	**san-mai**	さんまい	三枚
4	**yon-mai**	よんまい	四枚
5	**go-mai**	ごまい	五枚
6	**roku-mai**	ろくまい	六枚
7	**nana-mai**	ななまい	七枚
8	**hachi-mai**	はちまい	八枚
9	**kyū-mai**	きゅうまい	九枚
10	**jū-mai**	じゅうまい	十枚
11	**jūichi-mai**	じゅういちまい	十一枚
12	**jūni-mai**	じゅうにまい	十二枚

Small things (eggs, apples, dice, etc.)

-ko/～こ/～個

Q	**nan-ko**	なんこ	何個
1	**ik-ko**	いっこ	一個
2	**ni-ko**	にこ	二個
3	**san-ko**	さんこ	三個
4	**yon-ko**	よんこ	四個
5	**go-ko**	ごこ	五個
6	**rok-ko**	ろっこ	六個
7	**nana-ko**	ななこ	七個
8	**hak-ko**	はっこ	八個
9	**kyū-ko**	きゅうこ	九個
10	**juk-ko**	じゅっこ	十個
11	**jūik-ko**	じゅういっこ	十一個
12	**jūni-ko**	じゅうにこ	十二個

Long, slender objects (pens, bottles, umbrellas, belts, etc.)

-pon, hon, bon/
～ぽん、ほん、ぼん、/～本

Q	**nan-bon**	なんぼん	何本
1	**ip-pon**	いっぽん	一本
2	**ni-hon**	にほん	二本
3	**san-bon**	さんぼん	三本
4	**yon-hon**	よんほん	四本
5	**go-hon**	ごほん	五本
6	**rop-pon**	ろっぽん	六本
7	**nana-hon**	ななほん	七本
8	**hap-pon**	はっぽん	八本
9	**kyū-hon**	きゅうほん	九本
10	**jup-pon**	じゅっぽん	十本
11	**jūip-pon**	じゅういっぽん	十一本
12	**jūni-hon**	じゅうにほん	十二本

Person, people

Machines, vehicles (TVs, PCs, cameras, cars, bicycles, etc.)

-nin/〜にん/〜人

-dai/〜だい/〜台

Q	**nan-nin**	なんにん	何人		Q	**nan-dai**	なんだい	何台
1	**hitori**	ひとり	一人		1	**ichi-dai**	いちだい	一台
2	**futari**	ふたり	二人		2	**ni-dai**	にだい	二台
3	**san-nin**	さんにん	三人		3	**san-dai**	さんだい	三台
4	**yo-nin**	よにん	四人		4	**yon-dai**	よんだい	四台
5	**go-nin**	ごにん	五人		5	**go-dai**	ごだい	五台
6	**roku-nin**	ろくにん	六人		6	**roku-dai**	ろくだい	六台
7	**nana-nin**	ななにん	七人		7	**nana-dai**	ななだい	七台
	shichi-nin	しちにん						
8	**hachi-nin**	はちにん	八人		8	**hachi-dai**	はちだい	八台
9	**kyū-nin**	きゅうにん	九人		9	**kyū-dai**	きゅうだい	九台
	ku-nin	くにん						
10	**jū-nin**	じゅうにん	十人		10	**jū-dai**	じゅうだい	十台
11	**jūichi-nin**	じゅういちにん	十一人		11	**jūichi-dai**	じゅういちだい	十一台
12	**jūni-nin**	じゅうににん	十二人		12	**jūni-dai**	じゅうにだい	十二台

Floors of a house or building

Frequency, times

-kai/〜かい/〜階

-kai/〜かい/〜回

Q	**nan-gai**	なんがい	何階		Q	**nan-kai**	なんかい	何回
1	**ik-kai**	いっかい	一階		1	**ik-kai**	いっかい	一回
2	**ni-kai**	にかい	二階		2	**ni-kai**	にかい	二回
3	**san-gai**	さんがい	三階		3	**san-kai**	さんかい	三回
4	**yon-kai**	よんかい	四階		4	**yon-kai**	よんかい	四回
5	**go-kai**	ごかい	五階		5	**go-kai**	ごかい	五回
6	**rok-kai**	ろっかい	六階		6	**rok-kai**	ろっかい	六回
7	**nana-kai**	ななかい	七階		7	**nana-kai**	ななかい	七回
8	**hak-kai**	はっかい	八階		8	**hak-kai**	はっかい	八回
	hachi-kai	はちかい						
9	**kyū-kai**	きゅうかい	九階		9	**kyū-kai**	きゅうかい	九回
10	**juk-kai**	じゅっかい	十階		10	**juk-kai**	じゅっかい	十回
11	**jūik-kai**	じゅういっかい	十一階		11	**jūik-kai**	じゅういっかい	十一回
12	**jūni-kai**	じゅうにかい	十二階		12	**jūni-kai**	じゅうにかい	十二回

12 Time expressions

Minutes

-fun, pun/～ふん、ぷん/～分

Q	nan-pun	なんぶん	何分
1	ip-pun	いっぷん	一分
2	ni-fun	にふん	二分
3	san-pun	さんぶん	三分
4	yon-pun	よんぷん	四分
5	go-fun	ごふん	五分
6	rop-pun	ろっぷん	六分
7	nana-fun	ななふん	七分
8	hap-pun	はっぷん	八分
9	kyū-fun	きゅうふん	九分
10	jup-pun	じゅっぶん	十分
11	jūip-pun	じゅういっぷん	十一分
12	jūni-fun	じゅうにふん	十二分

Hours

-jikan/～じかん/～時間

Q	nan-jikan	なんじかん	何時間
1	ichi-jikan	いちじかん	一時間
2	ni-jikan	にじかん	二時間
3	san-jikan	さんじかん	三時間
4	yo-jikan	よじかん	四時間
5	go-jikan	ごじかん	五時間
6	roku-jikan	ろくじかん	六時間
7	nana-jikan	ななじかん	七時間
8	hachi-jikan	はちじかん	八時間
9	ku-jikan	くじかん	九時間
10	jū-jikan	じゅうじかん	十時間
11	jūichi-jikan	じゅういちじかん	十一時間
12	jūni-jikan	じゅうにじかん	十二時間

Days

-nichi/～にち/～日

Q	nan-nichi	なんにち	何日
1	ichi-nichi	いちにち	一日
2	futsu-ka	ふつか	二日
3	mik-ka	みっか	三日
4	yok-ka	よっか	四日
5	itsu-ka	いつか	五日
6	mui-ka	むいか	六日
7	nano-ka	なのか	七日
8	yō-ka	ようか	八日
9	kokono-ka	ここのか	九日
10	tō-ka	とおか	十日
11	jūichi-nichi	じゅういちにち	十一日
12	jūni-nichi	じゅうににち	十二日

Weeks

-shūkan/～しゅうかん/～週間

Q	nan-shūkan	なんしゅうかん	何週間
1	is-shūkan	いっしゅうかん	一週間
2	ni-shūkan	にしゅうかん	二週間
3	san-shūkan	さんしゅうかん	三週間
4	yon-shūkan	よんしゅうかん	四週間
5	go-shūkan	ごしゅうかん	五週間
6	roku-shūkan	ろくしゅうかん	六週間
7	nana-shūkan	ななしゅうかん	七週間
8	has-shūkan	はっしゅうかん	八週間
9	kyū-shūkan	きゅうしゅうかん	九週間
10	jus-shūkan	じゅっしゅうかん	十週間
11	jūis-shūkan	じゅういっしゅうかん	十一週間
12	jūni-shūkan	じゅうにしゅうかん	十二週間

	Months				*Years*		
	-kagetsu/～かげつ/～か月				**-nen**/～ねん/～年		
Q	nan-kagetsu	なんかげつ	何ヶ月	Q	nan-nen	なんねん	何年
1	ik-kagetsu	いっかげつ	一ヶ月	1	ichi-nen	いちねん	一年
2	ni-kagetsu	にかげつ	二ヶ月	2	ni-nen	にねん	二年
3	san-kagetsu	さんかげつ	三ヶ月	3	san-nen	さんねん	三年
4	yon-kagetsu	よんかげつ	四ヶ月	4	yo-nen	よねん	四年
5	go-kagetsu	ごかげつ	五ヶ月	5	go-nen	ごねん	五年
6	rok-kagetsu	ろっかげつ	六ヶ月	6	roku-nen	ろくねん	六年
7	nana-kagetsu	ななかげつ	七ヶ月	7	nana-nen	ななねん	七年
8	hachi-kagetsu	はちかげつ	八ヶ月	8	hachi-nen	はちねん	八年
	hak-kagetsu	はっかげつ					
9	kyū-kagetsu	きゅうかげつ	九ヶ月	9	kyū-nen	きゅうねん	九年
10	juk-kagetsu	じゅっかげつ	十ヶ月	10	jū-nen	じゅうねん	十年
11	jūik-kagetsu	じゅういっか げつ	十一ヶ月	11	jūichi-nen	じゅういち ねん	十一年
12	jūni-kagetsu	じゅうにか げつ	十二ヶ月	12	jūni-nen	じゅうに ねん	十二年

	Past ⟵		Present ⟶		Future
Day	**ototoi** おとどい 一昨日 the day before yesterday	**kinō** きのう 昨日 yesterday	**kyō** きょう 今日 today	**ashita** あした 明日 tomorrow	**asatte** あさって 明後日 the day after tomorrow
Week	**sensenshū** せんせんしゅう 先々週 the week before last	**senshū** せんしゅう 先週 last week	**konshū** こんしゅう 今週 this week	**raishū** らいしゅう 来週 next week	**saraishū** さらいしゅう 再来週 the week after next
Month	**sensengetsu** せんせんげつ 先々月 the month before last	**sengetsu** せんげつ 先月 last month	**kongetsu** こんげつ 今月 this month	**raigetsu** らいげつ 来月 next month	**saraigetsu** さらいげつ 再来月 the month after next
Year	**ototoshi** おととし 一昨年 the year before last	**kyonen** きょねん 去年 last year	**kotoshi** ことし 今年 this year	**rainen** らいねん 来年 next year	**sarainen** さらいねん 再来年 the year after next

13 Additional vocabulary

Food

tabemono/たべもの		
aisukurīmu	アイスクリーム	ice cream
bēkon	ベーコン	bacon
butaniku	ぶたにく	pork
chokorēto	チョコレート	chocolate
gyūniku	ぎゅうにく	beef
hamu	ハム	ham
karēraisu	カレーライス	curry and rice
kēki	ケーキ	cake
pan	パン	bread
piza	ピザ	pizza
potato chippusu	ポテトチップス	crisps
sandoitchi	サンドイッチ	sandwich
sōsēji	ソーセージ	sausage
supagetti	スパゲッティー	spaghetti
toriniku	とりにく	chicken

Vegetables

yasai/やさい		
daikon	だいこん	Japanese radish
hakusai	はくさい	Chinese leaves
hōrensō	ほうれんそう	spinach
jagaimo	じゃがいも	potato
kinoko	きのこ	mushroom
kyabetsu	キャベツ	cabbage
kyūri	きゅうり	cucumber
mame	まめ	beans
moyashi	もやし	beansprouts
nasu	なす	aubergine
negi	ねぎ	leek
ninjin	にんじん	carrot
retasu	レタス	lettuce
tamanegi	たまねぎ	onion
tomato	トマト	tomato
tōmorokoshi	とうもろこし	(sweet) corn

Fruit

kudamono/くだもの

banana	バナナ	banana
budō	ぶどう	grape
gurēpufurūtsu	グレープフルーツ	grapefruit
ichigo	いちご	strawberry
kiui	キウイ	kiwi fruit
meron	メロン	melon
mikan	みかん	mandarin
momo	もも	peach
nashi	なし	pear
painappuru	パイナップル	pineapple
remon	レモン	lemon
ringo	りんご	apple
sakuranbo	さくらんぼ	cherry
suika	すいか	watermelon
sumomo	すもも	plum

Drinks

nomimono/のみもの

bīru	ビール	beer
gyūnyū	ぎゅうにゅう	milk
jūsu	ジュース	juice
kakuteru	カクテル	cocktail
kōcha	こうちゃ	English tea
kōhī	コーヒー	coffee
kōra	コーラ	coke, cola
mizu	みず	water
nihon-cha	にほんちゃ	green tea
orenji jūsu	オレンジジュース	orange juice
(o)sake	おさけ	Jap. rice wine
ringo jūsu	りんごジュース	apple juice
uisukī	ウイスキー	whisky
wain	ワイン	wine
wokka	ウォッカ	vodka

Buildings

tatemono/たてもの

depāto	デパート	department store
eki	えき	station
jinja	じんじゃ	shrine
kēsatsusho	けいさつしょ	police station
kōban	こうばん	police box
kūkō	くうこう	airport
kyōkai	きょうかい	church
mosuku	モスク	mosque
(o)tera	(お)てら	temple
pūru	プール	swimming pool
shōbōsho	しょうぼうしょ	fire station
taīkukan	たいいくかん	gymnasium
taishikan	たいしかん	embassy
yūenchi	ゆうえんち	amusement park

Occupations

shigoto/しごと

bengoshi	べんごし	lawyer
chōrishi	ちょうり	cook
dezainā	デザイナー	designer
enjinia	エンジニア	engineer
haiyū	はいゆう	actor/actress
isha	いしゃ	doctor
kaishain	かいしゃいん	office worker
kangoshi	かんごし	nurse
kashu	かしゅ	singer
kēsatsukan	けいさつかん	policeman
kōmuin	こうむいん	civil servant
kyōshi	きょうし	teacher
sakka	さっか	author/writer
sējika	せいじか	politician
shufu	しゅふ	housewife
ten'in	てんいん	shop assistant

Sports

supōtsu/スポーツ		
badominton	バドミントン	badminton
barēbōru	バレーボール	volleyball
basukettobōru	バスケットボール	basketball
bodībiru	ボディービル	body-building
bokushingu	ボクシング	boxing
bōringu	ボウリング	bowling
gorufu	ゴルフ	golf
kakutōgi	かくとうぎ	martial arts
marason	マラソン	marathon
ragubī	ラグビー	rugby football
resuringu	レスリング	wrestling
sakkā	サッカー	football/soccer
suiē	すいえい	swimming
takkyū	たっきゅう	table tennis
yakyū	やきゅう	baseball

Music and film

ongaku to ēga/おんがく と えいが		
jazu	ジャズ	jazz
kurashikku	クラシック	classical
myūjikaru	ミュージカル	musical
opera	オペラ	opera
poppusu	ポップス	pop
rokku	ロック	rock and roll
akushon	アクション	action film
dokyumentarī	ドキュメンタリー	documentary film
esuefu	SF	SF film
horā	ホラー	horror film
iyashi	いやし	soothing film
komedī	コメディー	comedy film
misuterī	ミステリー	mystery film
ren'ai	れんあい	romance film

Appendix

i-adjectives

i-adjective	non-past affirmative	non-past negative	past affirmative	past negative	English	Unit
akai	akai desu	akakunai desu	akakatta desu	akakunakatta desu	red	12
akarui	akarui desu	akarukunai desu	akarukatta desu	akarukunakatta desu	bright	11
amai	amai desu	amakunai desu	amakatta desu	amakunakatta desu	sweet	11
atarashī	atarashī desu	atarashikunai desu	atarashikatta desu	atarashikunakatta desu	new	5
atatakai	atatakai desu	atatakakunai desu	atatakakatta desu	atatakakunakatta desu	warm	11
atsui	atsui desu	atsukunai desu	atsukatta desu	atsukunakatta desu	hot	5
chikai	chikai desu	chikakunai desu	chikakatta desu	chikakunakatta desu	near	11
chīsai	chīsai desu	chīsakunai desu	chīsakatta desu	chīsakunakatta desu	small	5
furui	furui desu	furukunai desu	furukatta desu	furukunakatta desu	old	5
hayai	hayai desu	hayakunai desu	hayakatta desu	hayakunakatta desu	fast	10
hikui	hikui desu	hikukunai desu	hikukatta desu	hikukunakatta desu	low	5
hiroi	hiroi desu	hirokunai desu	hirokatta desu	hirokunakatta desu	spacious	11
hoshī	hoshī desu	hoshikunai desu	hoshikatta desu	hoshikunakatta desu	want	10
ī/yoi	ī/yoi desu	yokunai desu	yokatta desu	yokunakatta desu	good	5
isogashī	isogashī desu	isogashikunai desu	isogashikatta desu	isogashikunakatta desu	busy	9
itai	itai desu	itakunai desu	itakatta desu	itakunakatta desu	painful	10
karai	karai desu	karakunai desu	karakatta desu	karakunakatta desu	spicy, hot	11
karui	karui desu	karukunai desu	karukatta desu	karukunakatta desu	light	11
kawaī	kawaī desu	kawaikunai desu	kawaikatta desu	kawaikunakatta desu	pretty	10
kowai	kowai desu	kowakunai desu	kowakatta desu	kowakunakatta desu	scary	11
kurai	kurai desu	kurakunai desu	kurakatta desu	kurakunakatta desu	dark	11

i-adjectives (cont'd)

i-adjective	non-past affirmative	non-past negative	past affirmative	past negative	English	Unit
kuroi	kuroi desu	kurokunai desu	kurokatta desu	kurokunakatta desu	black	12
mazui	mazui desu	mazukunai desu	mazukatta desu	mazukunakatta desu	tasteless	5
muzukashī	muzukashī desu	muzukashikunai desu	muzukashikatta desu	muzukashikunakatta desu	difficult	5
ōi	ōi desu	ōkunai desu	ōkatta desu	ōkunakatta desu	many	11
oishī	oishī desu	oishikunai desu	oishikatta desu	oishikunakatta desu	delicious	5
ōkī	ōkī desu	ōkikunai desu	ōkikatta desu	ōkikunakatta desu	big	5
omoi	omoi desu	omokunai desu	omokatta desu	omokunakatta desu	heavy	11
omoshiroi	omoshiroi desu	omoshirokunai desu	omoshirokatta desu	omoshirokunakatta desu	interesting	5
osoi	osoi desu	osokunai desu	osokatta desu	osokunakatta desu	slow, late	10
samui	samui desu	samukunai desu	samukatta desu	samukunakatta desu	cold (temperature)	5
semai	semai desu	semakunai desu	semakatta desu	semakunakatta desu	narrow	11
shiroi	shiroi desu	shirokunai desu	shirokatta desu	shirokunakatta desu	white	12
sugoi	sugoi desu	sugokunai desu	sugokatta desu	sugokunakatta desu	great	14
sukunai	sukunai desu	sukunakunai desu	sukunakatta desu	sukunakunakatta desu	few, a little	11
takai	takai desu	takakunai desu	takakatta desu	takakunakatta desu	expensive/high	5
tanoshī	tanoshī desu	tanoshikunai desu	tanoshikatta desu	tanoshikunakatta desu	enjoyable	5
tōi	tōi desu	tōkunai desu	tōkatta desu	tōkunakatta desu	far	6
tsumaranai	tsumaranai desu	tsumaranakunai desu	tsumaranakatta desu	tsumaranakunakatta desu	boring	5
tsumetai	tsumetai desu	tsumetakunai desu	tsumetakatta desu	tsumetakunakatta desu	cold (touch)	5
ureshī	ureshī desu	ureshikunai desu	ureshikatta desu	ureshikunakatta desu	happy	9
urusai	urusai desu	urusakunai desu	urusakatta desu	urusakunakatta desu	noisy	11
utsukushī	utsukushī desu	utsukushikunai desu	utsukushikatta desu	utsukushikunakatta desu	beautiful	11
wakai	wakai desu	wakakunai desu	wakakatta desu	wakakunakatta desu	young	12
warui	warui desu	warukunai desu	warukatta desu	warukunakatta desu	bad	5
yasashī	yasashī desu	yasashikunai desu	yasashikatta desu	yasashikunakatta desu	easy	5
yasui	yasui desu	yasukunai desu	yasukatta desu	yasukunakatta desu	cheap	5
yawarakai	yawarakai desu	yawarakakunai desu	yawarakakatta desu	yawarakakunakatta desu	soft	11

na-adjectives

na-adjective	non-past affirmative	non-past negative	past affirmative	past negative	English	Unit
anzen(na)	anzen **desu**	anzen **dewa/ja arimasen**	anzen **deshita**	anzen **dewa/ja arimasen deshita**	safe	11
benri(na)	benri **desu**	benri **dewa/ja arimasen**	benri **deshita**	benri **dewa/ja arimasen deshita**	convenient	5
daijōbu(na)	daijōbu **desu**	daijōbu **dewa/ja arimasen**	daijōbu **deshita**	daijōbu **dewa/ja arimasen deshita**	all right, OK	10
daisuki(na)	daisuki **desu**	daisuki **dewa/ja arimasen**	daisuki **deshita**	daisuki **dewa/ja arimasen deshita**	like very much	5
fuben(na)	fuben **desu**	fuben **dewa/ja arimasen**	fuben **deshita**	fuben **dewa/ja arimasen deshita**	inconvenient	5
genki(na)	genki **desu**	genki **dewa/ja arimasen**	genki **deshita**	genki **dewa/ja arimasen deshita**	vigorous, active	5
hade(na)	hade **desu**	hade **dewa/ja arimasen**	hade **deshita**	hade **dewa/ja arimasen deshita**	showy, gaudy	12
heta(na)	heta **desu**	heta **dewa/ja arimasen**	heta **deshita**	heta **dewa/ja arimasen deshita**	poor at	5
hima(na)	hima **desu**	hima **dewa/ja arimasen**	hima **deshita**	hima **dewa/ja arimasen deshita**	free (time)	5
iroiro(na)	iroiro **desu**	iroiro **dewa/ja arimasen**	iroiro **deshita**	iroiro **dewa/ja arimasen deshita**	various	8
jiyū(na)	jiyū **desu**	jiyū **dewa/ja arimasen**	jiyū **deshita**	jiyū **dewa/ja arimasen deshita**	free (freedom)	11
jōzu(na)	jōzu **desu**	jōzu **dewa/ja arimasen**	jōzu **deshita**	jōzu **dewa/ja arimasen deshita**	good at	5
kantan(na)	kantan **desu**	kantan **dewa/ja arimasen**	kantan **deshita**	kantan **dewa/ja arimasen deshita**	easy (for, to/of)	15
kenkō(na)	kenkō **desu**	kenkō **dewa/ja arimasen**	kenkō **deshita**	kenkō **dewa/ja arimasen deshita**	healthy	11
kirai(na)	kirai **desu**	kirai **dewa/ja arimasen**	kirai **deshita**	kirai **dewa/ja arimasen deshita**	dislike	5
kirē(na)	kirē **desu**	kirē **dewa/ja arimasen**	kirē **deshita**	kirē **dewa/ja arimasen deshita**	beautiful/clean	5
nigiyaka(na)	nigiyaka **desu**	nigiyaka **dewa/ja arimasen**	nigiyaka **deshita**	nigiyaka **dewa/ja arimasen deshita**	lively	5
shinsetsu(na)	shinsetsu **desu**	shinsetsu **dewa/ja arimasen**	shinsetsu **deshita**	shinsetsu **dewa/ja arimasen deshita**	kind	5
shizuka(na)	shizuka **desu**	shizuka **dewa/ja arimasen**	shizuka **deshita**	shizuka **dewa/ja arimasen deshita**	quiet	5
suki(na)	suki **desu**	suki **dewa/ja arimasen**	suki **deshita**	suki **dewa/ja arimasen deshita**	like	5
suteki(na)	suteki **desu**	suteki **dewa/ja arimasen**	suteki **deshita**	suteki **dewa/ja arimasen deshita**	wonderful	12
tanoshimi(na)	tanoshimi **desu**	tanoshimi **dewa/ja arimasen**	tanoshimi **deshita**	tanoshimi **dewa/ja arimasen deshita**	look forward to	5
yūmē(na)	yūmē **desu**	yūmē **dewa/ja arimasen**	yūmē **deshita**	yūmē **dewa/ja arimasen deshita**	famous	5

Verb conjugation: Group 1 verbs

masu-form	dictionary form	te-form	ta-form	nai-form	English	Unit
aimasu	au	atte	atta	awanai	to meet	9
araimasu	arau	aratte	aratta	arawanai	to wash	16
arimasu	aru	atte	atta	*nai	to be/there's something (exist)	8
arimasu	aru	atte	atta	*nai	to have/own	10
asobimasu	asobu	asonde	asonda	asobanai	to play	13
ganbarimasu	ganbaru	ganbatte	ganbatta	ganbaranai	to do (try) one's best	13
hairimasu	hairu	haitte	haitta	hairanai	to enter	9
hakimasu	haku	haite	kaita	hakanai	to wear (shoes, trousers, etc.)	13
hanashimasu	hanasu	hanashite	hanashita	hanasanai	to talk/speak	9
haraimasu	harau	haratte	haratta	harawanai	to pay	13
hashirimasu	hashiru	hashitte	hashitta	hashiranai	to run	9
hatarakimasu	hataraku	hataraite	hataraita	hatarakanai	to work	14
hikimasu	hiku	hīte	hīta	hikanai	to play (keyboard and stringed instruments)	16
ikimasu	iku	itte	itta	ikanai	to go	6
isogimasu	isogu	isoide	isoida	isoganai	to hurry	10
kaburimasu	kaburu	kabutte	kabutta	kaburanai	to wear (hat, cap, etc.)	15
kaerimasu	kaeru	kaette	kaetta	kaeranai	to go back/return	6
kaimasu	kau	katte	katta	kawanai	to buy	7

An explanation of how to make the **nai**-form and its usages can be found in the additional chapters which are downloadable at www.routledge.com/cw/colloquials

Verb conjugation: Group 1 verbs (*cont'd*)

masu-*form*	*dictionary form*	**te**-*form*	**ta**-*form*	**nai**-*form*	*English*	*Unit*
kakarimasu	kakaru	kakatte	kakatta	kakaranai	to take (time, cost)	6
kakimasu	kaku	kaite	kaita	kakanai	to write	7
kikimasu	kiku	kite	kita	kikanai	to listen (to), hear	7
kirimasu	kiru	kitte	kitta	kiranai	to cut	16
machimasu	matsu	matte	matta	matanai	to wait	13
magarimasu	magaru	magatte	magatta	magaranai	to turn	14
migakimasu	migaku	migaite	migaita	migakanai	to polish/brush	14
mochimasu	motsu	motte	motta	motanai	to have/own/hold	14
moraimasu	morau	moratte	moratta	morawanai	to receive	10
motte ikimasu	motte iku	motte itte	motte itta	motte ikanai	to take (something to somewhere)	13
narimasu	naru	natte	natta	naranai	to become	11
noborimasu	noboru	nobotte	nobotta	noboranai	to climb	14
nomimasu	nomu	nonde	nonda	nomanai	to drink	7
norimasu	noru	notte	notta	noranai	to get on/ride	14
odorimasu	odoru	odotte	odotta	odoranai	to dance	15
okimasu	oku	oite	oita	okanai	to put (something)	13
okurimasu	okuru	okutte	okutta	okuranai	to send (e.g. an email)	13
omoidashimasu	omoidasu	omoidashite	omoidashita	omoidasanai	to recall, remember	13
oyogimasu	oyogu	oyoide	oyoida	oyoganai	to swim	15
shirimasu	shiru	shitte	shitta	shiranai	to get to know	14
sumimasu	sumu	sunde	sunda	sumanai	to live	14
suwarimasu	suwaru	suwatte	suwatta	suwaranai	to sit down	14
tabako o suimasu	tabako o sū	tabako o sutte	tabako o sutta	tabako o suwanai	to smoke a cigarette	13
tachimasu	tatsu	tatte	tatta	tatanai	to stand up	14

Verb conjugation: Group 1 verbs (cont'd)

masu-form	dictionary form	te-form	ta-form	nai-form	English	Unit
tomarimasu	tomaru	tomatte	tomatta	tomaranai	to stay overnight	9
torimasu	toru	totte	totta	toranai	to take (a photo)	9
tsukurimasu	tsukuru	tsukutte	tsukutta	tsukuranai	to make, cook	15
tsurete ikimasu	tsurete iku	tsurete itte	tsurete itta	tsurete ikanai	to take (someone to somewhere)	13
utaimasu	utau	utatte	utatta	utawanai	to sing	11
watarimasu	wataru	watatte	watatta	wataranai	to cross	14
yasumimasu	yasumu	yasunde	yasunda	yasumanai	to rest	9
yobimasu	yobu	yonde	yonda	yobanai	to call (e.g. a taxi)	13
yomimasu	yomu	yonde	yonda	yomanai	to read	7

Verb conjugation: Group 2 verbs

masu-form	dictionary form	te-form	ta-form	nai-form	English	Unit
abimasu	abiru	abite	abita	abinai	to take	14
agemasu	ageru	agete	ageta	agenai	to give	11
akemasu	akeru	akete	aketa	akenai	to open (transitive verb)	13
atsumemasu	atsumeru	atsumete	atsumeta	atsumenai	to collect	16
dekimasu	dekiru	dekite	dekita	dekinai	can (do)	16
demasu	deru	dete	deta	denai	to leave/get out	14
denwa o kakemasu	denwa o kakeru	denwa o kakete	denwa o kaketa	denwa o kakenai	to make a phone call	15

Verb conjugation: Group 2 verbs *(cont'd)*

*masu-*form	*dictionary form*	*te-*form	*ta-*form	***nai-*form**	*English*	*Unit*
imasu	iru	ite	ita	inai	to be/there is someone (exist)	8
iremasu	ireru	irete	ireta	irenai	to put (something) in	14
kaemasu	kaeru	kaete	kaeta	kaenai	to change	9
kakemasu	kakeru	kakete	kaketa	kakenai	to wear (glasses)	15
karimasu	kariru	karite	karita	karinai	to borrow	13
ki o tsukemasu	ki o tsukeru	ki o tsukete	ki o tsuketa	ki o tsukenai	to be careful	13
kimasu	kiru	kite	kita	kinai	to wear (clothes)	15
mimasu	miru	mite	mita	minai	to watch/see	7
misemasu	miseru	misete	miseta	misenai	to show	13
motte imasu	motte iru	motte ite	motte ita	motte inai	to own, possess	14
nemasu	neru	nete	neta	nenai	to go to bed/sleep	7
norikaemasu	norikaeru	norikaete	norikaeta	norikaenai	to change/transfer	14
oboemasu	oboeru	oboete	oboeta	oboenai	to remember, memorize	13
okimasu	okiru	okite	okita	okinai	to wake up. get up	7
orimasu	oriru	orite	orita	orinai	to get off	13
oshiemasu	oshieru	oshiete	oshieta	oshienai	to teach, tell	13
shimemasu	shimeru	shimete	shimeta	shimenai	to close, to shut	13
shirabemasu	shiraberu	shirabete	shirabeta	shirabenai	to investigate/examine/ check/study	16
tabemasu	taberu	tabete	tabeta	tabenai	to eat	7
tasukemasu	tasukeru	tasukete	tasuketa	tasukenai	to help/rescue	13
tatemasu	tateru	tatete	tateta	tatenai	to build	16
todokemasu	todokeru	todokete	todoketa	todokenai	to deliver	13
tomemasu	tomeru	tomete	tometa	tomenai	to pull up (a car)/stop	13
tsukemasu	tsukeru	tsukete	tsuketa	tsukenai	to turn on/switch on	16

Verb conjugation: Group 3 verbs

masu-form	dictionary form	te-form	ta-form	nai-form	English	Unit
kimasu	kuru	kite	kita	konai	to come	6
shimasu	suru	shite	shita	shinai	to do	7
benkyō shimasu	benkyō suru	benkyō shite	benkyō shita	benkyō shinai	to study	7
chūmon shimasu	chūmon suru	chūmon shite	chūmon shita	chūmon shinai	to order	9
jogingu shimasu	jogingu suru	jogingu shite	jogingu shita	jogingu shinai	to jog	14
kaimono shimasu	kaimono suru	kaimono shite	kaimono shita	kaimono shinai	to go shopping	7
kankō shimasu	kankō suru	kankō shite	kankō shita	kankō shinai	to go sightseeing	9
kekkon shimasu	kekkon suru	kekkon shite	kekkon shita	kekkon shinai	to get married	14
kurikku shimasu	kurikku suru	kurikku shite	kurikku shita	kurikku shinai	to click	13
kyanseru shimasu	kyanseru suru	kyanseru shite	kyanseru shita	kyanseru shinai	to cancel	9
motte kimasu	motte kuru	motte kite	motte kita	motte konai	to bring (something to somewhere)	13
ryōri shimasu	ryōri suru	ryōri shite	ryōri shita	ryōri shinai	to cook	7
sanpo shimasu	sanpo suru	sanpo shite	sanpo shita	sanpo shinai	to go for a walk	11
sentaku shimasu	sentaku suru	sentaku shite	sentaku shita	sentaku shinai	to wash (clothes)	14
shigoto shimasu	shigoto suru	shigoto shite	shigoto shita	shigoto shinai	to work	7
shokuji shimasu	shokuji suru	shokuji shite	shokuji shita	shokuji shinai	to have a meal	14
sōji shimasu	sōji suru	sōji shite	sōji shita	sōji shinai	to clean (a room, house, park, etc.)	14
sotsugyō shimasu	sotsugyō suru	sotsugyō shite	sotsugyō shita	sotsugyō shinai	to graduate	15
tsuretekimasu	tsuretekuru	tsuretekite	tsuretekita	tsuretekonai	to bring (someone to somewhere)	13
undō shimasu	undō suru	undō shite	undō shita	undō shinai	to exercise	9
unten shimasu	unten suru	unten shite	unten shita	unten shinai	to drive	7
urusaku shimasu	urusaku suru	urusaku shite	urusaku shita	urusaku shinai	to make noise	13
yoyaku shimasu	yoyaku suru	yoyaku shite	yoyaku shita	yoyaku shinai	to reserve/book	9

Key to exercises

Unit 1

Exercise 1

1 (*Watashi wa*) Igirisu-jin desu. 2 Watashi wa gakusē desu.
3 Watashi wa kaishain desu. 4 Watashi wa Nihon-jin dewa arimasen.
(Watashi wa) Chūgoku-jin desu.

Exercise 2

1 e.g. Tanaka Tokiko 2 e.g. Nihon 3 e.g. gakusē 4 e.g. yoroshiku
(onegai shimasu)

Exercise 3

1 watashi no namae 2 anata no (o)shigoto 3 Sasaki-san no (o)shigoto
4 sensē no (o)namae

Exercise 4

1 Yamada-san wa kaishain desu ka. 2 Sasaki-san no (o)shigoto wa
nan desu ka. 3 (o)namae wa nan desu ka. 4 Teirā-san no sensē wa
Nihon-jin desu ka.

Exercise 5

1 e.g. Watashi (no namae) wa Tanaka Masae desu. 2 e.g. Watashi wa
Nihon-jin desu. 3 e.g. Watashi (no shigoto) wa kaishain desu.

Exercise 6

1 a 2 b 3 b

Exercise 7

1 e.g. Watashi no denwa-bangō wa 012-345-6789 desu. 2 Hai,
sō desu. / Hai, Howaito-san no denwa-bangō wa 784-0394 desu.
3 Katō-san no denwa-bangō wa 021-6658 desu.

Exercise 8

1 ✗ 2 ✓ 3 ✗

Exercise 9

2 a i 3 i ke 4 u e 5 a go 6 ka o 7 ki i (ro) 8 o ka (ne) 9 ko (mu) gi ko

Unit 2

Exercise 1

1 32 2 14 3 17 4 85 5 60 6 99

Exercise 2

1 e.g. Watashi wa nijūhas-sai desu. 2 e.g. Watashi no haha wa gojū-roku-sai desu. 3 e.g. Watashi no otōto wa nijū-go-sai desu.

Exercise 3

1 Satoshi-san no otōsan wa nan-sai desu ka. (59) 2 Satoshi-san no okāsan wa nan-sai desu ka. (56) 3 Satoshi-san no onēsan wa nan-sai desu ka. (30) 4 Satoshi-san no otōtosan wa nan-sai desu ka. (25)

Exercise 4

1 e.g. Watashi no tanjōbi wa jūni-gatsu jūsan-nichi desu. 2 e.g. Watashi no haha/chichi no tanjōbi wa ni-gatsu yokka desu. 3 Jon-san no imōtosan no tanjōbi wa jūni-gatsu nijūku-nichi desu. 4 Jon-san no otōsan no tanjōbi wa jūichi-gatsu tōka desu. 5 Ie, sō dewa arimasen. (Jon-san no onīsan no tanjōbi wa) shi-gatsu jūhachi-nichi desu.

Exercise 5

1 21st July 2 10th April

Exercise 6

1 ✓ 2 ✗ 3 ✓ 4 ✗ 5 ✓

Exercise 7

1 kotoshi 2 ashita 3 moku-yōbi 4 kinō

Exercise 8

1 ✗ 2 ✓ 3 ✓ 4 ✗

Exercise 9

1 su shi 2 sa shi (mi) 3 to (mo) da chi 4 a shi ta 5 chi zu 6 su i e i 7 chi ka te tsu 8 ka ze 9 so u de su ka

Unit 3

Exercise 1

1 koko 2 soko, Asoko 3 doko 4 achira 5 dochira

Exercise 2

1 Ueda-san wa byōin desu. 2 Kimura-san wa eki desu. 3 Otearai wa asoko desu.

Exercise 3

1 konbini 2 depāto

Exercise 4

1 ichi-ji nijup-pun 2 yo-ji sanjūgo-fun 3 hachi-ji gojup-pun 4 roku-ji han 5 gogo ni-ji yonjup-pun/gogo san-ji nijup-pun mae 6 gozen ku-ji go-fun 7 gogo jūichi-ji jūgo-fun 8 gogo go-ji gojūgo-fun/gogo roku-ji go-fun mae

Exercise 5

1 3:30 2 10:25 3 4:00 a.m. 4 5:50 p.m.

Exercise 6

1 Chūgoku wa ima gozen 7-ji 50-pun (shichi-ji gojup-pun) desu. 2 Nihon wa ima gogo 8-ji 25-fun (hachi-ji nijūgo-fun) desu. 3 Amerika

wa ima gozen 6-ji 10-pun (roku-ji jup-pun) desu. 4 Ōsutoraria wa ima gogo 3-ji (san-ji) desu. 5 Indo wa ima gozen 5-ji 40-pun (go-ji yonjup-pun) desu./Indo wa ima gozen 6-ji 20-pun (roku-ji nijup-pun) mae desu.

Exercise 7

1 (Café in the hotel) 6:00 a.m. – 9:00 p.m. 2 (Sakura library) 9:30 a.m. – 6:30 p.m. 3 (Sakura supermarket) 8:00 a.m. – 11:30 p.m.

Exercise 8

1 doko 2 itsu 3 nan-ji 4 nani-jin 5 nan-ji 6 nan-sai

Exercise 9

1 na ni 2 ha ne 3 ni ku 4 ne ko 5 hi no de 6 ho u se ki 7 se i fu ku 8 bo u shi 9 he bi

Unit 4

Exercise 1

1 Kore wa watashi no saifu desu. 2 Are wa Jōnzu-san no Nihon (or Nihon-go) no hon desu. 3 Anata no jisho wa dochira desu ka. 4 Are wa nan desu ka. 5 Kore wa watashi no kasa dewa arimasen.

Exercise 2

1 Ano 2 Sore 3 dono 4 Kore

Exercise 3

1 (Kore) wa dare no jūsu desu ka. 2 Sono hito wa dare desu ka. 3 Ano jisho wa watashi no desu.

Exercise 4

1 denchi [a] Sumisu-san 2 megane [d] Honda-san 3 tokē [b] Yamamoto-san

Exercise 5

1 hyaku gojū kyū 2 sanbyaku hachijū ni 3 nanahyaku kyūjū 4 sen roppyaku gojū yon 5 sanzen nanahyaku nijū go 6 kyūman hassen kyūhyaku

Exercise 6

1	YOU	Sumimasen. Kono kaban wa ikura desu ka.
	SHOP CLERK	Sono kaban wa niman nisen kyūhyaku-en desu.
	YOU	Sō desu ka. Jā, kono kaban o kudasai.
2	YOU	Sumimasen. Sono kētai denwa wa ikura desu ka.
	SHOP CLERK	Kono kētai denwa wa sanman gosen-en desu.
	YOU	Sō desu ka. Jā, sore o kudasai.

Exercise 7

1 nan 2 dore 3 dare 4 doko no 5 dochira 6 doko 7 ikura

Exercise 8

1 Personal computer 2 Mr/Mrs/Miss Kimura 3 120,000 yen 4 Mr/Mrs/Miss Johnson's mobile phone 5 UK 6 27,000 yen

Exercise 9

1 mo ya shi 2 yu mi 3 wa ni 4 wa ta shi 5 yo zo ra 6 ya ma 7 mu ka shi 8 yu u me i 9 ho u re n so u 10 wa ta shi wa ni ho n go no ga ku se i de su

Unit 5

Exercise 1

1 na 2 i 3 i 4 na 5 i 6 i 7 na 8 na 9 na 10 i 11 na 12 i

Exercise 2

1 atarashikunai desu 2 atarashikatta desu 3 atarashikunakatta desu 4 takakunai desu 5 takakatta desu 6 takakunakatta desu 7 samukunai desu 8 samukatta desu 9 samukunakatta desu 10 hima dewa arimasen

11 hima deshita 12 hima dewa arimasendeshita 13 genki dewa arimasen 14 genki deshita 15 genki dewa arimasendeshita 16 benri dewa arimasen 17 benri deshita 18 benri dewa arimasendeshita

Exercise 3

1 samukatta desu 2 yokunai desu 3 yasukunai desu 4 nigiyaka deshita 5 takakunakatta desu

Exercise 4

1 Īe, (kinō no tenki wa) zenzen yokunakatta desu. 2 Hiragana wa amari muzukashikunai desu. 3 Nihon no tabemono wa chotto takai desu.

Exercise 5

1 a 2 b 3 a 4 b 5 a 6 b

Exercise 6

1 Karen-san wa ongaku ga suki desu. 2 Karen-san wa terebi ga kirai desu. 3 Karen-san wa piano ga jōzu desu. 4 Karen-san wa supōtsu ga heta desu.

Exercise 7

1 Tarō likes Friday but dislikes Saturday. 2 Mariko is good at English but poor at French.

Exercise 8

1 ✓ 2 ✗ 3 ✗

Exercise 9

1 ka shu 2 kyo u 3 sha cho u 4 gyu u nyu u 5 kyo u ka sho 6 chu u sha jo u

Unit 6

Exercise 1

1 kimashita 2 ikimasendeshita 3 kaerimashita 4 kimasu 5 kimasen 6 kaerimasu

Exercise 2

1 Watashi wa maitoshi Nihon e ikimasu. 2 Watashi no tomodachi wa kinō (watashi no) uchi e kimasendeshita. 3 Suzuki-san wa (konshū no) shūmatsu, hakubutsukan e ikimasu. 4 Akita-san wa mainichi gakkō e ikimasu ka.

Exercise 3

1 a) New York (USA) b) Spring next year 2 a) London, Birmingham and Oxford (UK) b) Summer this year

Exercise 4

1 Densha de ikimasu. 2 Tomodachi to ikimasu. 3 Natsu-yasumi ikimasu. 4 Hikōki de ikimasu. 5 Kazoku to ikimasu.

Exercise 5

1 I went to the post office on my own on foot yesterday. 2 Mr Tanaka goes to school with friends by train every day.

Exercise 6

1 doko 2 dare 3 itsu 4 nani 5 donokurai

Exercise 7

1 to (or no) 2 to, de 3 de 4 ✗ 5 to, e

Exercise 8

1 b 2 a 3 c 4 b 5 c 6 a

Unit 7

Exercise 1

1 yomimasu, kakimasu 2 nomimasu, kaimasu 3 yomimasu, kakimasu 4 kikimasu, kaimasu 5 kaimasu, unten shimasu 6 yomimasu, kikimasu, kakimasu, benkyō shimasu

Exercise 2

1 Yamada-san wa ashita terebi o mimasu. 2 Yamada-san wa ashita gozen 9-ji kara gogo 5-ji made shigoto shimasu. 3 Yamada-san wa ashita tomodachi to hiru-gohan o tabemasu. 4 Yamada-san wa ashita ongaku o kikimasu. 5 Yamada-san wa ashita gogo 10-ji han ni nemasu.

Exercise 3

1 ✗ 2 ✗ 3 ✓

Exercise 4

1 hashi 2 Watashi wa te de hanbāgā o tabemasu. 3 Shinkansen wa ēgo de "bullet train/super express" desu. 4 "Family" wa Nihon-go de "kazoku" desu.

Exercise 5

1 Watashi wa kissaten de kōhī o nomimasu. 2 Pākā-san wa uchi de terebi o mimasen. 3 Anata wa doko de kaimono shimasu ka.

Exercise 6

1 de 2 a ✗ b o 3 de 4 ni 5 mo

Exercise 7

1 last month 2 ate Japanese ramen noodle soup 3 bought (a) beautiful (pair of) chopsticks 4 Japanese (language)

Exercise 8

1 a i su 2 ko i 3 ka ki 4 su i ka 5 ki u i 6 ku i zu 7 a sa ga o 8 ji gu za gu

Unit 8

Exercise 1

1 a 2 b 3 a 4 b

Exercise 2

1 Resutoran, onna no hito, imasu 2 niwa, ga 3 Daidokoro, daremo 4 Genkan, nani, ka

Exercise 3

1 go-ko 2 yo-nin 3 ip-pon 4 ni-mai 5 yon-dai 6 nana-hon

Exercise 4

1 Kyōto no chizu o 3-mai (san-mai) kudasai. 2 Watashi wa mainichi Nihon-go o 2-jikan (ni-jikan) benkyō shimasu. 3 Watashi no uchi ni otoko no hito ga 3-nin (san-nin) imasu.

Exercise 5

1 4tsu (yottsu) 2 5-nin (go-nin) 3 2-dai (ni-dai) 4 8-pon (hap-pon)

Exercise 6

1 (Hito) no ushiro ni otoko no ko ga futari imasu. 2 (Kaban) no naka ni kētai denwa ga ichi-dai arimasu. 3 (Biru) no tonari ni ōkī uchi ga arimasu.

Exercise 7

1 (Watashi wa) eki no naka ni imasu. 2 (Hon-ya wa) ginkō no hidari ni arimasu. 3 (Kōen wa) konbini to hoteru no aida ni arimasu. 4 (Takushī noriba wa) toshokan no chikaku ni arimasu.

Exercise 8

1 ✓ 2 ✗ 3 ✓

Exercise 9

1 i nu 2 ne ko 3 do i tsu 4 te ni su 5 po te to 6 ka na da 7 ne ku ta i 8 pi a ni su to

Unit 9

Dialogue 1 exercise

1 ✓ 2 ✗

Exercise 1

1 Hai, mō (kippu o) kaimashita. 2 Īe, mada desu. 3 Īe, mada desu.

Exercise 2

1 yasumitai desu 2 yasumitakunai desu 3 yasumitakunakatta desu
4 (shashin o) torimasu 5 toritakunai desu 6 toritakatta desu 7 hairimasu
8 hairitai desu 9 hairitakatta desu 10 hairitakunakatta desu

Exercise 3

1 Watashi wa tomodachi to hanashitai desu. 2 Watashi wa kazoku ni
aitai desu. 3 Watashi wa kōen de undō shitai desu.

Dialogue 2 exercise

1 ✗ 2 ✓

Exercise 4

1 Watashi wa asa (ni) toshokan e hon o yomi ni ikimasu. 2 Watashi
wa hiru (ni) kōen e hashiri ni ikimasu. 3 Watashi wa ban/yoru (ni)
ēgakan e ēga o mi ni ikimasu.

Dialogue 3 exercise

1 ✗ 2 ✓

Exercise 5

1 Masako-san, watashi no uchi de issho ni DVD o mimasen ka.
2 Masako-san, raigetsu issho ni onsen e ikimasen ka. 3 Masako-san,
maiasa issho ni hashirimasen ka.

Exercise 6

1 d 2 e

Exercise 7

1 Because this person wants to see Yuki matsuri (the snow festival). 2 Yuki matsuri is a very famous snow festival in Hokkaido. 3 She wants to take a lot of photos of Yuki matsuri and eat delicious food.

Exercise 8

1 wa i n 2 me da ru 3 a me ri ka 4 ro n do n 5 pa so ko n 6 ra i o n 7 de ji ta ru ka me ra 8 re su to ra n

Unit 10

Dialogue 1 exercise

1 ✗ 2 ✓

Exercise 1

1 Watashi wa tanjōbi ni Nihon-go no jisho ga hoshī desu. 2 Watashi wa hayai kuruma ga hoshī desu. 3 Watashi wa (kekkon iwai ni) kawaī shashin tate ga hoshī desu.

Exercise 2

1 Watashi wa kinō no ban/yoru byōki deshita kara. 2 Watashi wa furui (o)tera ga/o mitai desu kara. 3 Watashi no kazoku wa Rondon ni imasu kara.

Dialogue 2 exercise

1 ✓ 2 ✗

Exercise 3

1 d 2 a 3 e 4 c

Dialogue 3 exercise

1 ✓ 2 ✗

Exercise 4

1 a 2 b 3 b, c 4 a

Exercise 5

1 b 2 e 3 a

Exercise 6

1 ga 2 kara 3 ni 4 de 5 a) ga b) ✗

Exercise 7

1 ✓ 2 ✗

Exercise 8

A) 1 e 2 a 3 f 4 c 5 b B) 1 c 2 e 3 a 4 b 5 d

Unit 11

Dialogue 1 exercise

1 ✓ 2 ✗

Exercise 1

1 b 2 b 3 c 4 c 5 a

Exercise 2

1 chikakute 2 chikakunakute 3 yokute 4 yokunakute 5 suki de 6 suki dewanakute 7 kenkō de 8 kenkō dewanakute 9 kaisha de 10 kaisha dewanakute

Exercise 3

1 omoshirokute 2 yokute 3 nigiyaka de 4 jōzu de 5 watashi no tokē de

Dialogue 2 exercise

1 ✓ 2 ✗

Exercise 4

1 samuku 2 suki ni 3 25-sai (nijū go-sai) ni 4 hima ni

Exercise 5

1 hayaku 2 jōzu ni 3 osoku 4 jiyū ni

Exercise 6

1 ✓ 2 ✗

Exercise 7

1 K 2 O 3 O 4 K 5 K 6 O 7 K 8 O

Exercise 8

1 ひゃくえん 2 さんじゅう　きゅう 3 せんよんひゃく　ごじゅう　えん
4 じゅうなな 5 いちまん　はっせん　えん 6 にじゅうまん　えん
7 ろっぴゃく　にじゅう　えん 8 ひと (つ) 9 ふた (つ) 10 やっ (つ)

Unit 12

Dialogue 1 exercise

1 ✓ 2 ✗

Exercise 1

1 (kami) nagai desu. 2 (me) kuroi desu. 3 (te) chīsai desu. 4 (atama)
ī desu.

Exercise 2

1 Nihon wa Fujisan ga yūmē desu. 2 Kyōto wa furui (o)tera ga ōi desu.
3 Nihon (no tabemono) wa (o)sushi ga oishī desu. 4 e.g. Watashi no
kuni wa Rondon ai (London Eye) ga yūmē desu.

Exercise 3

1 Ichi-nen no naka de 8-gatsu (hachi-gatsu) ga ichi-ban atsui desu.
2 Is-shūkan no naka de sui-yōbi ga ichi-ban isogashī desu. 3 Supein-go
to Nihon-go to Furansu-go no naka de Furansu-go ga ichi-ban jōzu desu.

Dialogue 2 exercise

1 ✓ 2 ✗

Exercise 4

1 a 2 a 3 b 4 a

Exercise 5

1 Getsu-yōbi no hō ga hima desu. 2 katakana no hō ga muzukashī
desu. 3 (Umi mo yama mo) dochira mo suki desu.

Exercise 6

1 c 2 b 3 a

Exercise 7

1 a. de b. ga 2 yori 3 a. wa b. ga 4 a. to b. to c. ga d. ga 5 a. to
b. to c. ga d. mo

Exercise 8

1 おんな、 ひと、 くち 2 さん、 やま 3 ちい 4 うえ、 した
5 ひと、 じん、 じん 6 ひとり、 おお 7 かわ

Unit 13

Dialogue 1 exercise

1 ✗ 2 ✓

Exercise 1

1 [2] 2 [1] 3 [1] 4 [3] 5 [1] 6 [3] 7 [3] 8 [2]

Exercise 2

1 あそんで (asonde) 2 つれてきて (tsurete kite) 3 いって (itte) 4 がんばって (ganbatte) 5 おぼえて (oboete) 6 みせて (misete) 7 もっていって (motte itte) 8 いそいで (isoide) 9 おくって (okutte) 10 クリックして (kurikku shite)

Exercise 3

1 kaite kudasai (please write) かいてください 2 kyanseru shite kudasai (please cancel) キャンセルしてください 3 ki o tsukete kudasai (please be careful) きをつけてください 4 oshiete kudasai (please teach/tell) おしえてください 5 okite kudasai おきてください 6 oite kudasai おいてください

Exercise 4

1 a 2 b

Exercise 5

1 Sumimasen ga, (o)hashi no tsukaikata o oshiete kudasai. 2 Sumimasen ga, Fuji hoteru no ikikata o oshiete kudasai.

Dialogue 2 exercise

1 ✗ 2 ✓

Exercise 6

1 (Kurejitto) Kādo de haratte mo ī desu ka. 2 Kono pen o tsukatte mo ī desu ka. 3 Koko de (o)sake o nonde wa ikemasen.

Exercise 7

1 a 2 d 3 b

Exercise 8

Hikōki (no naka)/In an aeroplane

Exercise 9

1 きょう、 か (よう) び、 げつ (よう) び 2 すこ、 みず 3 き、 した、 とも (だち) 4 ど (よう) び 5 わ 6 にほん、 いま、 ふん 7 こんげつ

Unit 14

Dialogue 1 exercise

1 ✗ 2 ✓

Exercise 1

1 f 2 b

Exercise 2

1 Watashi wa kinō toshokan e itte, hon o karimashita. 2 Watashi wa kyō 7-ji (shichi-ji) ni okite, shawā o abite, terebi o mimashita. 3 Watashi wa rainen Nihon e itte, Fujisan ni noboritai desu.

Exercise 3

1 Watashi wa shokuji shite kara, shawā o abimasu. 2 Watashi wa heya o sōji shite kara, yasumimashita. 3 Watashi wa Nihon ni tsuite kara, Mori-san ni denwa shimashita.

Dialogue 2 exercise

1 ✓ 2 ✗

Exercise 4

1 ha o migaite imasu. 2 mēru o kaite imasu. 3 shigoto shite imashita. 4 shawā o abite imashita.

Exercise 5

1 Mori-san wa kuruma no naka ni suwatte imasu. 2 Okada-san wa pasokon o 2-dai (ni-dai) motte imasu. 3 Takeda-san wa kekkon shite imasu. 4 Watashi wa kono uta o shirimasen ga, sono uta wa shitte imasu.

Dialogue 3 exercise

1 ✓ 2 ✗

Exercise 6

1 Kimu-san wa mainichi Nihon no ongaku o kīte imasu. 2 Kimu-san wa mainichi (Nihon no) kotoba o oboete imasu. 3 Kimu-san wa mainichi Nihon no terebi o mite imasu. 4 Kimu-san wa mainichi (ichi-ban) sukina Nihon no uta o utatte imasu.

Exercise 7

1 ちち、　はは、　がい（こく）2 やまだ、　め 3 たなか、　とう、　なか 4 じょうず 5 て 6 ぶん、7 みぎ、　ひだり

Unit 15

Dialogue 1 exercise

1 ✗ 2 ✓

Exercise 1

1 きた 2 きた 3 した 4 かけた 5 はなした 6 いった 7 およいだ 8 かりた 9 はいた 10 かぶった

Exercise 2

1 a) sōji shita b) sentaku shita 2 a) katta b) karita 3 a) itta b) odotta 4 a) chekku shita b) kaketa

Exercise 3

a ✗ b ✓ c ✓ d ✗ e ✓ f ✓

Dialogue 2 exercise

1 ✓ 2 ✗

Exercise 4

1 (Inoue-san wa) yasunda ato de, shawā o abimasu. 2 (Inoue-san wa) kōcha o nonda ato de, asa-gohan o tsukurimasu. 3 (Inoue-san wa) asa-gohan o tabeta ato de, ha o migakimasu. 4 (Inoue-san wa) ha o migaita ato de, fuku o kimasu.

Dialogue 3 exercise

1 ✓ 2 ✓

Exercise 5

1 Watashi wa Fujisan ni nobotta koto ga arimasu. 2 Watashi no imōto wa kimono o kita koto ga arimasen. 3 Hankokku-san wa (o)sushi o tabeta koto ga arimasu ka. 4 Watashi wa (o)sushi o tsukutta koto ga arimasu.

Exercise 6

1 ✓ 2 ✓ 3 ✗ 4 ✓ 5 ✗ 6 ✓

Exercise 7

1 にほん（ご）、　せんせい 2 にほん（ご）、　がくせい、（かん）じ 3 なに 4 いちねん、　にほん 5 にほんじん、　ほん 6 にほん、　くるま　す（き） 7 まいにち、　（でん）しゃ

Unit 16

Dialogue 1 exercise

1 ✗ 2 ✓

Exercise 1

1 よむ yomu 2 する suru 3 いく iku 4 ひく hiku 5 もってくる motte kuru 6 しらべる shiraberu

Exercise 2

1 ひくこと playing (keyboard or stringed) instruments 2 およぐこと swimming 3 すること doing, playing 4 テレビを　みること watching TV 5 しゃしんを とること taking photographs 6 ほんを　よむこと reading books 7 きってを あつめること collecting (postage) stamps

Exercise 3

1 Honda-san no shumi wa ryōri (o) suru koto desu. 2 Howaito-san no yume wa ēga o tsukuru koto desu. 3 Watashi no tomodachi no shumi

wa shashin o toru koto desu. 4 Watashi no otōto no yume wa yakyū senshu ni naru koto desu. 5 e.g. Watashi no shumi wa hon o yondari, e o kaitari suru koto desu.

Exercise 4

1 b 2 a 3 a

Exercise 5

1 Watashi wa Nihon no ēga o miru koto ga suki desu. 2 Watashi no tomodachi wa gitā o hiku koto ga jōzu desu. 3 Watashi wa kuruma o unten suru koto ga amari suki dewa arimasen. 4 Watashi no imōto wa e o kaku koto ga jōzu desu.

Dialogue 2 exercise

1 ✓ 2 ✗

Exercise 6

1 kekkon suru mae ni 2 yomu mae ni 3 kiru mae ni 4 neru mae ni 5 5-nen (go-nen) mae ni

Exercise 7

1 Tomu-san wa Furansu-go o hanasu koto ga dekimasu ka. 2 Tomu-san wa Nihon no uta o utau koto ga dekimasu ka. 3 Tomu-san wa sukī o suru koto ga dekimasu ka. 4 Tomu-san wa kanji o kaku koto ga dekimasu ka.

Exercise 8

1 ✓ 5 ✓ 6 ✓ 7 ✓

Exercise 9

1 ✓ 2 ✗ 3 ✓

Exercise 10

1 いもうと、 まえ 2 おとうと 3 まいしゅう、 きんようび 4 おとこ、 あに 5 かね 6 あと 7 きょうだい、 しまい

Japanese–English glossary

A

ā	ah, oh
abimasu	to shower, bathe, saturate
abunai (i-adj.)	dangerous
achira (Unit 3)	that place over there (polite equivalent of **asoko**)
achira (Unit 4)	that one over there (polite equivalent of **are**)
agemasu	to give
aida	between
aimasu	to meet, see
Airurando	Ireland
Ajia	Asia
aka	red (n.)
akai (i-adj.)	red (adj.)
akarui (i-adj.)	bright
akemasu	to open
aki	autumn, fall
amai (i-adj.)	sweet
amari	not so much (used with negatives)
ame	rain
Amerika	USA
Amerika-jin	American (nationality)
anata	you
ane	(one's own) elder sister
ani	(one's own) elder brother
annaijo	information (desk, agency, office)
ano (Unit 4)	that one over there
anō (Unit 3)	ah, er, uh, um, etc.

anzen(na) (na-adj.)	safe
ao	blue (n.)
aoi (i-adj.)	blue (adj.)
araimasu	to wash
are (Unit 4)	that one (thing) over there
are (Unit 13)	Look!, Oh no!
arigatō	thank you
arigatō gozaimasu	thank you very much
arimasu (Unit 8)	to be, exist, there is something
arimasu (Unit 10)	have, own
asa	morning
asagohan	breakfast
Asakusa	Asakusa district in Tokyo
ashi	leg, foot
ashita	tomorrow
asobimasu	to play, enjoy doing something
asoko	that place over there
atama	head
atama ga itai	have a headache
atarashī (i-adj.)	new
atatakai (i-adj.)	warm
ato	after, behind
. . . ato de	after . . .
atsui (i-adj.)	hot
atsumemasu	to collect
atsumeru koto	collecting (n.)

B

ban	evening, night
ban-gohan	supper, dinner, evening meal
bangō	number

basho	place
basu	bus
basukettobōru	basketball
basutē	bus stop
beddo	bed
benkyō	study, studying (n.)
benkyō shimasu	to study
benri(na) (na-adj.)	convenient
bijutsukan	art gallery, art museum
biru	building
bīru	beer
-bon (counter suffix)	counter for long, slender objects
bōnasu-bi	bonus day
bōrupen	ball-point pen
bōshi	hat, cap
Burajiru	Brazil
byōin	hospital
byōki	sickness, illness

C

chairo	brown (n.)
chairoi (i-adj.)	brown (adj.)
chichi	(one's own) father
chikai (i-adj.)	near, close
chikaku	near
chikaku no (+ noun)	nearby (+ noun)
chikatetsu	underground, subway
chīsai (i-adj.)	small
chizu	map
chōjō	top, summit (of a mountain)
chokorēto	chocolate
chotto . . . (Unit 9)	a little, a bit (inconvenient)
chotto (Unit 12)	a little, slightly
chūgakusē	secondary/junior high school student
Chūgoku	China
Chūgoku-go	Chinese (language)
Chūgoku-jin	Chinese (nationality)
chūmon shimasu	to order

D

-dai (counter suffix)	counter for machinery object
daidokoro	kitchen
daigaku	university
daigakusē	university student
daijōbu	all right, ok
daisuki(na) (na-adj.)	like . . . very much
dake	only
dare	who
dare no	whose (+ noun)
dare to	with whom
daremo	no one
de (particle, Units 6 and 7)	by means of transportation, with (tool), in (language)
de (particle, Unit 7)	at (indicating location)
dejikame	digital camera
dekimasu	can
demasu	to leave, get out
demo	but, however
denchi	battery
denki	electricity, light
densha	electric train
denwa	telephone
denwa-bangō	telephone number
depāto	department store
deshita	was, were
desu	am, are, is
dewa arimasen	am not, aren't, isn't
DVD (dībuidī)	DVD
dō	how
dō itashimashite	you are welcome, my pleasure
dōbutsuen	zoo
dochira (Unit 3)	where, which way (polite equivalent of doko)
dochira (Unit 4)	which one (out of two)
Doitsu	Germany
doko	where
doko de	(at) where

doko no	from where?	**F**
	(e.g. which	**fōku**	fork
	company's/	**fuben(na)** (na-adj.)	inconvenient
	country's)	**Fujisan**	Mt. Fuji
doko(e)mo	(to) nowhere,	**fuku**	clothes
	(to) anywhere	**-fun** (suffix)	minute
dokusho	reading books (n.)	**-fun(kan)** (suffix)	minute(s)
dōmo	thanks	**Furansu**	France
donata	who (polite	**Furansu-go**	French (language)
	equivalent of	**furui** (i-adj.)	old (things)
	dare)	**futari**	two people
donata no	whose (polite	**futatsu**	two (small things)
	equivalent of	**futsū**	usually, normally
	dare no)	**futsuka**	2nd of the month
donna	what kind of?	**fuyu**	winter
	(+ noun)		
dono	which? (+ noun)	**G**
donokurai	how long?	**ga** (conjunction,	but, however
dore	which one? (out of | Unit 5)	
	more than two	**ga** (particle,	subject marker
	things)	Unit 5)	(used with **suki**,
dōshite	why?		**kirai**, **jōzu**, etc.)
do-yōbi	Saturday	**gaikoku**	foreign country
dōzo	please, here you	**gakusē**	student
	are, if you	**ganbarimasu**	to work hard to do,
	please		do/try one's best
dōzo yoroshiku	pleased to meet	**-gatsu** (suffix)	month
	you	**geki**	theatre play
		gēmu	game
E		**genkan**	entrance hall
e (Unit 5)	dear, to (used for	**genki desu ka**	How are you?
	letters, emails,	**genki(na)** (na-adj.)	vigorous, active
	etc.)	**getsu-yōbi**	Monday
e (particle, Unit 6)	to (direction marker)	**ginkō**	bank
e	picture	**ginkōin**	bank clerk
eakon	air conditioning	**Girisha**	Greece
ēga	film, movie	**gitā**	guitar
ēgakan	cinema	**go**	five
Ē-go	English (language)	**-go** (suffix)	language
eki	station	**go-gatsu**	May
-en	yen (Japanese	**gogo**	p.m., in the
	currency)		afternoon
enjinia	engineer	**gohan**	meal, cooked rice
enpitsu	pencil	**go-ji**	five o'clock
ēto	let me see . . . ,	**gokazoku**	(someone's) family
	well . . .	**goro**	about, around

gorufu	golf	**hayai** (i-adj.)	fast, early
goryōshin	(someone's) parents	**heta(na)** (na-adj.)	poor at
gozen	a.m., in the morning	**heya**	room
-guchi	exit, entrance,	**hidari**	left
	doorway (e.g.	**hikimasu**	to play (keyboard
	south exit)		and string
gyūnyū	milk		instruments)
		hikōki	plane, aeroplane
H		**hiku koto**	playing (keyboard
ha	teeth		and string
ha ga itai	have a toothache		instruments) (n.)
hachi	eight	**hikui** (i-adj.)	low
hachi-gatsu	August	**hima(na)** (na-adj.)	free (time), have
hachi-ji	eight o'clock		time
hade(na) (na-adj.)	showy, gaudy,	**hiragana**	the Japanese
	loud		cursive syllabary
haha	(one's own) mother	**hiroi** (i-adj.)	spacious, wide
hai	yes	**hiru**	noon, day
hairimasu	to enter, come in,	**hiru-gohan**	lunch
	go in, go into,	**hito**	person
	get in	**hitori**	one person
haite mo ī desu	(one) may wear	**hitori de**	on one's own, by
	(e.g. shoes,		oneself
	slippers)	**hitotsu**	one (small item)
hajimemashite	how do you do?	**Hokkaidō**	Hokkaido prefecture
hajimete	for the first time	**hon**	book
hakimasu	to wear (shoes,	**-hon, -pon, -bon**	counter for long,
	trousers, socks,	(counter suffix)	slender objects
	etc.)	**Honkon**	Hong Kong
hakubutsukan	museum	**hontō**	true, really, sure
han	half	**hontō desu ka**	really, is that true?
hana (Unit 5)	flower	**hon-ya**	bookshop,
hana (Unit 12)	nose		bookstore
hanashimasu	to talk, speak, chat	**hoshī** (i-adj.)	want (an object)
hanasu koto ga	can speak	**hoteru**	hotel
dekimasu		**hyaku**	(one) hundred
hanbāgā	hamburger	**hyaku-man**	one million
haraimasu	to pay		
hare	sunny, fair weather	**I**	
haru	spring	**ī** (i-adj.)	good
hashi (Units 1	chopsticks	**ichi**	one
and 7)		**ichi-ban**	best, first, top, most
hashi (Unit 14)	bridge	**ichi-gatsu**	January
hashirimasu	to run, to jog	**ichi-ji**	one o'clock
hatarakimasu	to work, labour	**ichi-nen**	a year
hatsuka	20th of the month	**īe**	no

Igirisu	UK	**J**	
Igirisu-jin	British (nationality)	**jā**	then, well then
ikebana	(Japanese) flower	**-ji** (suffix)	o'clock
	arrangement	**-jikan** (suffix,	hour(s)
ikimasen	do not go, does	Unit 6)	
	not go	**jikan** (Unit 10)	time
ikimasen ka	won't you go?	**jikoshōkai**	self-introduction
ikimasu	to go	**-jin** (suffix)	-ese, -ian, -sh, etc.
ikitai desu	want to go		(nationality)
ikura	how much?	**jisho**	dictionary
ikutsu	how many? (small	**jitensha**	bicycle
	objects)	**jiyū(na)** (**na**-adj.)	liberty, free
ikutsume	how many?	**jogingu shimasu**	to jog
ima (Unit 3)	now	**jōzu(na)** (**na**-adj.)	good at
ima (Unit 8)	living room	**jū**	ten
imasu	to be, exist, there is	**jūdō**	Judo (Japanese
	someone		martial art)
īmēru	email	**jū-gatsu**	October
imōto	(one's own) younger	**jūichi-gatsu**	November
	sister	**jūichi-ji**	eleven o'clock
imōtosan	(someone else's)	**jū-ji**	ten o'clock
	younger sister	**jū-man**	one hundred
Indo	India		thousand
intānetto	Internet	**jūni-gatsu**	December
inu	dog	**jūni-ji**	twelve o'clock
irasshaimase	welcome, may I help	**jūsu**	juice
	you? (at a shop	**jūyokka**	14th of the month
	or restaurant)		
iremasu	to put (something)	**K**	
	in	**ka** (particle)	question marking
iro	colour		particle
iroiro na	various (+ noun)	**kaban**	bag
isha	doctor	**kabin**	vase
isogashī (**i**-adj.)	busy	**kabuki**	classical Japanese
isogimasu	to hurry		dance-drama
issho ni	together	**kaburimasu**	to wear (hat, cap,
is-shūkan	a week		helmet, etc.)
isu	chair	**kado**	corner
itai (**i**-adj.)	sore, painful	**kādo**	card
Itaria	Italy	**kādo de**	by card
itsu	when	**kaemasu**	to change
itsuka (Unit 2)	5th of the month	**kaerimasu**	to go back, return
itsuka (Unit 14)	some time, some	**-kagetsu(kan)**	month(s)
	day, one day	(suffix)	
itsumo	always	**-kai** (counter	counter for times
itsutsu	five (small items)	suffix, Unit 8)	

kaimasu	to buy	**kashu**	singer
kaimono	shopping	**~kata**	how to ~
kaimono shimasu	to go shopping	**katakana**	katakana script
kaisha	company	**kawaī** (i-adj.)	pretty, cute, lovely
kaishain	office worker,	**ka-yōbi**	Tuesday
	company	**kaze**	wind
	employee	**kazoku**	family
kakarimasu	to take (time, cost)	**kekkon iwai**	celebration or gift
(denwa o)	to make a phone		for one's wedding
kakemasu	call	**kekkon shimasu**	to get married
(Unit 15)		**kenchō**	prefectural office
kakemasu	wear (glasses)	**kenkō(na)** (na-adj.)	healthy
(Unit 15)		**kesa**	this morning
kakimasu	to write	**keshiki**	view, scenery
kami	hair	**kētai denwa**	mobile phone
Kanada	Canada	**ki o tsukemasu**	to be careful
Kanada-jin	Canadian	**kikimasu**	to listen to
	(nationality)	**kimasu** (Unit 6)	to come
kanji	Japanese Chinese	**kimasu** (Unit 15)	to wear (clothes)
	characters	**kimochi ga warui**	feel unwell, feel sick
kankō	sightseeing	**kimono**	Japanese traditional
kankō annaijo	tourist information		clothes
kankō shimasu	to go sightseeing	**kin'en**	non-smoking
Kankoku	South Korea	**kinō**	yesterday
kankōkyaku	tourist	**kin-yōbi**	Friday
kantan(na)	easy	**kippu**	ticket
(na-adj.)		**kirai(na)** (na-adj.)	dislike
kao	face	**kirē(na)** (na-adj.)	beautiful, clean
kappu-rāmen	instant (cup)	**kirimasu**	to cut
	noodles	**kīro**	yellow (n.)
kara (Unit 10)	because	**kīroi** (i-adj.)	yellow
kara (particle,	from	**kissaten**	coffee shop, café
Unit 3)		**kitte**	(postage) stamp
karada	body, health	**-ko** (counter	counter for small
karada ni ī	healthy (*lit.* "good	suffix)	objects
	for one's body")	**kōban**	police box, koban
karai (i-adj.)	hot, spicy		(neighbourhood
karaoke	karaoke		police station)
karate	karate (Japanese	**kōcha**	black tea, English
	martial art)		tea
karita koto ga	have borrowed	**kochira** (Unit 3)	this place, this way
arimasu			(polite equivalent
karui (i-adj.)	light		of **koko**)
kasa	umbrella	**kochira** (Unit 4)	this, this one (polite
kashikoma-	certainly		equivalent of **kore**)
rimashita		**kodomo**	child, children, kid(s)

kōen	park	**kusuri**	medicine, drug
kōhī	coffee	**kutsu**	(a pair of) shoes
koko	here, this place	**kutsushita**	sock, a pair of
kokonoka	9th of the month		socks
kokonotsu	nine	**kyanseru**	to cancel
kōkōsē	high school student	**shimasu**	
konbanwa	good evening	**kyō**	today
konbini	convenience store	**kyonen**	last year
kondo	next time	**kyōshi**	teacher
kongetsu	this month	**Kyōto**	Kyoto prefecture
konnichiwa	good afternoon,	**kyū**	nine
	hello	**kyūjitsu**	off-duty day,
kono	this (precedes noun)		day off
konsāto	concert		
konshū	this week	**M**	
kore	this, this one (thing)	**machi**	town, city
kōsaten	crossroads,	**machimasu**	to wait
	intersection	**mada**	not yet
-koto ga arimasu	have done	**-made** (particle)	until, to, up to
(Unit 15)	(expressing one's	**mado**	window
	experience)	**mae** (Unit 3)	before, front
-koto ga	can	**mae** (Unit 8)	in front of
dekimasu		**-mae ni** (Unit 16)	before doing
(Unit 16)		**magarimasu**	to turn
kōto	coat	**mai-** (prefix,	every . . .
kotoba	word	Unit 6)	
kotoshi	this year	**-mai** (counter	counter for thin,
kowai (i-adj.)	scary, afraid,	suffix, Unit 8)	flat objects
	frightening	**maiasa**	every morning
kubi	neck	**maiban**	every evening,
kuchi	mouth		every night
kudamono	fruit	**mainichi**	every day
ku-gatsu	September	**maishū**	every week
ku-ji	nine o'clock	**maishūmatsu**	every weekend
kūkō	airport	**maitoshi**	every year
kumori	cloudy	**maitsuki**	every month
kuni	country	**māmā**	quite, so-so,
-kurai (Unit 6)	about, around		reasonably
kurai (i-adj,	dark	**-man**	ten thousand
Unit 12)		**-masen ka**	won't you?, would
kurikku shimasu	to click		you like to?
kurisumasu	Christmas	**-mashō**	let's
kuro	black (n.)	**massugu**	straight
kuroi (i-adj.)	black (adj.)	**mata**	again
kuru mae ni	before coming	**matsuri**	festival
kuruma	car, vehicle	**mazui** (i-adj.)	tasteless

me (Unit 12)	eye
~me (counter suffix, Unit 14)	order in numbers
megane	(a pair of) glasses
Mekishiko	Mexico
mēru	email
michi	street, road
midori	green (n.)
migakimasu	to polish, brush
migi	right
mikka	3rd of the month
mimasu	to watch, look at, see
mimi	ear
minagara	while watching/ seeing
minami	south
minami-guchi	south exit
minna	everybody, everyone
mise	shop, store
misemasu	to show
mittsu	three (small items)
mizu	water
mo (particle)	also, too
mō	already
mō ichido	once more
mochimasu	to have, hold, carry, own, possess
mochiron	of course
moku-yōbi	Thursday
mono	thing(s)
moraimashita	received
moraimasu	to receive
motte imasu	to own, possess
motte ikimasu	to take (something to somewhere)
motte kimasu	to bring (something to somewhere)
motte kite kudasai	please bring (something)
motto	more
muika	6th of the month
musuko	son
muttsu	six (small items)
muzukashī (i-adj.)	difficult

N

nagai (i-adj.)	long
-nagara	while doing
naifu	knife
naitokurabu	nightclub
naka	inside
namae	name
nan	what
nan de	by what, how, why
nana	seven
nanatsu	seven (small items)
nan-ban	what number
nan-gatsu	what month
nani	what
nani de	by what, how to
nani-jin	what nationality
nanimo	nothing
nan-ji	what time
nan-nichi	what day
nanoka	7th of the month
nan-pun	what (time)
nan-sai	how old
nan-yōbi	what day (of the week)
narimasu	to become
natsu	summer
natsu yasumi	summer holiday
ne (particle)	isn't it?, aren't they?, aren't you?, etc.
nekkuresu	necklace
neko	cat
nekutai	tie, necktie
nemasu	to go to bed, sleep
-nen(kan) (suffix)	year(s)
netsu	fever
netsu ga arimasu	have a fever
ni	two
ni (particle, Unit 7)	at, on, in (particle indicating time)
ni (particle, Unit 8)	at, in (location in/at which something exists)
ni (particle, Unit 9)	(particle indicating purpose)

ni (particle, Unit 10) — to, for (indirect object marker; *receiver* of the action)

-nichi (suffix) — day (of the month)

-nichi(kan) (suffix) — day(s)

nichi-yōbi — Sunday

ni-gatsu — February

nigiyaka(na) (**na**-adj.) — lively

Nihon — Japan

Nihon-go — Japanese (language)

Nihon-jin — Japanese (nationality)

ni-ji — two o'clock

nijūyokka — 24th of the month

nikki — diary

niku — meat

-nin (counter suffix) — counter for people

ninki — popularity

. . . ni shimasu — I will take . . .

nite imasu — be similar, alike

niwa — garden

no (particle) — of, 's (possessive marker)

noborimasu — to climb, go up

nodo ga itai — have a sore throat

. . . no hō ga . . . yori — be more (adjective) than . . .

nomimasu — to drink

nomimono — (something to) drink, beverage

no naka de — among

-noriba — stop, stand, rank, station, etc.

norikaemasu — to change, transfer

norimasu — to get on, ride

. . . no tame ni — for the benefit of . . .

Nyūjīrando — New Zealand

Nyūyōku — New York

O

o (particle) — object marker (indicating object)

. . . o kudasai — please give me . . . , I will have . . .

. . . o tabemashita — (I/you/she/he) ate . . .

obāsan — (someone else's) grandmother

oboemasu — to remember, memorize

ocha — Japanese tea, green tea

odorimasu — to dance

ohashi (Units 1 and 7) — chopsticks (polite equivalent of **hashi**)

ohayō (gozaimasu) — good morning

ōi (**i**-adj.) — many

oisha-san — (medical) doctor

oishī (**i**-adj.) — delicious, tasty

ojīsan — (someone else's) grandfather

okāsan — (someone else's) mother

okashi — confectionery

ōkī (**i**-adj.) — big

okimasu (Unit 7) — to wake up

okimasu (Unit 13) — to put (something)

okonomiyaki — Japanese pizza

okuni — country (polite equivalent of **kuni**)

okurimasu — to send

okyakusan — visitor, customer

omatsuri — festival

omedetō (gozaimasu) — congratulations

omise — shop, store (polite equivalent of **mise**)

omiyage — souvenir, gift

omizu — water (polite equivalent of **mizu**)

omoi (**i**-adj.) — heavy

omoidashimasu — to recollect, recall, remember

omoshiroi (**i**-adj.) — interesting, funny

onaka ga itai	have a stomachache	**otoko no ko**	boy
onamae	name (polite equivalent of **namae**)	**otōsan**	(someone else's) father
		otōto	(one's own) younger brother
onegai shimasu	please	**otōtosan**	(someone else's) younger brother
onēsan	(someone's) elder sister		
ongaku	music	**oyogimasu**	to swim
onīsan	(someone else's) elder brother	**P**	
onna	female	**pasokon**	personal computer
onna no hito	woman	**pasupōto**	passport
onna no ko	girl	**pātī**	party
onsen	hot spring, spa	**piano**	piano
Oranda	The Netherlands	**pinku**	pink (n.)
orimasu	to get off	**-pon** (counter suffix)	counter for long, slender objects
Ōsaka	Osaka, second city of Japan		
		Porutogaru	Portugal
osake	alcoholic drink, liquor, Japanese rice wine	**-pun** (suffix)	minute (see **-fun**)
		-pun(kan) (suffix)	minute(s) (see **-fun(kan)**)
oshiemasu	to teach	**purezento**	present
oshiete kudasai	please tell (me), please teach (me)	**R**	
		raigetsu	next month
		rainen	next year
oshigoto	work, job, occupation (polite equivalent of **shigoto**)	**raishū**	next week
		rāmen	Japanese noodle soup
oshiro	castle (polite equivalent of **shiro**)	**resutoran**	restaurant
		rimokon	remote control
		ringo	apple
osoi (i-adj.)	slow, late	**robī**	lobby
osushi	Japanese sushi (polite equivalent of **sushi**)	**roku**	six
		roku-gatsu	June
		roku-ji	six o'clock
Ōsutoraria	Australia	**rōmaji**	Roman alphabet
otearai	toilet	**Rondon**	London, capital of the UK
otera	temple (polite equivalent of **tera**)		
		Roshia	Russia
		ryokan	Japanese style inn/ hotel
ōtobai	motorcycle, motorbike	**ryokō**	travel, trip
		ryōri	cooking (n.)
otoko	male	**ryōri shimasu**	to cook
otoko no hito	man	**ryōshin**	(one's own) parents

S

sadō	(Japanese) tea ceremony
-sai	years old (suffix)
saifu	wallet
saikin	recently, lately
sakana	fish
sake	alcoholic drink, liquor, Japanese rice wine
sakkā	football, soccer
samui (i-adj.)	cold (temperature)
san	three
-san	Mr, Miss, Mrs, Ms (title)
san-gatsu	March
san-ji	three o'clock
sanpo	walk, stroll (n.)
sanpo shimasu	to go for a walk
se	stature, height
se ga takai	tall
sēkatsu	life, living
semai (i-adj.)	narrow
sen	(one) thousand
senchi	centimetre
sengetsu	last month
sensē	teacher
-sensē (Unit 1)	title for teacher, doctor, professor, lawyer etc.
senshū	last week
sentaku shimasu	to wash (laundry)
sētā	sweater
shashin	photograph
shashin tate	photo frame
shatsu	shirt(s)
shawā	shower
shi	four
shichi	seven
shichi-gatsu	July
shichi-ji	seven o'clock
shi-gatsu	April
shigoto	work, job, occupation
shikashi	but, however
shimashita	did (something)

shimasu	to do
shimemasu	to close, shut
shinbun	newspaper
shingō	traffic lights, signal
Shinjuku Gyoen	Shinjuku Gyoen, one of the parks in Tokyo
shinkansen	Japanese bullet train, super express train
shinsetsu(na) (na-adj.)	kind
shinshitsu	bedroom
shirabemasu	to investigate, examine, check, study
shirimasu	to get to know
shiro (Unit 8)	castle
shiro (Unit 12)	white (n.)
shiroi (i-adj.)	white (adj.)
shita	under, below
shitagi	underwear, underclothes
shite imashita	was/were doing
shiyakusho	city hall, town hall
shizuka(na) (na-adj.)	quiet
shodō	calligraphy
shōgakusē	primary school student
shokuji shimasu	to have a meal
-shū(kan) (suffix)	week(s)
shufu	housewife
shukudai	homework
shūmatsu	weekend
shumi	hobby
sō desu ne	that is true, I agree with you
sō desu ka	really?, is that so?, I see
sobo	(one's own) grandmother
sochira (Unit 3)	that place near you, that way (polite equivalent of soko)

sochira (Unit 4)	that, that one (polite equivalent of sore)	supūn	spoon
		surippa	(a pair of) slippers
		sushi	Japanese sushi
sofu	(one's own) grandfather	suteki(na) (na-adj.)	wonderful, splendid
sōji shimasu	to clean (a room, house, park, etc.)	sūtsu	suit
		suwarimasu	to sit down
sokkuri(na) (na-adj.)	to closely resemble someone	**T**	
		tabako	tobacco, cigarette
soko	that place, there	tabemashita	ate
sono	that (+ noun)	tabemasu	to eat
sore	that, that one (thing)	tabemono	food
		tabun	maybe, probably
sore wa ikemasen	that is bad	tachimasu	to stand up
		-tai desu	to want to do
sorekara	also, in addition, and then	taishikan	embassy
		takai (i-adj.)	expensive, high (in height), tall
soreni	besides		
soshite	and (sentence link)	takusan	a lot of, many
soto	outside	takushī	taxi
sotsugyō shimasu	to graduate	takushī noriba	taxi rank
		tamani	not so often, occasionally
sugoi (i-adj.)	great		
suiē	swimming (n.)	tanjōbi	birthday
(tabako o) suimasu	to smoke a cigarette	tanoshī (i-adj.)	enjoyable, pleasant, delightful
Suisu	Switzerland	tanoshimi(na) (na-adj.)	look forward to
sui-yōbi	Wednesday		
suizokukan	aquarium	tanoshimini shimasu	to look forward to
sukāto	skirt		
sukēto	ice skating	tasukemasu	to help, rescue
sukī	skiing	tatemasu	to build
suki(na) (na-adj.)	like	te	hand(s)
sukoshi	a little, few	-te imasu (Unit 14)	be (verb)-ing (present progressive), a state of someone or something, be (verb)-ing (habitual action)
sukunai (i-adj.)	few		
sumimasen	excuse me, I am sorry		
sumimasu	to live, reside		
sumō	Japanese sumo wrestling		
sūpā	supermarket	-te kudasai	please (do)
Supein	Spain	tegami	letter
Supein-go	Spanish (language)	-te mo ī desu	may
supōtsu	sports	ten'in	shop clerk, shop assistant
sūpu	soup		

tenisu — tennis
tenki — weather
tenpura — tempura (Japanese food)
tera — temple
terebi — television
-te wa ikemasen — must not
tō — ten (small items)
to (conjunction, Unit 2) — and (connecting nouns)
-to (particle, Unit 6) — with, together with
todokemasu — to deliver
tōi (i-adj.) — far
tōka — 10th of the month
tokē — clock, watch
tokidoki — sometimes
tokorode — by the way
Tōkyō — Tokyo, capital of Japan
Tōkyō sukai tsurī — Tokyo Sky Tree (new Tokyo tower)
tomarimasu — to stay overnight
tomemasu — to pull up (a car), stop
tomodachi — friend
tonari — next to
torimasu — to take (a photograph)
Toruko — Turkey
toshokan — library
toshokan kādo — library card
totemo — very (much)
-tsu (counter suffix) — counter for material things in general
tsugi — next
tsugō ga warui desu — (time/schedule) is inconvenient for me
tsuitachi — the first (of the month)
tsukaimasu — to use
tsukemasu — to turn on, switch on
tsukimasu — to arrive
tsūkōnin — passer-by

tsukue — desk
tsukurimasu — to make, produce, create
tsumaranai (i-adj.) — boring, uninteresting
tsumetai (i-adj.) — cold (touch)
tsurete ikimasu — to take (someone to somewhere)
tsuretekimasu — to bring (someone to somewhere)

U

uchi — home, house
udedokē — wristwatch
udon — Japanese noodles made from (wheat) flour
ue — on, above, top
umi — sea, ocean
undō shimasu — to exercise
unten — drive (n.)
unten shimasu — to drive
ureshī (i-adj.) — happy, glad, grateful
urusai (i-adj.) — noisy, loud
usagi — rabbit
ushiro — behind, back
uta — song
utaimasu — to sing
utsukushī (i-adj.) — beautiful

V

[V-dic.] **mae ni** — before doing
[V-stem] **nagara** — while doing
[V-**ta**] **koto ga arimasu** — have done
[V-**te**] **imasu 1** — be (verb)-ing (present progressive)
[V-**te**] **imasu 2** — a state of someone or something
[V-**te**] **imasu 3** — habitual action
[V-**te**] **kudasai** — Please (verb) . . .
[V-**te**] **mo ī desu** — may
[V-**te**] **wa ikemasen** — must not

[V-stem] **masen**
   ka
	won't you (do
	   something)
		yoi (**i**-adj.)
		yo-ji
			good
			four o'clock

[V-stem] **mashō**	let's (do something)	**yōka**	8th of the month
[V-stem] **tai desu**	want to (do something)	**yokka** **yoku**	4th of the month often, frequently
		yomikata	how to read
W		**yomimashita**	read (past tense)
wa (particle)	topic marker particle	**yomimasu** **yon**	to read four
wain	wine	**yori** (Unit 12)	than, rather . . .
wakai (**i**-adj.)	young		than . . . ,
wakarimashita	understood		more . . . than . . .
wakarimasu	to understand	**yori** (Unit 5)	from (used for
warui (**i**-adj.)	bad		letters, emails, etc.)
washitsu	Japanese-style room	**yōroppa** **yoru**	Europe evening, night
watarimasu	to cross	**yōshitsu**	Western-style room
watashi	I	**yottsu**	four (small items)
		yoyaku shimasu	to reserve, book
Y		**yubi**	finger

ya (particle,
   Unit 8)
	and (among other
	   things)
		yūbinkyoku
		yuki
			post office
			snow

-ya (suffix, Unit 8)	shop, store	**yukkuri**	slowly
yakyū senshu	baseball player	**yume**	dream
yama	mountain	**yūmē(na)** (**na**-adj.)	famous
yasai	vegetable		

yasashī (**i**-adj.)	easy (to do),
	   kind, gentle
	   (personality)
		Z
		zannen desu ga
			it is regrettable/
			   unfortunate but

yasui (**i**-adj.)	inexpensive, cheap	**zasshi** **zehi**	magazine by all means,
yasumi	holiday, rest (n.)		please, definitely
yasumimasu	to rest	**zenbu de**	in total, all together
yattsu	eight (small items)	**zenzen**	(not) at all
yawarakai (**i**-adj.)	soft	**zero**	zero
-yōbi (suffix)	day (of the week)	**zō**	statue
yobimasu	to call (e.g. a taxi)	**zubon**	(a pair of) trousers

English-Japanese glossary

You can find a full list of particles, counters, time phrases, interrogatives and months/dates in the Grammar Summary. You can also find a full list of verb conjugations and adjective inflections in the Appendix.

A

a little	chotto . . .
about	goro (for time), kurai/gurai (duration of time, etc.)
again	mata
air conditioning	eakon
airport	kūkō
alcoholic drink	(o)sake
all right	daijōbu
alone	hitori de
already	mō
also	mo (particle)
always	itsumo
a.m.	gozen
and	to (for nouns), ya (for nouns), soshite (for sentences)
and then	sorekara
apple	ringo
aquarium	suizokukan
arrive	tsukimasu
art gallery	bijutsukan
at	de (for places), ni (for items and places)
autumn	aki

B

bad	warui
bag	kaban
ball-point pen	bōrupen
bank	ginkō
bank clerk	ginkōin
baseball player	yakyū senshu
basketball	basukettobōru
battery	denchi
be	arimasu, imasu, desu
be careful	ki o tsukemasu
be similar	nite imasu
beautiful	utsukushī, kirē(na)
because	kara
become	narimasu
bed	beddo
bedroom	shinshitsu
beer	bīru
before (verb)	mae, mae ni
behind	ushiro
besides	soreni
best	ichi-ban
between	aida
bicycle	jitensha
big	ōkī
birthday	tanjōbi
black	kuro (n.), kuroi (adj.)
black tea	kōcha
blue	ao (n.), aoi (adj.)
body	karada
bonus day	bōnasu-bi
book	hon
bookshop	hon-ya
boring	tsumaranai
boy	otoko no ko
breakfast	asagohan
bridge	hashi
bright	akarui

bring	tsurete kimasu (someone), **motte kimasu** (something)	clothes	fuku
		cloudy	kumori
		coat	kōto
brown	chairo (n.), chairoi (adj.)	coffee	kōhī
		coffee shop	kissaten
brush	migakimasu	cold	samui (for temperature), tsumetai (for touch)
build	tatemasu		
building	biru		
bus	basu	collect	atsumemasu
bus stop	basutē	colour	iro
busy	isogashī	come	kimasu
but	demo, ga, shikashi	company	kaisha
buy	kaimasu	concert	konsāto
by	de	confectionery	okashi
by all means	zehi	congratulations	omedetō (gozaimasu)
by the way	tokorode	convenience store	konbini
C		convenient	benri(na)
call	yobimasu	cook	ryōri shimasu
calligraphy	shodō	cooking	ryōri
can	dekimasu	corner	kado
cancel	kyanseru shimasu	country	(o)kuni
car	kuruma	cross	watarimasu
card	kādo	crossroads	kōsaten
castle	(o)shiro	cut	kirimasu
cat	neko		
centimetre	senchi	**D**	
certainly	kashikomarimashita	dance	odorimasu
chair	isu	dangerous	abunai
change	kaemasu, norikaemasu	dark	kurai
		dear	e (used for letters)
cheap	yasui		
child	kodomo	December	jūni-gatsu
chocolate	chokorēto	definitely	zehi
chopsticks	(o)hashi	delicious	oishī
Christmas	kurisumasu	deliver	todokemasu
cigarette	tabako	department store	depāto
cinema	ēgakan		
city	machi	desk	tsukue
city hall	shiyakusho	diary	nikki
clean	kirē(na) (adj.), sōji shimasu (v.)	dictionary	jisho
		difficult	muzukashī
click	kurikku shimasu	digital camera	dejikame
climb	noborimasu	dinner	ban-gohan
clock	tokē	dislike	kirai(na)
close	shimemasu	do	shimasu

doctor	(o)isha(-san)	**F**	
dog	inu	face	kao
dream	yume	family	kazoku
drink	nomimasu	famous	yūmē(na)
(something to)	nomimono	far	tōi
drink		fast	hayai
drive	unten shimasu	father	chichi (one's own),
driving	unten (n.)		otōsan (someone
DVD	DVD (read as dībuidī)		else's)
		February	ni-gatsu
E		feel unwell	kimochi ga warui
ear	mimi	female	onna
early	hayai	festival	(o)matsuri
easy	kantan(na), yasashī	fever	netsu
eat	tabemasu, shokuji	few	sukunai, chotto
	shimasu	film	ēga
eight	hachi	finger	yubi
elder brother	ani (one's own),	fish	sakana
	onīsan (someone	five	go
	else's)	flower	hana
elder sister	ane (one's own),	(Japanese)	ikebana
	onēsan (someone	flower	
	else's)	arrangement	
electric train	densha	food	tabemono
electricity	denki	football	sakkā
email	īmēru	for the first time	hajimete
embassy	taishikan	foreign country	gaikoku
engineer	enjinia	fork	fōku
English	Ē-go	four	shi, yon
(language)		free (time)	hima(na), jiyū(na)
enjoyable	tanoshī	Friday	kin-yōbi
enter	hairimasu	friend	tomodachi
entrance hall	genkan	from	kara, yori (used for
evening	ban, yoru		letters)
every day	mainichi	fruit	kudamono
every evening	maiban		
every month	maitsuki	**G**	
every morning	maiasa	game	gēmu
every week	maishū	garden	niwa
every weekend	maishūmatsu	get off	orimasu
every year	maitoshi	get on	norimasu
everyone	minna	girl	onna no ko
excuse me	sumimasen	give	agemasu
exercise	undō shimasu	glad	ureshī
expensive	takai	(a pair of)	megane
eye	me	glasses	

go	**ikimasu**	hot spring	**onsen**
go back	**kaerimasu**	hotel	**hoteru, ryokan**
go for a walk	**sanpo shimasu**		(Japanese-style inn)
go to bed	**nemasu**	housewife	**shufu**
golf	**gorufu**	how?	**dō**
good	**ī, yoi**	how long?	**donokurai** (time)
good afternoon	**konnichiwa**	how many?	**ikutsu** (small objects),
good at	**jōzu(na)**		**ikutsume** (bus/train
good evening	**konbanwa**		stops), **nan-dai**
good morning	**ohayō (gozaimasu)**		(machines), **nan-ko**
graduate	**sotsugyō shimasu**		(small objects),
grandfather	**sofu** (one's own),		**nan-mai** (long
	ojīsan (someone		objects), **nan-nin**
	else's)		(people)
grandmother	**sobo** (one's own),	how much?	**ikura**
	obāsan (someone	how old?	**nan-sai**
	else's)	how to . . .	**-kata**
great	**sugoi**	hundred	**hyaku**
green	**midori** (n.)	hundred	**-jū-man**
guitar	**gitā**	thousand	
		hurry	**isogimasu**
H			
hair	**kami**	**I**	
half	**han**	I	**watashi**
hamburger	**hanbāgā**	ice skating	**sukēto**
hand(s)	**te**	in front of	**mae**
happy	**ureshī**	in total	**zenbu de**
hat	**bōshi**	inconvenient	**fuben(na)**
have	**arimasu, mochimasu,**	information	**annaijo**
	motte imasu	(desk, agency,	
head	**atama**	office)	
healthy	**kenkō(na), karada**	inside	**naka**
	ni ī	instant (cup)	**kappu-rāmen**
heavy	**omoi**	noodles	
help	**tasukemasu**	interesting	**omoshiroi**
here	**koko**	Internet	**intānetto**
high school	**kōkōsē**	investigate	**shirabemasu**
student			
hobby	**shumi**	**J**	
holiday	**yasumi**	January	**ichi-gatsu**
home	**uchi**	Japan	**Nihon**
homework	**shukudai**	jog	**jogingu shimasu**
hospital	**byōin**	juice	**jūsu**
hot	**atsui** (temperature),	July	**shichi-gatsu**
	karai (spicy)	June	**roku-gatsu**

K

kind	**shinsetsu(na), yasashī**
kitchen	**daidokoro**
knife	**naifu**
know	**shirimasu, shitte imasu**

l

last month	**sengetsu**
last week	**senshū**
last year	**kyonen**
leave	**demasu**
left	**hidari**
leg	**ashi**
let me see . . .	**ēto**
letter	**tegami**
library	**toshokan**
life	**sēkatsu**
light	**denki** (n.), **karui** (adj.)
like	**suki(na), daisuki(na)**
liquor	**(o)sake**
listen to	**kikimasu**
(a) little	**sukoshi**
live	**sumimasu, sunde imasu**
lively	**nigiyaka(na)**
living room	**ima**
lobby	**robī**
long	**nagai**
look	**mimasu**
look forward to	**tanoshimi(na)** (adj.), **tanoshimi ni shimasu** (v.)
low	**hikui**
lunch	**hiru-gohan**

M

magazine	**zasshi**
make	**tsukurimasu**
man	**otoko, otoko no hito**
many	**ōi, takusan**
map	**chizu**
March	**san-gatsu**
marry	**kekkon shimasu**
May	**go-gatsu**

maybe	**tabun**
meal	**gohan**
meat	**niku**
medicine	**kusuri**
meet	**aimasu**
milk	**gyūnyū**
million	**hyaku-man**
minute(s)	**-fun(kan), -pun(kan)**
Miss	**-san**
mobile phone	**kētai denwa**
Monday	**getsu-yōbi**
month(s)	**-gatsu, -kagetsu(kan)**
more	**motto**
morning	**asa**
most	**ichiban**
mother	**haha** (one's own), **okāsan** (someone else's)
motorcycle, motorbike	**ōtobai**
mountain	**yama**
mouth	**kuchi**
movie	**ēga**
Mr, Mrs, Ms	**-san**
Mt. Fuji	**Fujisan**
museum	**hakubutsukan**
music	**ongaku**

N

name	**(o)namae**
narrow	**semai**
near	**chikai** (adj.), **chikaku no** (+ noun)
neck	**kubi**
necklace	**nekkuresu**
new	**atarashī**
newspaper	**shinbun**
next	**tsugi**
next month	**raigetsu**
next time	**kondo**
next to	**tonari**
next week	**raishū**
next year	**rainen**
night	**ban, yoru**
nine	**kyū**
no	**īe**

no one	**daremo**	photograph	**shashin**
noisy	**urusai**	piano	**piano**
non-smoking	**kin'en**	picture	**e**
noon	**hiru**	pink	**pinku** (n.)
nose	**hana**	place	**basho** (n.), **iremasu**
not at all	**zenzen**		(v.), **okimasu** (v.)
not so much	**amari**	plane	**hikōki**
not so often	**tamani**	play (v.)	**asobimasu, hikimasu**
not yet	**mada**		(stringed
nothing	**nanimo**		instrument),
November	**jūichi-gatsu**		**shimasu** (game,
now	**ima**		sport)
nowhere	**dokomo**	please	**onegai shimasu,**
number	**bangō**		**[V-te] kudasai**
		p.m.	**gogo**
O		(neighbourhood)	**kōban**
October	**jū-gatsu**	police station	
of course	**mochiron**	poor at	**heta(na)**
off-duty day	**kyūjitsu, yasumi**	popularity	**ninki**
office worker	**kaishain**	post office	**yūbinkyoku**
often	**yoku**	present	**purezento**
OK	**daijōbu, ī**	pretty	**kawaī**
old (things)	**furui**	primary school	**shōgakusē**
on	**ue**	pupil	
once more	**mō ichido**		
one	**ichi**	**Q**	
only	**dake**	quiet	**shizuka(na)**
open	**akemasu**	quite	**māmā**
order	**chūmon shimasu**		
outside	**soto**	**R**	
		rabbit	**usagi**
P		rain	**ame**
painful	**itai**	read	**yomimasu**
parents	**ryōshin** (one's own),	reading books	**dokusho**
	goryōshin	really?	**sō desu ka, hontō**
	(someone else's)		**desu ka**
park	**kōen**	recall	**omoidashimasu**
party	**pātī**	receive	**moraimasu**
passer-by	**tsūkōnin**	recently	**saikin**
passport	**pasupōto**	red	**aka** (n.), **akai** (adj.)
pay	**haraimasu**	remember	**oboemasu**
pencil	**enpitsu**	remote control	**rimokon**
person	**hito**	reserve	**yoyaku shimasu**
personal	**pasokon**	rest	**yasumimasu**
computer		restaurant	**resutoran**
photo frame	**shashin tate**	right	**migi**

ring	**kakemasu**	soft	**yawarakai**
room	**heya, washitsu**	some day	**itsuka**
	(Japanese-style),	sometimes	**tokidoki**
	yōshitsu	son	**musuko**
	(Western-style)	song	**uta**
run	**hashirimasu**	sore	**itai**
		soup	**sūpu**
S		south	**minami**
safe	**anzen(na)**	souvenir	**omiyage**
Saturday	**do-yōbi**	spacious	**hiroi**
scary	**kowai**	spoon	**supūn**
sea	**umi**	sports	**supōtsu**
secondary	**chūgakusē**	spring	**haru**
school		(postage) stamp	**kitte**
student		stand	**tachimasu, tatte**
send	**okurimasu**		**imasu**
September	**ku-gatsu**	station	**eki**
seven	**nana, shichi**	statue	**zō**
shirt(s)	**shatsu**	stature	**se**
(a pair of) shoes	**kutsu**	stay overnight	**tomarimasu**
shop	**(o)mise, -ya**	stop	**-noriba** (n.),
shop clerk /	**ten'in**		**tomemasu** (v.)
assistant		straight	**massugu**
shopping	**kaimono**	street	**michi**
go shopping	**kaimono shimasu**	student	**gakusē**
show	**misemasu**	study	**benkyō** (n.), **benkyō**
shower (n.)	**shawā**		**shimasu** (v.)
shower (v.)	**abimasu**	suit	**sūtsu**
showy	**hade(na)**	summer	**natsu**
sickness	**byōki**	Sunday	**nichi-yōbi**
sightseeing	**kankō**	sunny	**hare**
go sightseeing	**kankō shimasu**	supermarket	**sūpā**
sing	**utaimasu**	supper	**ban-gohan**
singer	**kashu**	sweater	**sētā**
sit down	**suwarimasu**	sweet	**amai**
six	**roku**	swim	**oyogimasu**
skiing	**sukī**	swimming	**suiē**
skirt	**sukāto**		
slipper	**surippa**	**T**	
slow	**osoi**	take	**torimasu** (a photo),
slowly	**yukkuri**		**kakarimasu**
small	**chīsai**		(time, cost), **tsurete**
smoke	**(tabako o) suimasu**		**ikimasu** (someone),
snow	**yuki** (n.), **yuki ga**		**motte ikimasu**
	furimasu (v.)		(thing)
socks	**kutsushita**	talk	**hanashimasu**

tall	**takai, se ga takai**	tobacco	**tabako**
tasteless	**mazui**	today	**kyō**
tasty	**oishī**	together	**issho ni**
taxi	**takushī**	toilet	**otearai**
tea	**kōcha** (black tea),	tomorrow	**ashita**
	ocha (green tea)	too	**-mo** (particle)
teach	**oshiemasu**	tourist	**kankōkyaku**
teacher	**kyōshi, sensē**	tourist	**kankō annaijo**
teeth	**ha**	information	
telephone	**denwa**	town	**machi**
telephone	**denwa-bangō**	traffic lights	**shingō**
number		transfer	**norikaemasu**
television	**terebi**	travel	**ryokō**
temple	**(o)tera**	trousers	**zubon**
ten	**jū**	true	**hontō**
ten thousand	**-man**	Tuesday	**ka-yōbi**
tennis	**tenisu**	turn	**magarimasu**
thank you	**(dōmo) arigatō**	turn on	**tsukemasu**
	(gozaimasu)	two	**ni**
that	**sore, sochira** (polite	two people	**futari**
	version)		
that (+ noun)	**sono**	**U**	
that over there	**are, achira** (polite	umbrella	**kasa**
	version)	under	**shita**
that (+ noun)	**ano**	underground	**chikatetsu**
over there		underwear	**shitagi**
that place	**soko, sochira** (polite	university	**daigaku**
	version)	university	**daigakusē**
that place over	**asoko, achira** (polite	student	
there	version)	until	**made** (time)
theatre play	**geki**	(to feel) unwell	**kimochi ga warui**
then, well then	**jā**	use	**tsukaimasu**
thing(s)	**mono**	usually	**futsū**
this (+ noun)	**kono-**		
this month	**kongetsu**	**V**	
this morning	**kesa**	various	**iroiro na**
this week	**konshū**	vase	**kabin**
this year	**kotoshi**	vegetable	**yasai**
thousand	**-sen**	very (much)	**totemo**
three	**san**	view	**keshiki** (n.)
Thursday	**moku-yōbi**	vigorous	**genki(na)**
ticket	**kippu**	visitor	**okyakusan**
tie	**nekutai**		
time	**jikan**	**W**	
to	**e** (particle), **made**	wait	**machimasu**
	(particle)	wake up	**okimasu**

walk, stroll	sanpo (n.), sanpo shimasu (v.)	who?	dare, donate (polite version)
wallet	saifu	whose?	dare no, donate no (polite version)
want	hoshī, -tai desu	why?	dōshite
warm	atatakai	wind	kaze
was, were	deshita	window	mado
wash	araimasu, sentaku shimasu (laundry)	wine	wain
		winter	fuyu
watch	tokē (n.), mimasu (v.)	with	to (particle)
water	(o)mizu	woman	onna no hito
wear	kimasu (clothes), hakimasu (shoes), kakemasu (glasses), kaburimasu (hat)	wonderful	suteki(na)
		word	kotoba
		work	(o)shigoto (n.), hatarakimasu (v.)
weather	tenki	work hard	ganbarimasu
Wednesday	sui-yōbi	wristwatch	udedokē
week(s)	-shū(kan)	write	kakimasu
weekend	shūmatsu		
what?	nan, nani	**Y**	
what day?	nan-nichi	year(s)	-nen(kan)
what day (of the week)?	nan-yōbi	. . . years old	-sai
		yellow	kīro (n.), kīroi (adj.)
what kind of . . .?	donna	yen	-en
what? (time)	nan-pun	yes	hai
what month?	nan-gatsu	yesterday	kinō
what nationality?	nani-jin	you	anata
		young	wakai
what number?	nan-ban	younger brother	otōto (one's own), otōto-san (someone else's)
what time?	nan-ji		
when?	itsu		
where?	doko, dochira (polite version)	younger sister	imōto (one's own), imōto-san (someone else's)
which?	dore (out of more than two), dochira (out of two)		
		Z	
which (+noun)?	dono, dochira no	zero	zero
white	shiro (n.), shiroi (adj.)	zoo	dōbutsuen

Index of language points

www.routledge.com/languages

Also available...

Modern Japanese
Grammar Workbook

By **Naomi McGloin, M. Endo Hudson, Fumiko Nazikian** and **Tomomi Kakegawa**

Series: Modern Grammar Workbooks

The *Modern Japanese Grammar Workbook* is an innovative book of exercises and language tasks for all learners of Japanese. The book is divided into two parts:

- Section A provides exercises based on essential grammatical structures

- Section B practices everyday functions (e.g. making introductions, apologizing, expressing needs).

All sentences are written both in Romanization and in the Japanese script and a comprehensive answer key at the back enables the learner to check on their progress.

Key features of the book include:

- Exercises graded on a 3-point scale according to their level of difficulty

- Cross-referencing to the related *Modern Japanese Grammar*

- Topical exercises to help learners develop their vocabulary

Modern Japanese Grammar Workbook is an ideal practice tool for learners of Japanese at all levels. No prior knowledge of grammatical terminology is assumed and it can be used both independently and alongside the *Modern Japanese Grammar* (ISBN 978-0-415-57201-9), which is also published by Routledge.

2014 | 200 Pages | HB: 978-0-415-60864-0 | PB: 978-0-415-27093-9
Learn more at: www.routledge.com/9780415270939

Available from all good bookshops

www.routledge.com/languages

Also available...

Modern Japanese Grammar

A Practical Guide

By **Naomi McGloin, M. Endo Hudson, Fumiko Nazikian** and **Tomomi Kakegawa**

Series: Modern Grammars

This reference guide to Japanese combines traditional and function-based grammar in a single volume. It covers grammatical categories, such as nouns, verbs and adjectives, and also language functions covering major communication situations.

Features include: clear, jargon-free explanations; extensive cross-referencing; a detailed index of forms and topics; grammar points and functions selected on frequency and usefulness; examples given in Romanization and Japanese script; glossary of grammatical terms.

Both reference grammar and practical usage manual, this will be essential for learners of Japanese at all levels. No prior knowledge of grammatical terminology or Japanese script is required.

This *Grammar* is accompanied by the *Modern Japanese Grammar Workbook* (ISBN 978-0-415-27093-9) which features related exercises and activities.

2013 | 432 Pages | HB: 978-0-415-57199-9 | PB: 978-0-415-57201-9
Learn more at: www.routledge.com/9780415572019

Available from all good bookshops